LIBRARY ETHICS

Jean Preer

LIBRARIES
U N L I M I T E D
A Member of the Greenwood Publishing Group
Westport, Connecticut • London

Library of Congress Cataloging-in-Publication Data

Preer, Jean L.
  Library ethics / Jean L. Preer.
      p. cm.
  Includes bibliographical references and index.
  ISBN 978-1-59158-636-4 (alk. paper)
  1. Librarians—Professional ethics. 2. Library science—Moral and ethical aspects. I. Title.
  Z682.35.P75P74   2008
  174.902092—dc22   2008021122

British Library Cataloguing in Publication Data is available.

Library of Congress Catalog Card Number: 2008021122
ISBN: 978-1-59158-636-4

First published in 2008

Libraries Unlimited, 88 Post Road West, Westport, CT 06881
A Member of the Greenwood Publishing Group, Inc.
www.lu.com

Printed in the United States of America

The paper used in this book complies with the
Permanent Paper Standard issued by the National
Information Standards Organization (Z39.48–1984).

10   9   8   7   6   5   4   3   2   1

Dedicated to the memory of Dr. Elizabeth W. Stone

CONTENTS

ETHICAL EXAMPLES

ACKNOWLEDGMENTS

I wish to thank those who made this volume possible: Blanche Woolls of Libraries Unlimited, for her suggestion that I write about library ethics, and Laura Smith of Cadmus Communications for her editorial oversight; Marilyn Irwin, Associate Dean of the Indiana University School of Library and Information Science-Indianapolis for support, and Kimberly Kramer for teaching and grading help that gave me time to write. Special thanks go to Kathy Mulder, my IU SLIS graduate assistant, for outstanding work in locating sources and compiling the Library Ethics Timeline. Thanks also to the many students over the years who have grappled with ethical issues in my classes and who demonstrate such pride in their new profession. While the text echoes with many voices and reflects the work of many hands, the responsibility for any errors is mine alone.

INTRODUCTION

In planning for library service, librarians face ethical issues before the first patron comes through the door or visits the library's Web site. Basic choices about the library's location, its hours and collections, the qualifications of its staff, policies about who can use the library and under what conditions, choices about what information can be accessed and how, all require not only professional competence but ethical judgment. Our need for ethical awareness has grown as the practice of librarianship has become more professional, our roles and services more complex, and information technologies faster and more pervasive.

This book will examine how our understanding of library ethics has evolved along with the development of librarianship itself. It grows out of the foundations course I have taught for many years at the schools of library and information science at The Catholic University of America in Washington, D.C., and at Indiana University in Indianapolis. The course was designed as an introduction to the profession of librarianship, its history, values, and the issues and challenges that librarians face. It is organized around six major themes: identity, ethics, issues, access, funding, and future. While the content of the course has changed continuously as our world and our work have been transformed, the framework has remained the same, giving students a way to view the world over the course of their careers.

While it has never been solely an ethics course, it has functioned in that way. Students often call it the "ethics course." Beginning with professional identity, it explores the role of libraries and librarians in various settings and over time. We distinguish professional identity from "image." Professional identity is what we do; image is someone else's idea of what librarians are about. To a large extent, we can shape our identity, and ethics is an important element in this. So we move from what librarians do to what they stand for. We explore ethics near the start of the course so that every dimension of librarianship, how we approach social issues, how we interpret access, and how we seek funding, can all be viewed through an ethical lens.

Students and those who are not librarians are often surprised that librarians have ethics. They say, "I didn't know that librarians have ethics," but then they quickly correct themselves and say, "I thought that all librarians have ethics." But many have not considered that librarians face particular ethical dilemmas arising from their users' needs for information. I believe that a measure of a profession's development is its understanding of the values that govern its practice. A central element of professional education is acquiring the knowledge, skills, and values that help librarians identify and then address ethical issues. In law school, students learn to "think like a lawyer." In my foundations class, students learn to "think like a librarian." This means absorbing the traditions, outlook, and values that have evolved as generations of practitioners have sought to provide information to expanding audiences, in changing formats, using ever-new technologies. It means separating personal views from professional responsibilities, and responding to the obligations of service and access.

The goal of this book is to provide an ethical framework that will remain constant while we subject our values to constant scrutiny, reexamination, and reformulation. The intent is to provide clarity. We are particularly interested in those values that are the hallmark of our profession and that cut across all areas of specialization: providing service, ensuring access to information, avoiding conflicts of interests, and protecting patron confidentiality. This book is grounded in the belief that professional education matters and that professional spirit, while important, must be informed by historical precedent, technological know-how, and ethical understanding. And because I am trained as a librarian, a lawyer, and a historian, I approach the themes in my course and the ethical values explored in this book from those three perspectives.

Ethics is not the same as good customer service or efficient management, although ethical issues arise in both service and management contexts. Where librarianship shares ethical values with other professions, as with our concern to protect confidentiality and to avoid conflicts of interest, we will focus on how those values apply in a library context. Though ethics involves a choice between alternative actions, ethics is not the same as law. We will see, however, that ethical obligations may over time become legal requirements, and, in some cases, that legal standards may be incorporated into codes of ethics.

Ethical conduct does not mean adherence to strict rules of behavior but rather the application of values in situations where there is no fixed rule or clear right answer. Ethical conduct requires imagination to envision alternatives that both address a problem and honor a professional value. It means making exceptions in a principled way.

This book argues that there is a presumption in favor of responses based on professional values, and that these values will be overridden only when circumstances clearly and convincingly indicate the appropriateness of a contrary course of action. Thus, the starting point of professional conduct is adherence to the core ethical values of librarianship: providing service and access, avoiding philosophical and financial conflicts of interest, and protecting patron confidentiality. The burden is on those who would ignore these values to present evidence why. This is not a balancing test. It means that conduct is governed by ethical values unless an overwhelming case can be made to act otherwise.

Just as practice changes, ethical standards evolve to encompass new understandings of our role. Meeting a new ethical dilemma, the professional librarian should apply this accumulated wisdom and experience to addressing an unforeseen and perhaps unforeseeable dilemma. Everyday practice adds to our ethical understanding and helps reshape our standards for ethical conduct. This book honors those practitioners whose work over generations has deepened our ethical commitment to new users, new services, and new technologies. As we work within today's codes of library ethics, we continue this process of redefining our professional response to challenges and issues yet unknown.

1

PROFESSIONALISM, IDENTITY, AND VALUES

One of the deepest problems with the library profession's sense of itself is, I believe, its failure to come to terms with what it means to make decisions as a professional. For myself, I define that decision-making process by borrowing a favorite view of intelligence: "Intelligence is measured not by what you know but what you do when you don't know." We librarians know a lot, as we must, but we tend to distrust and avoid the large questions and dilemmas that hover not very far over our heads and concentrate exclusively on the endless clerical, technical, technological, and managerial details of our work, as if we will solve all the problems worth solving by rooting out clear answers and procedures.[1]

—John Swan

THE MEANING OF ETHICS

The evolution of ethical standards is a central element in the professionalization of librarianship. The recognition of a common professional identity and the quest for professional status require external tangible signs of profession and internal intangible values shared by practitioners. Ethical understanding and standards grow out of practice. Once codified, these standards inform and change practice. The circle is complete when further experience demonstrates the need for changes in those ethical standards and our ethical codes. What we do shapes what we stand for. And what we stand for influences what we do. Ethics is about choices. As a system of principles determining right or wrong conduct, ethics defines the parameters of those choices. How we see the choices we have evolves along with changes in our society, its values, and the introduction of new technology.

Before there was a profession of librarianship or articulated ethical standards, those who maintained collections nonetheless made choices about materials to acquire, patrons to be served, and services to be provided. Values were implicit in many of these decisions: when printed material was scarce or expensive, protection of the physical item was paramount; rules developed in practice to control access to those materials and establish conditions for their use. Without academic training to inculcate professional values or professional organizations to promulgate, promote, or enforce them, librarians developed rules in practice that were determined by institutions, customs, and local needs. Indeed, ethics relates to "custom," the word deriving from ethos, the way things are done.

While the history of libraries stretches back centuries and across continents, early "librarians" were scholars, bibliographers, or clerks, without a separate identity or professional status. As keepers of books, librarians were responsible for the protection of their collections. Since most libraries were in private hands or in universities, academies, or religious institutions, librarians were also responsible to those bodies and to the users of their collections. In the years before publicly funded libraries, librarians had no transcendent obligation to the local community, to the larger society, to their profession, or to the values it embodied.

THE MEANING OF PROFESSION

We now recognize the essential elements of a profession as a base of generalized and systematized knowledge, means of practice or technique, and shared values derived from that practice. Writing about librarians as professionals in 1979, Lester Asheim quoted the three-part formulation offered by Louis Brandeis in 1914, a discussion of professionalism in business that emphasized the learned and altruistic aspects of a profession.

First, a profession is an occupation for which the necessary preliminary training is intellectual in character, involving knowledge and to some extent learning as distinguished from mere skill. Second, it is an occupation which is pursued largely for others and not merely for one's self. Third, it is an occupation in which the amount of financial return is not the accepted measure of success.[2]

In a 1946 talk on the ethics of librarianship, library educator and author Helen Haines described three attributes of a profession:

A profession, it seems to me, must have three distinctive characteristics: it must have a discipline (a system of training), an ethic (a formulation of rules of conduct, of moral obligation), and a vision (the outcome, or essence of philosophy). Rarely born ready-made, it takes shape slowly in evolutionary growth.

Haines described the ethics of librarianship as "collective, impersonal formulations of beliefs and conclusions rather than individual distillations."[3]

The growth of professionalism is manifested externally by the organization of professional associations, a move away from apprenticeships to formal academic preparation, and the formulation of ethical standards of conduct. In the last quarter of the nineteenth century, librarians, along with other learned practitioners, sought to cloak their activities in the mantle of professionalism. Meeting in Philadelphia in 1876, the founding members of the American Library Association (ALA) sought not just to establish a professional organization for librarians but to lay the groundwork for the modern profession of librarianship. The creation of an autonomous association of practitioners was only the first step to professional status, but one that many were taking at the time. Within a decade on either side of the establishment of the ALA, doctors, lawyers, social workers, and others formed professional organizations to distinguish themselves from crafts- and tradespeople who were less skilled and less highly trained. The organization of professional associations asserted and promoted common interests.

Formal academic training assumes a core of generalized and systematized knowledge. Professionals draw on this intellectual capital as the store of their competence and informed judgments. If a professional is one who is paid to make informed decisions, then this academic preparation is what distinguishes the professional from the layperson and justifies the higher compensation and societal respect that follows professional status. The establishment by Melvil Dewey of the School of Library Economy at Columbia College in 1887 confirmed, at least outwardly, the intellectual nature of the profession of librarianship.

Despite the tangible benefits of professional status, however, the essence of profession is service to society, a commitment not to self-interest but to the community's well-being. Thus, in promoting their members, professional organizations also advance the good of society. Animated by a spirit of service, professionals share a worldview shaped by their common professional training and experience. Moving from practical training to the academy, future professionals learn to view problems through the particular lens of shared expertise and values. Society allows professions a high degree of autonomy but expects them in return to set and enforce appropriate standards of conduct. The process of becoming professional requires the identification and articulation of these values and their adoption in spirit and practice.

While centuries of practice had honed the idea of librarianship as a scholarly and altruistic enterprise, this accumulated experience had not produced a set of core values, though it had determined the context for those values. A statement of ethics remained the third essential element to define and secure the professional status of librarians. Ethical values are rooted in practice, and in late-nineteenth-century America, the practice that would produce what we now consider the core ethical values of librarianship was just beginning.

VALUES FROM PRACTICE

While the ALA established the institutional framework for librarianship, the profession itself was shaped by societal currents of the new Industrial Age. Librarians organized as a profession before the spread of public libraries across the United States. For nearly a century and a half, beginning with Benjamin Franklin and his cronies in the Junto who pooled their books for all to use, in 1731, literate Americans relied on private and subscription libraries for books. The demand for library service grew along with the mid-nineteenth century spread of literacy and the availability of cheaper books printed on pulp paper and secured by machine-stitched bindings. In 1876, few communities had free, tax-supported public library services but relied instead on private collections, subscription libraries, and libraries of donated books organized and staffed by volunteers. The establishment of tax-supported public libraries in smaller communities, like Peterborough, New Hampshire, in 1833, and in urban centers such as Boston in 1852, marked the beginning of America's public library movement. Following the Civil War, it regained momentum thanks to the activities of local women's clubs and the beneficence of industrialist and philanthropist Andrew Carnegie.

By the turn of the century, librarianship had acquired two of the three essential elements that characterize a profession: a professional association and educational preparation. However, librarianship still fell short of true professional status. Although law and medicine were undergoing similar transitions to fuller professional status, the power of the courts and the state to determine licensing standards drew a clear line between those who had professional status and those who did not. In contrast, the ALA lacked the power to define and enforce professional standing, and while academic training was increasingly desirable, many librarians lacked any formal library education. Writing in 1951, Pierce Butler observed that the early founding of the ALA may have held back the development of professional identity.

For the purposes of membership, anyone who worked in a library or was interested in libraries was regarded as a librarian. Hence the organization has always been what the American Medical Association would be if it enrolled druggists, nurses, hospital clerks as well as physicians, gave them all an equal vote, and evaded ill-advised majority decisions by political manipulations.[4]

Furthermore, the ALA had not yet assumed responsibility for accrediting the numerous library science programs that were established after 1876. Even after Dewey moved library training to academia, many librarians continued to take classes in the training schools conducted in major public libraries, as in New York, Atlanta, Los Angeles, and Pittsburgh. Butler lamented the effect of these early schools as well. Noting that they had been established in an era when librarians thought too much in terms of technology and process, their emphasis on cataloging and classification, he observed, crystallized the curriculum in a form that proved hard to dissolve.

Finally, while both law and medicine had formally stated and enforceable standards of professional practice, librarianship had yet to articulate its own professional values and standards. Librarians establishing the ALA did not formulate or even suggest a set of professional values. It was not until December 1938 that the ALA adopted its first official code of ethics, almost sixty years after its founding and nearly thirty years after the publication of Charles Knowles Bolton's canon of ethics on which it was based.[5] The final tangible piece in librarianship's quest for professional status, the code was a mix of professional definition, obligation, and etiquette that reflected a nineteenth-century view of libraries as repositories of collections and librarians as their keepers. Outdated even before it appeared, it nonetheless served as an indicator of librarianship's continuing efforts to establish itself among the professional ranks, enhance the education of its practitioners, and expand the expectations of those it served. In declaring what librarians do, it also helped shape what librarians stand for. As an early effort to proclaim the core values of library ethics, it is the benchmark against which librarianship's past progress and future evolution can be measured.

The ALA's 1938 code served multiple purposes. It asserted librarianship's claim to professional status, defined the identity of its practitioners, recorded their manifold obligations, and set standards for ethical practice. In this the code resembled the central tenets of other professional codes while it furthered the process of identifying the unique values that characterize librarianship.

THE PURPOSE OF AN ETHICS CODE

Assertion of Professional Status

The earliest draft codes of ethics for librarianship sought to advance the professional status of the field rather than to distinguish the particular values on which it stood. Mary Plummer's remarks to the Illinois Library Association in 1903 are generally cited as one of the earliest statements of ethical standards for librarians. Director of the library school at Pratt Institute, Plummer sought to promote librarianship as a profession and saw a code as a measure of professional status. Comparing professions to trades, she noted that the codes of doctors, lawyers, college professors, and military officers presupposed their status as gentlemen; a breach of etiquette was described as striking at the foundation of this order. In contrast, codes governing trades were largely unwritten but no-less-binding debts of honor. Noting that librarians and educators had yet to make their own code, Plummer asked what elements a code for librarians would have to include "to help that calling to rank among the professions."[6]

In Plummer's view, the professional training of librarians included knowledge of the field (a history of learning), library technique, administration, and personal preparation. This "fourth essential" encompassed ethics and such qualities as dignity, humility, a willingness to learn, and an unostentatious belief in the work of the library. In Plummer's view, librarians who prepared in library school, rather than on the job, seemed to have more of this essential spirit and a broader view of their work than found in other library employees. Most dramatically, Plummer proposed that librarians ask themselves, "Am I personally a credit to librarianship and if not, what is wrong with me? Am I helping to make librarianship a profession, or am I hindering?" Those who could not work in the best interests of the profession should "be willing to give up the work for the good of the work."[7] In Plummer's hierarchy of values, duty to profession came first. A properly trained librarian, with knowledge of the field, bibliographic and administrative technique, and the right personal qualities, would validate librarianship's claim to professional status.

Statement of Professional Identity

A formal code of ethics promised not only to assert librarianship's claim to professional status but to define the duties and obligations of the profession. Plummer urged her listeners to take a longer and broader view beyond "our ordinary conception of librarianship as the administering economically and to the satisfaction of the public of a collection, large or small, of modern books."

Let us look back into our origins and examine into the claims of librarianship to be called a profession. We may say that the calling began as soon as there were two records of human thought to be kept together and preserved for use; and while mankind were still inscribing these records on clay tablets, there were collections which were called libraries, and which had keepers assigned them who were learned in material they had in charge and could make it serviceable to others.[8]

Building on Plummer's work, Charles Knowles Bolton, secretary and librarian of the Boston Athenaeum, proposed a Librarian's Canon of Ethics, published in *Public Libraries* in June 1909, and in a revised and expanded version in May 1922 in an issue of *Annals of the American Academy of Political and Social Science* devoted entirely to the ethics of the professions and business.[9] Its opening paragraph, too, depicted the librarian as the organizer and custodian of knowledge:

The librarian's profession is sometimes thought to be of recent origin whereas it is as old as learning itself. At the dawn of civilization we find the priesthood with temples and tablets; while the keeper of records stood from the first as the organizer and custodian of inscribed knowledge.... The librarian has ever been the scholar.... The American colonies and then the states, although absurdly modern as compared with the Old World, have outstripped the continent of Europe in developing tax-supported libraries for the benefit of the rank and file of the people. Organization and ideals of service have gone hand in hand.[10]

Recognition of Professional Obligations

Where Mary Plummer had been concerned about the development of librarianship as a profession and the personal qualities of librarians, Charles Knowles Bolton emphasized the multiple obligations of librarians. His advice was not surprising since many of those he consulted were library directors who viewed ethics from an institutional perspective.[11] In a vision of the profession that dominated thinking about ethics for three generations, Bolton's code outlined the duty of the librarian to serve trustees, staff, other librarians, and the public. Mixing the niceties of etiquette with the demands of administrative rationality and the obligations of public service, Bolton's canons were based on relationships rather than on values. To the trustees, the librarian owed loyalty and discretion. To the staff, the librarian was obliged to remain on the job. To the public, the librarian was to offer pleasant and courteous service. The librarian was to respect confidences and avoid conflicts of interest arising in the course of his (or her) work. The importance of good manners and wise administration resounds throughout, with many of its strictures applicable to various employment settings and work relationships, not just libraries.

Declaration of Professional Values

Nonetheless, a few of Bolton's canons captured the essence of values and practice that now characterize professional conduct in librarianship. Concerns about the censorship of library materials did not appear in the canons themselves but in a comment on "A Librarian's Province" suggesting that the librarian's duty was to protect readers from harmful material.

Censorship of reading is a perilous No Man's Land on the boundary of a librarian's province. How far an executive should go in exposing books which are in his opinion destructive of morals and society, and those issued frankly as propaganda, is a serious question.[12]

Fortunately for the librarian, this question was to be answered by the library's board of trustees.

Bolton came out strongly in favor of professional neutrality, an issue that would roil the profession in the 1960s. Regardless of personal beliefs, he argued, the librarian should refrain from voicing an opinion. Again in comments, he warned the librarian against taking sides, even "giving for publication a testimonial to a book is likely to lead to serious abuses. Standing on neutral ground, he should be all things to all men." In the matter of book selection, he urged the librarian to put community needs above personal taste or interests. Once again, the selection of books should be broad, and the librarian's "power to guide be exercised with discretion."

Educating Professionals and the Public

Mary Plummer's code focused on the personal conduct of librarians as a means to advance the profession of librarianship. Charles Knowles Bolton's canons promoted the smooth functioning of the library and honored the multiple obligations of librarians to the board, staff, and public. Both saw statements of ethics as raising the awareness of practitioners and the public to the nature of librarianship. Whether a proclamation of professional status, a statement of professional identity, a record of professional obligation, or a litany of professional values, early codes of library ethics contained no suggestion of enforcement. Indeed, Plummer's much-admired code of gentlemanly conduct and a librarian's own recognition of failure in meeting professional standards were sufficient to correct breaches of etiquette and lapses in professional judgment. Professional standards were to be commonly shared and individually internalized.

An approved and promoted statement of professional ethics can speed the acceptance and adoption of shared professional values. With the imprimatur of the profession's association, a code can function as an educational tool to practitioners, their staffs, trustees, and the public served by the library. In 1922, when Bolton published his "proposal for a revised code," he noted that the founders of the ALA were passing away. A professional canon would serve to pass along the high ideals of this pioneering generation, helping to educate and socialize new practitioners. "We assume that these canons of ethics stand in the position of counselor to the younger men and women of the profession," he wrote, "combining worldly wisdom with unworldly ideals."[13]

Viewing the tumultuous years between Bolton's original proposals in 1909 and the final adoption of the ALA Code of Ethics in 1938, it is surprising how little their essence changed over nearly three decades. From the years before World War I to the years immediately before World War II, new libraries, new communities of users, new technologies, and new challenges transformed the library landscape. A brief list shows the dimensions of this change: the remarkable spread of public libraries, more than 1,600, built across the United States with funds from Andrew Carnegie and support from local communities; the advent of county library service in California; the creation of separate professional associations for law librarians in 1906 and for special librarians in 1909; the provision of library service to recently arrived immigrants as part of the "Americanization" of the foreign born; the widespread censorship of books by German authors during World War I; and the participation of the ALA in the Army War Service, supplying books to troops at home and abroad. Bolton's canons, and in turn, the ALA Code of 1938, suggest a profession still devoted to collecting, protecting, and making books available in the confines of a library, yet somehow sheltered from the excitement and challenges of political and social upheaval.

CHANGING PRACTICE

Melvil Dewey: Changing the Librarian

In his article, "The Profession," published in the inaugural issue of *Library Journal* distributed at the founding meeting of the ALA in 1876, Melvil Dewey linked professional status with a more dynamic role for librarians. No longer just the keeper of books, the librarian, by selecting and promoting materials, was to be an influencer of thoughts like teachers and clergy, "positive, aggressive characters, standing in the front rank of the educators of their communities, side by side with the preachers and the teachers...." Preserving and protecting books was an insufficient professional role, Dewey concluded:

The time *was* when a library was very like a museum, and the librarian was a mouser in musty books, and visitors looked with curious eyes at ancient tomes and manuscripts. The time *is* when the library is a school, and the librarian is in the highest sense a teacher, and the visitor is a reader among the books as a workman among his tools. Will any man deny to the high calling of such a librarianship the title of profession?[14]

Further, in the mid-1920s, Dewey took librarians out of the realm of books and put them squarely in the world of information. At the fiftieth anniversary of the ALA in 1926, Dewey proclaimed that the book was not sacred and urged librarians to "give to the public in the quickest and cheapest way information and recreation in the highest plane," in whatever medium was most efficient.[15]

Alvin Johnson: Changing Library Service

While Melvil Dewey reminded the ALA that the definition of librarianship needed to be updated constantly, the Carnegie Corporation pushed librarians to higher levels of professional service. At the request of the corporation in 1914, Alvin Johnson, author, adult educator, and later president of the New School, visited Carnegie libraries across the United States to determine how well they were functioning. Johnson's anecdotal report, described later in his autobiography, contrasted the gap between library buildings constructed with Carnegie funds and the often insufficient, lackluster, or nonexistent library services offered inside. On the basis of first-hand observation, Johnson concluded that, "Not buildings nor even book collections, but trained, intelligent, enterprising library service makes a real library."[16] While the Carnegie Corporation did not acknowledge or publicize Johnson's findings, it formally concluded its support of library construction and turned its attention to promoting library service.

C. C. Williamson: Changing Library Education

In 1923, another report to the Carnegie Corporation continued the transition of librarianship from practice to profession with an emphasis on service, not facilities, and education, not construction.[17] C. C. Williamson's recommendations to move the preparation of librarians from practical training to academic study mirrored the earlier report of Abraham Flexner on the education of social workers and the transition of medical and legal education from practice-based to academic settings. While Williamson approved of training schools in public libraries for a library's own clerks, he advocated university education to prepare professionals for service anywhere, raising the sights from local occupation to transcendent profession. The organization of the American Association of Library Schools and the ALA Board of Library Education furthered this professionalization process. Library education, which followed the establishment of librarianship's professional organization, had been geared to technical practice, skills, and efficiency, and not to professional values. While the curriculum in library schools continued this practical focus, it offered the possibility of common professional values and goals.

William Learned: Changing Libraries

Commissioned by the Carnegie Corporation, William Learned's study, *The American Public Library and the Diffusion of Knowledge*, envisioned the public library as a community information center.[18] Not a passive repository, the public library would serve as a community resource hub, informing citizens about the issues they faced. Such a library required the dynamic leadership of professional librarians who were keys to the success of this new library model. At the same time, the Carnegie Corporation sponsored major efforts within the ALA to promote adult education within libraries and to extend library service to unserved areas. The library was to become the central community education agency providing resources to citizens of all ages.

L. R. Wilson: Changing the Librarian's Worldview

To become actively engaged professionals, Louis Round Wilson, dean of the graduate school at the University of Chicago, called on librarians to shed their interest in technical and bibliographic matters and become advocates for their libraries and library users. In an address in 1936, he declared:

A librarianship concerned largely with technical and bibliographical matters, as much of our earlier librarianship has been, is not sufficient to cope with the present situation which the Great War and an equally Great Depression have created. As a profession we are confronted with the inescapable duty of meeting the present and the future realistically, of restudying our functions, reshaping our methods and procedures, and readjusting our thinking in such ways that our libraries will serve society today and tomorrow in fundamentally desirable ways.[19]

He called on librarians to become more "legally minded," looking outward and adapting to new conditions.

1938 Code of Ethics for Librarians

Amid these currents of professional change, the ALA's committees attempted to formulate a code of ethics during the late 1920s and early 1930s that could be approved by the association. The Code of Ethics for Librarians formally adopted by the ALA Council on December 19, 1938, closely resembled the prewar, top-down perspective of Bolton's 1909 draft and 1922 revision. Nothing in its language or tone suggested the kind of dynamic professional envisioned by Dewey or the lively information center pictured by Learned. The same detailed mix of duty and etiquette, the code's twenty-eight points did not suggest that fast-paced world events and rapidly developing technologies were transforming the staid librarianship of the turn of the century.

The preamble to the 1938 code defined the library as "an institution that exists for the benefit of a given constituency, whether it be the citizens of a community, members of an educational institution, or some larger or more specialized group." It defined the librarian in terms of status and obligation, not function or values. "Those who enter the library profession assume an obligation to maintain ethical standards of behavior in relation to the governing authority under which they work, to the library constituency, to the library as an institution and to fellow workers on the staff, to other members of the library profession, and to society in general."[20]

Envisioning the library as an institution existing to benefit a given constituency, the code viewed the librarian's ethical obligations in relation to others. Standing at the hub of a wheel, the librarian had duties extending within the library to its governing authority, the library institution, and staff and beyond the library's walls to its constituency, the library profession, and society. The 1938 code retained the shape and viewpoint of Bolton's canons, covering the details of narrowly defined professional obligations. The librarian was to carry out policies loyally, follow procedures

for personnel changes, delegate responsibilities, encourage staff development, confine criticism to proper authority and only for the purpose of
improving the library, stay on the job long enough to repay the cost of hiring, and give adequate notice of leaving.

Between the requirements of personnel policy and professional etiquette,
the 1938 code contained a suggestion of the core values of service and
access that would emerge as characteristic of the profession. The librarian
had an obligation to the library's constituency to acquire materials on the
basis of their needs and to provide a wide a range of publications and varied
viewpoints consistent with library policy and available funds. Further, the
librarian was to make the library's resources and services known to potential
users and render impartial service to all those entitled to use the library.
And like other professionals, librarians were to treat as confidential any private information obtained through contact with patrons and avoid personal
gain through business dealings on behalf of the library or in the use of its
resources.

Perhaps because the process of consideration and adoption had gone on
for so long, or because the provisions had barely changed since Bolton proposed his canons, the 1938 code was greeted with little fanfare. This final
tangible piece in the triad of professionalism was long overdue, but having
adopted its code, the ALA did little to promote it or to suggest how it
might affect professional practice or ethical decision-making.

LIBRARIANSHIP'S ONE BIG IDEA

Looking back, we can see that the ALA adopted its first code of ethics
just before librarians realized that access to information is what library service is all about. The 1938 code left unanswered the question that perilous
times and changing values would bring into sharp relief. When the librarian's obligation to the governing authority or institution was in conflict
with his or her duty to the library's users, to the library profession, or to
society, what was to determine the ethical course of action? Librarians were
about to discover the transcendent value that would serve as the ethical
compass they had been lacking.

At the 1922 ALA conference in Detroit, Carl Roden, director of the
Chicago Public Library, had captured some of this longing for a higher
purpose in librarianship. Returning to the theme of profession that animated Mary Plummer's suggested code, Roden found librarianship in need
of an overarching commitment to a social good. While the clergy, doctors,
and lawyers served individuals, Roden observed, they also advanced the
larger causes of societal well-being, health, and justice. In contrast, librarianship assisted individuals without a greater sense of mission to serve
humanity, the most vital and dynamic element of professionalism. On the
one hand, Roden saw "service to men—highly satisfying service—to teach

the celebrated man in the street to earn more dollars, raise more hens, to win more and more of earthly prizes by using library books." On the other, service to humanity meant bringing books and the people together for a greater purpose.

Books and the Human Race; Librarianship to Humanity. That is a task of profession-al proportions, for the promotion of which we must contrive to save, to rescue, perhaps, a margin of professional ministry. And when we have all been brought to accept this commission, and have succeeded in gaining recognition from the world of men that our fulfillment of it is a vital contribution to its upward flight then we shall have accomplished our full duty to our profession, for then we shall have a profession.[21]

In Roden's view, this commitment to the service of humanity, not the outward trappings of association and education, was at the core of professionalism.

THE LIBRARY BILL OF RIGHTS AS AN ETHICAL COMPASS

On November 21, 1938, a month before the ALA adopted its first code of ethics, the board of trustees of the Des Moines Public Library approved the Library's Bill of Rights. Led by librarian Forrest Spaulding, the public library had welcomed divergent viewpoints in its collection and among its users. The city of Des Moines itself had been a leader in the public forum movement, supported by the Carnegie Corporation and then the U.S. Bu-reau of Education, hosting speakers and inviting discussion of the major issues of the day. In the late 1930s, Americans witnessed book burnings abroad as the Nazis gained control of Germany, and in 1939, protests over John Steinbeck's *The Grapes of Wrath* raised the possibility of book censor-ship close to home.[22] The four provisions of the Library's Bill of Rights reflected the situations faced in public libraries and suggested how, in facing these challenges, the public library served the common good. More than the generalized standards of service stated in the Code of Ethics, the Library's Bill of Rights demonstrated the unique role of libraries, the dilemmas they faced, and the values they represented. Its preamble pro-vided the context:

Now, when indications in many parts of the world point to growing intolerance, suppression of free speech and censorship, affecting the rights of minorities and individuals, the Board of Trustees of the Des Moines Public Library reaffirms these basic policies governing a free public library to serve the best interests of Des Moines and its citizens.[23]

To fulfill this role, the library was to purchase material of value and interest to the people of Des Moines, without regard to the race, nationality, political, or religious views of the authors. In selecting books on subjects where opinions differed, all sides of the controversy were to be represented equally. Library meeting rooms were to be made available on equal terms to all organized nonprofit groups for meetings that were open, where no admission fee was charged, and from which no one was excluded. Where values had been buried in the code, here they were for all to see: provision of service on equal terms, access to controversial ideas, and the inclusion of authors and groups regardless of their backgrounds or points of view.

Six months later, at the 1939 ALA conference in San Francisco, Ernestine Rose, of the New York Public Library and chair of the association's Adult Education Board, proposed that the council adopt its own Library Bill of Rights. With the coming of World War II, the ALA's executive secretary, Carl Milam, anticipated a rise in censorship and urged the consideration of policies that the ALA might support.[24] The ALA document closely followed Des Moines's preamble and provisions, with only a few changes in emphasis. The policies were to govern the *services* of free public libraries.

The first point calling for selection without regard to the author's face or views was virtually identical, but the second point varied slightly. Where Des Moines called for equal representation of all sides of a controversy, the ALA Library Bill of Rights stated that "all sides of questions on which differences of opinion exist should be represented fairly and adequately in the books and other reading matter purchased for public use." Equity rather than equality was to be the standard for including diverse points of view in collections. In the ALA version, the use of library meeting rooms was to be "for socially useful and cultural activities and the discussion of current public questions," linked to the library's role as "an institution to educate for democratic living." It declared that meeting rooms should be available on equal terms to all groups in the community regardless of their beliefs or affiliations but did not call for meetings that were free and open to the public. Finally, the ALA Library Bill of Rights omitted anything comparable to point 3 of the Des Moines policy, which called on the library to acquire free propaganda materials from various organizations, diversifying its collection and saving money at the same time.[25]

As with the adoption of the Code of Ethics, the ALA did little to publicize or promote its Library Bill of Rights beyond the conference proceedings. In its brevity and its focus on the values that animate library service, the Library Bill of Rights fulfilled the role of ethical code as the 1938 statement had not. And perhaps because it had been so difficult and taken so long to adopt its code, the ALA did not consider revising it again until the 1960s. In the meantime, the Library Bill of Rights was revised in 1948 and then supplemented with the Freedom to Read Statement adopted jointly with publishers and booksellers in 1953. In adopting the Library Bill of Rights, the ALA helped redefine what librarians do and what they stand for.

CODES AS STATEMENTS OF PROFESSIONAL IDENTITY

In the decades between the adoption of the Code of Ethics in 1938 and its next most significant revision in 1975, committees of the ALA tried to square the values embodied in the Library Bill of Rights with the multiple obligations that freighted the code with complexity and ambiguity. In 1960, the Library Administration Division proposed "A Librarian's Code" that sought to define service in terms of access and obligation in terms of service. Beginning with the affirmation that "The librarian serves in one of the essential professions in a good society," it identified the profession's higher purpose to make books and other records of man's experience readily accessible for the education, information, and recreation of all people." The four relationships of 1938 code were now described in terms of serving readers, serving the governing authority, serving colleagues, and serving the library world. Service was the defining shared value, with service to readers coming first. The preamble added an additional obligation to future generations.[26]

Discussion of the proposed revision encountered opposition not only to specific language but to the whole idea of a code of ethics. The Association of College and Research Libraries (ACRL) formally rejected the proposed draft on the basis of arguments articulated by Patricia Paylore, an ACRL board member and assistant librarian at the University of Arizona. Paylore's objections to ethical codes were multifaceted, somewhat contradictory, but also representative of continuing currents of dissatisfaction. The existing code was ineffectual, though well-meaning, she wrote, in part because nobody knew about it or abided by it. Further, most of what the code covered went without saying:

... except for the assertion that our librarian will "defend the library's freedom to select for its readers the books and other materials needed for a useful and representative collection." Yet this is more adequately and eloquently covered in the Library Bill of Rights, which is the most important counsel we need to govern ourselves in what *is* perhaps unique to our profession.

Perhaps most fundamentally, Paylore argued, as did Robert Hauptman a decade later, that right conduct was not governed by codes but by basic human instincts and individual judgment.

There is nothing here in this proposed code which should not be an instinctive and recognized part of our natural equipment as human beings. And I for one resent the implication that my behavior as a professional person of any kind must be codified for me. If I do not recognize my responsibilities to the structure of society by the time I am ready to face the world professionally, no formal code will ever provide this recognition.[27]

Preferring to rely on the power to be ethical that lay within each person's heart, Paylore urged that ACRL reject not only this draft but all such ethical codes in the future. This was not, however, to say the profession should ignore ethics.

Surely the proper place to emphasize ethics in the profession is in the library schools where the meaning of librarianship as well as of professionalism in its most ethical sense should be set forth unmistakably for all to understand. Superimpose this at this point on the basic structure of ethical human behavior in its wider social sense and you will not need a formal code. A man's behavior is better governed by his inner voice. This and this only can tell him what is right and good, and what is not. To this he will respond. To generalities designed to cover all of us erratic and infinitely variegated human beings, he will not.[28]

But indeed, it was this infinite variety of voices within the profession that called for a code of ethics to serve as a standard for all its practitioners and to identify shared values across increasingly diverse areas of specialization.

Subsequent drafts continued the process of defining the profession and identifying its core values. With each new proposal, the emphasis on access as the central dimension of service increased as the multiple obligations receded. Another attempt by the Library Administrative Division in 1968 was notable for its focus on values rather than roles, taken even further in 1970, with a much more concise version beginning, "The objective of the library profession is to serve society by the preservation, presentation, and dissemination of the record of the world's knowledge, experience, and aspirations."[29]

With the ALA's adoption of the Statement on Professional Ethics in 1975, the shift from service to access and from obligations to values was complete. The role of librarians in providing service was to promote access. The introduction established this transcendent professional value and sought by reference to incorporate the ALA's pronouncements on intellectual freedom.

The American Library Association has a special concern for the free flow of information and ideas. Its views have been set forth in such policy statements as the Library Bill of Rights and the Freedom to Read Statement where it has said clearly that in addition to the generally accepted legal and ethical principles and the respect for intellectual freedom which should guide the action of every citizen, membership in the library profession carries with it special obligations and responsibilities.[30]

Those obligations were not to institutions or constituencies or the profession but to the values of the Library Bill of Rights itself. Though it was shortly to be replaced by the 1981 Statement on Ethics, the 1975 statement was the watershed between the old ethical code and the new. The ALA had cast off Bolton's canons at last.

WHOSE CODE IS IT?

As the ALA continued to fine-tune its statement of professional ethics, it wavered in its answer to the question, "Whose code is it?" Plummer called on the individual librarian to meet the standards of the profession. Bolton's canons referred to the librarian but clearly had the library director in mind.

Amy Winslow's version of a code for the staff of the Indianapolis Public Library in 1928 focused on loyalty to the library's various constituencies and stated the personal responsibility of every librarian in the first person:

Since I have chosen to be a librarian there are certain loyalties which I owe to my profession, to my fellows, and to myself. Loyalty to my job, my library, library patrons, the community, my fellow workers, to myself, loyalty to books—the loyalty which is the "why" of all the others.[31]

The ALA's 1938 code set the ethical bar for the professional librarian but in a somewhat impersonal and legalistic way. "The term librarian in this code applies to any person who is employed by a library to do work that is recognized to be professional in character according to the standards established by the American Library Association."

In contrast, the revision proposed by the Library Administration Division in 1968 cast the preamble as a personal pledge to the profession, patrons, and society, and to the values of tradition, service, and freedom.

I pledge according to my best ability and judgment that I will practice my profession with conscience and dignity; the welfare of my patrons will be my first consideration; I will respect the confidences and responsibilities which are bestowed upon me. I will maintain the honor and traditions of the library profession. I will not permit considerations of race, religion, nationality, party politics, personal gain, or social standing to intervene between my duty to my profession and to society. I will maintain the utmost respect for service. Even under threat I will strive for the freedom to read and for the other basic freedoms inherent in a democracy.[32]

The pendulum swung back to the third person in the 1979 draft, but it was librarians, and not the ALA, who had "a special concern for the free flow of information and ideas." Heavily weighted to intellectual freedom, it identified "certain ethical norms which are basic to librarianship." While each citizen had an obligation to generally accepted legal and ethical principles and respect for intellectual freedom, "membership in the library profession carries with it special obligations and responsibilities." These were stated not as declaratives of what librarians do but of what they *should* do:

Know and execute the library's policies and change those conflicting with the spirit of the Library Bill of Rights.

Provide competent and complete professional service both to the individual user and to the clientele as a whole.

Recognize and protect user's right to privacy.

Recognize and avoid situations in which the librarian's personal interests are served or financial benefits are gained at the expense of the employing institution.[33]

After lengthy debate at ALA conferences and in the pages of *Library Journal*, the ALA in 1981 adopted a Statement on Professional Ethics that set the standard for professional conduct, with some revision in 1995, into the twenty-first century. Reverberating in its three-paragraph introduction, longer than its six provisions, were echoes of Plummer's draft, Bolton's canons, the 1938 code, and the endless drafts of the previous decade.

Paragraph one acknowledged these earlier efforts to adopt a code and to proclaim the profession's values both within the association and to society. Further, it declared for the first time in an ALA code that these values were not static, but were shaped by changes in librarianship in response to changes in society.

Since 1939 [sic], the American Library Association has recognized the importance of codifying and making known to the public and the profession the principles which guide librarians in action. This latest revision of the Code of Ethics reflects changes in the nature of the profession and in its social and institutional environment. It should be revised and augmented as necessary.

Perhaps the greatest of these changes had already taken place with the ascendancy of access to information as the central dimension of professional service. This might have been unintentionally acknowledged by a telling slip which gave 1939, the date of the adoption of the Library Bill of Rights, as the beginning of the ALA's recognition of the importance of codifying its ethical values, rather than 1938, when its first code of ethics was approved.

The second paragraph of the 1981 statement defined the profession in terms of access to information, from its selection to its dissemination, and implicitly linked the function of libraries to the maintenance of a democratic government. Information was not for personal growth and cultural enrichment envisioned by adult educators in the 1920s, or for recreational reading, or for practical help for jobseekers, parents, or hobbyists.

Librarians significantly influence or control the selection, organization, preservation, and dissemination of information. In a political system grounded in an informed citizenry, librarians are members of a profession explicitly committed to intellectual freedom and the freedom of access to information. We have a special obligation to ensure the free flow of information to present and future generations.

The third paragraph hinted at the way in which librarians were to provide this service and called for a general standard of personal ethics and professional competence:

Librarians are dependent upon one another for the bibliographical resources that enable us to provide information services, and have obligations for maintaining the highest level of personal integrity and competence.

The 1995 revisions to the 1981 Statement on Ethics were small but telling. First, although the overall shape and language were largely the same, the name was changed from a statement on ethics back to a code of ethics. Second, the introduction no longer talked about "librarians" but "we," that is, the members of the ALA. Rather than focusing on the profession, it represented the views of the profession's association. No longer a powerful statement of professional identity, it was now a description of what ALA members do.

We significantly influence or control the selection, organization, preservation, and dissemination of information. In a political system grounded in an informed citizenry we are members of a profession explicitly committed to intellectual freedom and the freedom of access to information. We have a special obligation to ensure the free flow of information and ideas to present and future generations.[34]

In contrast to the 1981 statement's emphatic call for adherence, with "librarians must" reiterated throughout, the 1995 code used more descriptive language, "we do this and that," suggesting that the standards had already been met. Since membership included professional and nonprofessional staff members, library trustees, and library supporters, the code weakened the primary purpose of the earliest statements of library ethics: to claim and define the unique professional identity and status of librarians.

The 1995 code added two provisions to the six formulated in the 1981 predecessor. Article IV stated that "we adhere to standards of intellectual property."* Article VIII stated that librarians take advantage of professional development opportunities. While representing important dimensions of professional conduct, neither embodied a central ethical value. Copyright is a legal obligation binding upon all users of information, with important implications for access. Professional development is a responsibility of all professionals, not uniquely that of librarians, with important implications for service.

SPECIALIZED CODES OF ETHICS

As the oldest and largest association supporting libraries and librarians, and with constituent parts representing various types of libraries, the ALA sets the standard for the profession as a whole merely because of its first claim, tradition, and size. Under the umbrella of the ALA and other library organizations, librarians at work in different settings serve varied constituencies and face diverse ethical challenges. Though Carl Roden sought the one big idea that would lift the profession to a higher calling, the process of professionalization inevitably led to specialization and fragmentation. Writing on the theme "Our Common, Unifying Objective" in 1947, Mary Utopia Rothrock, librarian of the Tennessee Valley Authority and president of the ALA, saw the library profession following a pattern similar to that of other professions.

---

*In 2008, this was modified to read, "We respect intellectual property rights and advocate balance between the interests of information users and rights holders."

A few individuals are moved to join together to address a social need, then organize to advance their interests, acquire technical skills, develop professional training and establish professional standards. As the profession grows, more specialized work leads to the creation of separate groups which repeat this evolutionary pattern.

Rothrock perceived hidden dangers in this apparent success.

With increasing specialization the inclusive, unifying objective around which the organization was formed tends to fade from consciousness; members within separate, specialized groups lose in some degree their sense of significant participation in the total effort. When this happens the members lose much of the satisfaction which comes from group accomplishment, and the organization loses forcefulness and vitality in advancing the objectives of the profession and in helping its individual members. The point of diminishing returns has been reached.[35]

This cycle repeated itself both in the establishment of specialized library organizations and in their formulation of codes of ethics applicable to their communities of practitioners. Where the ALA had once been the fount of ethical wisdom, specialization of the profession led inevitably to the adoption of ethical codes reflecting their unique professional identities, multifaceted responsibilities, and diverse obligations. Evolving from practice, these differences are reflected in variations in professional priorities and interpretations of the core values that continue to characterize and unite the library profession.

SPECIALIZED CODES FOR SPECIAL LIBRARIANS

More specialized codes of ethics followed the ALA code at an accelerated pace, reflecting division and compartmentalization within the profession. Having spurred the creation of more specialized library associations, the ALA continued to serve as a unifying presence for professional status and identity. The very success of librarians set in motion divisions within the newly established profession as subgroups sought to differentiate themselves and establish their own professional identity. While these subgroups did not initially create separate codes of ethics, after the adoption of the 1981 statement and the 1995 code, virtually all the constituent parts of the ALA as well as the specialized independent associations of librarians codified and publicized their ethical standards. Like their predecessors, these codes combined definitions of professional identity with statements of core values and reiterations of multiple obligations. While sharing the core values of the profession, their varying interpretations of service, access, conflicts of interest, and confidentiality demonstrate the diverse settings in which librarians work, the variety of materials they preserve and make available, and the different clienteles they serve. Here are some examples:

Law Librarians

The American Association of Law Libraries (AALL) specifically modeled its first professional code on that of the ALA, stating in its background information, "The Code of Ethics incorporates by reference the ALA Code of Ethics which has been revised twice since the AALL Code was adopted." The most recent statement of AALL Ethical Principles, adopted by the membership of the organization on April 5, 1999, identifies the professional role of law librarians with both public and private purposes and clientele. On the public and personal side, its preamble states that the members of AALL, by providing ready access to legal information, enable people to participate fully in the affairs of their government. On the private and institutional side, legal information professionals promote the interests and respect the values of their clientele, including law firms, corporations, and academic law libraries. Asserting the professional status of law librarians and the values underlying their practice, the preamble states that these diverse information needs

are best addressed by professionals committed to the belief that serving these information needs is a noble calling and that fostering the equal participation of diverse people in library services underscores one of our basic tenets, open access to information for all individuals.[36]

The AALL code is organized around both values and obligations. Service, to be discussed more fully later, includes open and effective access to legal information and the protection of confidentiality and privacy. At the same time, work within a legal setting imposes limits on that service to avoid the unauthorized practice of law. Business relationships require fair and ethical trade practices, avoidance of personal gain, and wise use of resources. Professional responsibilities include cooperative relationships with colleagues, respect for intellectual property, and the separation of personal conviction and professional duties. Thus, while it incorporates the four core values of librarianship, providing service, facilitating access, protecting privacy, and avoiding conflicts of interest, the AALL code organizes and states them in ways appropriate to the settings in which they work.

Health Sciences Librarians

Similarly, the Code of Ethics for Health Sciences Librarianship, adopted by the Medical Library Association in 1994, embraces the core values of librarianship within a web of relationships. To society, medical librarians owe access to medical information; to clients, they owe unbiased service, protection of privacy, and the best available information; to the institution, they provide leadership and expertise "in the design, development, and ethical management of knowledge-based information systems"; to the profession, they are obliged to respect its philosophy and ideals, advance its knowledge and standards, and demonstrate courtesy, respect, and professional integrity; and to self, they must be personally responsible for professional excellence.[37]

Special Collections Librarians

The code of ethics adopted by special collections librarians offers a further example of a specialized community of librarians identifying with shared professional goals while interpreting them in the distinct environment in which they practice.

"Standards for Ethical Conduct for Rare Book, Manuscript, and Special Collections Librarians" was formulated in 1987 by the Association of College and Research Libraries (ACRL) to amplify and supplement the Code of Ethics of the ALA of which it is a constituent part. Lengthy and detailed, it appeared in a second edition in 1993; recast as the ACRL Code of Ethics for Special Collections Librarians, it was approved in October 2003. The preamble highlights how librarians working in special collections share the values of their professional colleagues while carrying additional responsibilities imposed by the materials in their care.

In this case, professional identity dramatically influences professional priorities and obligations. On one hand, the preamble begins with commonalities:

Special collections librarians share fundamental values with the entire library profession. They should be thoroughly familiar with the ALA Code of Ethics and adhere to principles of fairness, freedom, professional excellence, and respect of individual rights expressed therein.

On the other hand, librarians working in special collections have obligations to their materials and to posterity that set them apart from their professional colleagues.

Furthermore, special collections librarians have extraordinary responsibilities and opportunities associated with the care of cultural property, the preservation of original artifacts, and the support of scholarship based on primary research materials.

Acknowledging that, "At times their commitment to free access to information may conflict with their mission to protect and preserve objects in their care," the code relies for resolution on the professional expertise of special collections librarians.

When values come into conflict, librarians must bring their experience and judgment to bear on each case in order to arrive at the best solution, always bearing in mind that the constituency for special collections includes future generations.[38]

A special collections librarian is defined as an employee of a special collections library or any staff member whose duties involve working with special collections materials. While the code applies primarily to professional staff, it asserts the need for all library staff to avoid potential and apparent conflicts of interest. Just as law librarians must eschew any unauthorized practice of law, special collections librarians must be ever attentive to potential conflicts of interest.

Archivists

Facing many of the same tensions between preservation and access, archivists have adhered to codes that recognize their multiple obligations. A succinct code formulated by Wayne C. Grover, archivist of the United States from 1948 to 1965, and reissued by the National Archives and Records Administration in 1985, began with the obligation to preserve records: "The Archivist has a moral obligation to society to take every possible measure to ensure the preservation of valuable records, not only those of the past but those of his own times, and with equal zeal."[39] A much more detailed Code of Ethics for Archivists, approved by the Council of the Society of American Archivists in 1992, began with a statement of professional definition: "Archivists select, preserve, and make available documentary materials of long-term value that have lasting values to the organization or public that the archivist serves."[40] Much like the 1938 Code of Ethics for Librarians, this code for archivists combined descriptions of what archivists do (transfer, organize, and appraise documents), with cautions about how to do it (answer questions courteously, avoid irresponsible criticism), with ethical values held in common with librarianship (the need to respect privacy and avoid conflicts of interest).

A much shortened Code of Ethics for Archivists, approved in 2005, defined archivist in the code's preamble. "The term 'archivist' as used in this code encompasses all those concerned with the selection, control, care, preservation, and administration of historical and documentary records of enduring value."[41] In contrast to the 1992 code, this version is briefly stated and organized around general attributes (professional relationships, judgment, and trust), with specifically professional values (protection of authenticity and integrity of the records, promoting equitable and open access, protecting the privacy rights of donors and users, and keeping documentary materials from harm).

To varying degrees, each of the ALA's codes and those of the more specialized library and archival organizations center around four values that librarians have in common: providing service, ensuring access to information, avoiding conflicts of interest, and protecting confidentiality. Of these, service, confidentiality, and avoidance of conflicts of interest are common to other professions, but they take on a particular meaning and ethical dimension in the context of library practice. The fourth, providing access to information, has become the central ethical value of librarianship and the one that is unique to the library profession.

In the following chapters, we will see how the ethical obligation to provide access to information shapes our understanding of each of the others. Although these values will be considered separately, we will note many ways in which they are interconnected and how often they are defined and measured in terms of one another. We will also look at how societal change, shifting demographics, and technological innovation require the constant reexamination and reinterpretation of the profession's core values. Finally, we will ask whether questions about the concept of professionalism itself threaten to undermine the basis for ethical standards applied to a defined professional group.

END NOTES

1. John Swan, "Lies, Damned Lies, and Democracy" in *The Freedom to Lie* by John Swan and Noel Peattie. Jefferson, NC: McFarland, 1989, 22.

2. Lester Asheim, "Librarians as Professionals," *Library Trends* 27 (Winter 1979): 227, quoting from Louis D. Brandeis, *Business—A Profession*. Boston: Small, Maynard and Co., 1914.

3. Helen E. Haines, "Ethics of Librarianship," *Library Journal* 71 (June 15, 1946): 848–851. Talk given for the Southern California Chapter of the Special Libraries Association at California Institute of Technology, Pasadena, March 20, 1946.

4. Pierce Butler, "Librarianship as a Profession," *Library Quarterly* 21 (October 1951): 238.

5. "Code of Ethics for Librarians [adopted by ALA Council, December 29, 1938]." *ALA Bulletin* 33 (February 1939): 128–130; *Intellectual Freedom Manual*, 7th ed. Chicago: American Library Association, 2006, 255–259. The manual refers to it as the 1939 code although it was adopted in 1938, and early commentators referred to it as the 1938 code (as does this volume).

6. Mary W. Plummer, "The Pros and Cons of Training for Librarianship," *Public Libraries* 8 (May 1903): 212. For more information on Plummer, see Mary Niles Maack, "No Philosophy Carries So Much Conviction as the Personal Life: Mary Wright Plummer as an Independent Woman," *Library Quarterly* 70 (January 2000): 1–46.

7. Ibid.

8. Plummer, "Pros and Cons," 208.

9. Charles Knowles Bolton, "The Librarian's Canon of Ethics," *Public Libraries* 14 (June 1909): 203; Charles Knowles Bolton, "The Ethics of Librarianship: A Proposal for a Revised Code," *Annals of the American Academy* 101 (May 1922): 138–146.

10. Bolton, "The Ethics of Librarianship," 138.

11. Bolton's advisers included Librarian of Congress Herbert Putnam, Josephine Rathbone of Pratt Institute, Azariah Root, librarian of Oberlin College, and Phineas Windsor, librarian of the University of Illinois.

12. Bolton, "The Ethics of Librarianship," 145.

13. Bolton, "The Ethics of Librarianship," 138.

14. Melvil Dewey, "The Profession," *Library Journal* 1, no. 1 (September 30, 1876); quoted in Helen E. Haines, "Ethics of Librarianship," *Library Journal* 71 (June 15, 1946): 848–851; reprinted in Dianne J. Ellsworth and Norman D. Stevens, *Landmarks of Library Literature, 1876–1976*. Metuchen, NJ: Scarecrow Press, 1976, 21–23.

15. Melvil Dewey, "Next Half-Century," *Library Journal* 51 (October 15, 1926): 888.

16. Alvin Johnson, *Pioneer's Progress*. New York: Viking Press, 1937, 237.

17. C. C. Williamson, *Training for Library Service: A Report Prepared for the Carnegie Corporation of New York*. Boston: 1923.

18. William S. Learned, *The American Public Library and the Diffusion of Knowledge*. New York: Harcourt, Brace, 1924.

19. Louis Round, "Restudying the Library Chart," *ALA Bulletin* 30 (June 1936): 484.

20. "Code of Ethics for Librarians [adopted by ALA Council, December 29, 1938]." *ALA Bulletin* 33 (February 1939): 128–130; *Intellectual Freedom Manual*, 7th ed. Chicago: American Library Association, 2006, 255–259.

21. Carl B. Roden, "The Librarian's Duty to His Profession," *Library Journal* 47 (July 1922): 597–598.

22. Marci Lingo, "Forbidden Fruit: The Banning of *The Grapes of Wrath* in the Kern County Free Library," *Libraries & Culture* 38 (Fall 2003): 351–377.

23. "The Library's Bill of Rights," *ALA Bulletin* 33 (January 1939) [inside back cover]. Adopted by the Des Moines [Public Library] Board of Trustees, November 21, 1938; *Intellectual Freedom Manual*, 7th ed., 57–58.

24. Peggy Sullivan, *Carl H. Milam and the American Library Association*. New York: H. W. Wilson, 1976, 276.

25. *Intellectual Freedom Manual*, 7th ed., 57–58.

26. "A Librarian's Code 1960," reprinted in Jonathan A. Lindsey and Ann E. Prentice, *Professional Ethics and Librarians*. Phoenix, AZ: Oryx Press, 1985, 45–46.

27. Patricia P. Paylore, "A Note on the Proposed 'A Librarian's Code'," *College and Research Libraries* 22 (March 1961): 163–164.

28. Paylore, "A Note," 164.

29. Code of Ethics Proposed Revision [1970], reprinted in Lindsey and Prentice, *Professional Ethics*, 52.

30. "Statement on Professional Ethics, 1975," Lindsey and Prentice, *Professional Ethics*, 53.

31. "A Librarian's Code: From the Practice Book of the Indianapolis Public Library," *Library Occurrent* 8, no. 7 (July–September 1928): 234–235.

32. "1968 Code of Ethics for Librarians—A Draft Proposal," reprinted in Lindsey and Prentice, *Professional Ethics*, 47.

33. "[1979] Draft Statement on Professional Ethics," reprinted in Lindsey and Prentice, *Professional Ethics*, 62–63.

34. American Library Association Code of Ethics adopted by ALA Council, June 28, 1995.

35. Mary U. Rothrock, "Our Common, Unifying Objective," *ALA Bulletin* 41 (January 1947): 12.

36. AALL Ethical Principles, approved by the AALL Membership, April 5, 1999, http://www.aallnet.org/about/policy_ethics.asp.

37. Code of Ethics for Health Sciences Librarianship, 1994, Medical Library Association, http://www.mlanet.org/about/ethics.html.

38. Code of Ethics for Special Collections Librarians adopted by the Association of College and Research Libraries, October 2003, http://www.rbms.info/standards/code_of_ethics.shtml.

39. The Archivist's Code, reissued by the National Archives and Records Administration, April, 1985.

40. Code of Ethics for Archivists, adopted by the Council of the Society of American Archivists, 1992.

41. Code of Ethics for Archivists, approved the Society of American Archivists Council, February 5, 2005, http://www.archivists.org/governance/handbook/app_ethics.asp.

2

SERVICE: BY WHOM

The librarian was the central figure in early codes of ethics, the key player in Mary Plummer's quest for professionalism and in Charles Knowles Bolton's canons for efficiently administered libraries. Early ethical obligations were defined in terms of the librarian's multiple relationships. Although Andrew Carnegie's gift of public libraries did not require communities to hire professional librarians, the Carnegie Corporation came to see that librarians, not just library buildings, are essential to professional service. The 1995 ethical code of the ALA calls for the "highest level of service" and "equitable service policies." In the age of the Internet, how do we define that service—by whom, for whom, of what kind?

In the constellation of ethical values, service is the polestar guiding the practice of librarians through generations of practice and across the profession. But when we speak of the ethics of library service, what do we mean? The ethical requirements of service are constantly in motion as our practice and our understanding change. We have noted that our understanding of ethics is constantly deepening. Similarly, our concept of service is continuously expanding as we meet the information needs of new groups of users and introduce new information technologies. Thus, any code merely captures the ethical obligations of the moment and represents an incomplete definition of "service." In this changing universe, what are the fundamental ethical obligations in providing service?

Service takes its meaning from the institutional setting in which librarians and other information professionals practice. While the codes of more specialized library organizations repeat the core values of service, access, protection of confidentiality, and avoidance of conflicts of interests, the ways in

which these values are interpreted, prioritized, and implemented vary
with institutional mission, collections, and clientele. But while the type and
level of service is determined by the library's mission, the presence of
professionally trained librarians makes a library more than a collection of information resources. So our discussion of the ethics of service starts with
the question—service by whom? Then, in Chapter Three—service for
whom?

THE "WE" IN LIBRARY SERVICE

In 1879, Melvil Dewey formulated a motto for the ALA that might be
taken as its first statement of the ethics of service: "The best reading for the
largest numbers, at the least expense."[1] Modified slightly in 1892 to declare,
"The best reading for the largest number at the least cost,"[2] the motto
defined a threefold obligation for librarians: to determine what was "best"
for readers, to extend the reach of the library to serve the greatest number,
and to exercise stewardship over what was viewed in the late nineteenth century as a public trust. Formulated at the very beginning of the public library
movement, this definition of service was sufficiently broad to accommodate
the professionalization of librarianship, the spread of Carnegie libraries, the
investment of the Carnegie Corporation in library adult education and
library extension, and the beginnings of the quest for federal aid to support
public libraries in unserved areas, all before the ALA adopted its first code of
ethics in 1938.

Despite Dewey's emphasis on library education as an aspect of professionalism, and the establishment of a number of library schools following
Columbia in 1887, the spread of public libraries far outstripped the supply
of trained librarians and the ability of small public libraries to hire them. As
we saw in Chapter One, Alvin Johnson's 1914 report on the impact of Carnegie library buildings highlighted deficiencies in libraries that lacked
trained librarians.[3] By the time the 1938 code was adopted, the ALA had a
half century of experience demonstrating that professional staff was the
essential component of quality library service. The presence of a professional librarian promised to enhance the ability of the entire staff and library
board to address issues in an ethical way.

Nonetheless, none of the codes of ethics adopted by the ALA has linked
professional training with the ethical standard of service. When the 1995
ALA Code of Ethics declared that "we provide the highest level of service,"
it suggested rather than required the presence of a professional librarian. It
assumed that the "we," that is, ALA members who are librarians, along
with library staff and library board members, would be adequately trained
and supported to assure "appropriate and usefully organized resources;
equitable service policies; equitable access; and accurate, unbiased, and

courteous responses to all requests."[4] Similarly, though each of the codes of specialized library associations speaks to the nature of service within their institutional settings, the presence of a professional librarian is assumed rather than required.

Decisions concerning the qualifications for staff and continued professional development create the framework for quality service. Since the professionalization of librarianship took place over a period of decades, larger and more affluent libraries were able to offer the higher salaries commanded by librarians with both college training and master's degrees. When the code of ethics calls for the highest level of service, at what point does the failure to hire a professional librarian become an ethical issue?

QUESTIONS

- Is it ethical to say that library service is just as good in a library without a professionally trained librarian?

- Is it ethical to set lower standards for professional positions in smaller libraries?

- Is it ethical to employ paraprofessionals to provide reference service, readers' advisory, and develop library collections?

CREDENTIALS

Despite the growth of library schools, the recommendations of the Williamson report, the move from practical training to academic preparation of librarians, and the role of the ALA in accrediting library programs, the ALA has not supported a consistent definition of "librarian." As late as 1940, Ralph Munn, director of the Carnegie Library in Pittsburgh and president of the ALA, declared:

Some people are librarians; others just work in libraries. This division has nothing to do with the importance of the position; a junior assistant may be a librarian, while his chief may just work in a library. Attitude is the sole basis of distinction.

The librarian thinks of himself as a member of a professional group whose work is important to society. His interest is automatically extended far beyond his own daily duties; all of the factors which influence library service as a whole are of concern to him, even though some of them may seem to have little bearing on his own immediate welfare.[5]

Reviewing the status of library development in the United States, Munn concluded "that we have too few librarians and too many people who just work in libraries."

In 1995, *Library Journal* editor John N. Berry III objected to the "exclusionary elitism" that would focus efforts of the ALA on behalf of librarians to the detriment of library support staff. Commenting on the decision of the Virginia Library Association to change its name from *Virginia Librarian* to *Virginia Libraries*, Berry wrote:

It cheapens our claim to "professional" status when we try to validate it by closing our institutions or organizations to other classes of library workers. The class we most often mistreat, support staff, has been our most productive source of new recruits. That posturing has gained us very little, and almost always it has carried a petty elitist tone. Much of it seems to stem from a defensive reaction, from the notion that we must protect the gates of our calling to prevent entry to our practice by hordes of inferior people who we imagine are dying to work as librarians, without the benefit of an MLS![6]

Instead, all who support libraries should be welcomed, especially support staff. "To exclude them," declared Berry, "is misguided discrimination against our natural allies, other library workers."

In several notable cases, the ALA has taken a strong public stand, insisting that libraries be headed by professionally trained librarians. As part of its quest for professional status and recognition, the ALA opposed the appointment of Archibald MacLeish to succeed Herbert Putnam as Librarian of Congress in 1939 because MacLeish, a lawyer, poet, and New Dealer, was "not a librarian." Putnam, also a lawyer, was not a library school graduate when he was named Librarian of Congress in 1899, but he had directed public libraries in Minneapolis and Boston. Similar objections arose over the appointments of Daniel Boorstin as Librarian of Congress in 1975 and James Billington in 1987. Herbert Putnam had envisioned the Library of Congress as a sort of university where librarians with subject expertise functioned as the institution's faculty. In the academic world, the tradition of appointing a scholar to head university libraries is well-established, as at Harvard, where political scientist Sidney Verba and historian Robert Darnton have recently headed the university library. More often the position requires both professional library training, management experience, and a doctoral degree.

Despite its public protestations, the ALA itself has not adopted a consistent stand in defending the master of library science (MLS) as the professional qualification. The *Merwine* case[7] raised the question of whether a university could require an MLS degree from an ALA-accredited school as one of the qualifications for an academic library position. Librarians testified on both sides, with a personnel officer from the Library of Congress asserting, on behalf of the plaintiff, that an MLS was not required for professional positions at the Library of Congress, while Edward Holley, dean of the library school at the University of North Carolina, representing library educators, appeared for the defendant university. Claiming that the issues were too complex, the ALA did not take a position. The large number of school library media specialists in the ALA who are not required to have an MLS has complicated the ALA's ability to take a stand.

THE *MERWINE* CASE (1980)

In 1980, Glenda Merwine applied for a faculty librarian position at Mississippi State University (MSU) in the College of Veterinary Medicine branch. The job announcement specified that applicants should hold a master's degree in library science from an ALA-accredited school. At the time, Merwine was completing a master's degree in education with a major in secondary education and library science. The search committee, however, did not consider any candidates who did not hold a library degree from an accredited program, and when a male applicant was hired, Merwine sued Mississippi State University and George Lewis, director of the university's Mitchell Memorial Library. She alleged sex discrimination and challenged the appropriateness of the requirement of an ALA-MLS degree for an entry-level position. MSU had adopted that as the hiring standard for professional library positions in 1978 as a means to upgrade its staff.

At trial, Merwine introduced expert witnesses to make the case that her qualifications and expertise were equivalent to those applicants who held an ALA-MLS degree, although the position announcement did not provide for equivalent experience. Glen Zimmerman, from the personnel office at the Library of Congress (LC), testified that LC did not require its professional librarians to hold an ALA-accredited master's degree, nor in fact, any library degree. Job announcements for positions at LC included an educational requirement of an MLS degree, not necessarily from an accredited program, and allowed applicants to substitute relevant experience, a practice throughout the federal government. In a later letter to *American Libraries*, Zimmerman wrote, "In the case of professional librarian positions in the library, some individuals with a high school education with the requisite related experience meet LC's basic minimum educational qualifications."

Appearing for the university, Dean Edward Holley, of the University of North Carolina School of Information and Library Science, testified to the appropriateness of requiring a MLS degree from an ALA-accredited school for an entry-level position in an academic library. The jury heard evidence that 80 to 90 percent of all academic libraries had such a requirement, that the requirement assured that the applicant had received appropriate instruction from an institution of recognized academic standards, and that those holding degrees from ALA-accredited programs were superior in reliability and dependability compared to those without such degrees.

After hearing both sides, the jury found for Merwine and against the university and George Lewis, director of the library. It found that Merwine was qualified for the position and that she had been denied the job because of favored treatment to a male applicant. She was awarded $5,000 in actual damages and $5,000 in punitive damages. On a motion by Lewis, however, the magistrate entered a judgment notwithstanding the verdict and dismissed the plaintiff's claims on the grounds that no reasonable jury could have concluded that Merwine was qualified for the job.

Merwine appealed directly to the 5th Circuit Court of Appeals, which upheld the magistrate's judgment. The appellate court found that

The uncontradicted evidence establishes that the ALA-MLS degree is a legitimate nondiscriminatory standard for hiring academic librarians. It is a standard widely recognized and utilized by academic and professional employers, including the United States Supreme Court. [638]

Regardless of Merwine's education or experience, the court held that they did not meet the published minimum requirements for the position. The court considered such an objective educational standard to be a business necessity that relieved the university of the burden of subjective judgments concerning the academic qualifications of job applicants.

Since the central question in the Merwine case dealt with the appropriateness of requiring an ALA-accredited degree for an entry-level job, what role did the ALA play in the litigation? After some consideration, the ALA declined to take a position, claiming that the issues were "too complex." Its failure to defend its own degree was noted and criticized in the library press. Writing in *American Libraries*, J. Periam Danton, former dean of the Graduate School of Librarianship at the University of California at Berkeley, commended Edward Holley's willingness to testify in the case and chastised the ALA for its unwillingness to take a stand. He asked, "Does ALA *really* stand behind the requirement of an ALA-accredited MLS for most professional positions in most libraries?" If so, he declared, the ALA must be prepared to back up its commitment in the court. Otherwise, repeated undefended challenges will erode the status and the effect of the degree and, ultimately, the profession.

QUESTIONS

- What are the ethical implications of decisions about hiring standards for library positions?
- When defining job qualifications, do library employers have an ethical obligation to the profession as well as to their institutions?
- What might be the consequences of a decision to set a higher educational standard for professional employees?

- Does a professional organization such as the ALA have a stake in the hiring qualifications for librarians?

SOURCES

Coe, Polly. [rebuttal of Edward Holley] *American Libraries* 15 (June 1984): 376–377.
Coe was a member of the ALA Office for Library Personnel Resources (OLPR) Advisory Committee.
Danton, Periam J. [Reader Forum] "Will ALA Defend Its MLS?" *American Libraries* 15 (July/August1984): 484.
Holley, Edward. "The Merwine Case and the MLS Degree: Where Was ALA?" *American Libraries* 15 (May 1984): 327–330.
Merwine v. Board of Trustees for State Institutions of Higher Learning, 754 F. 2d 631 (5th Cir. 1985).
Zimmerman, Glen. [Reader Forum] "LC Personnel Policies re MLS," *American Libraries* 15 (July/August 1984): 482, 484.

The ALA has since taken the position that the MLS is the basic professional qualification. Nonetheless, it has sent mixed signals as to whether it is most interested in promoting librarians or libraries. Its National Library Week celebration most often focuses on libraries and only occasionally on librarians, as it did in with the slogan, "When you absolutely have to know, ask a librarian." More recently, the ALA has celebrated National Library Workers Day, honoring not just librarians but all who work in libraries. Seeking to support the interests of paraprofessionals, the ALA established the American Library Association Allied Professional Association, "the organization for the advancement of library workers."[8] Though it provides data on salaries and offers resources to improve benefits for both MLS librarians and support staff, it also illustrates the blurred line separating professional from nonprofessional. The hiring in 1999 of Emily Sheketoff, a public relations specialist, to head the ALA's Washington office raised similar questions. In the past, this position had been held by library practitioners who, drawing on their experience and connections, represented the interests of the library community before Congress. While work with government agencies and media experience are valuable skills for the position, the ALA seemed to undermine its own claims for professional education and library experience in shaping the values and worldview of librarianship.[9]

This trend mirrors what has happened in other professions, with paralegals assisting lawyers in research and filing, nurse practitioners and physician's assistants taking over tasks from doctors, and dental hygienists doing routine work for dentists. In each of these cases, however, the professional status of lawyer, dentist, doctor, and nurse is protected by licensing requirements. The line remains clearly drawn between professionals on one side and all the rest on the other. The use of such titles as chief executive officer of a public library, executive director of a library system, or dean of the university library, in an academic setting, rather than librarian, further obscures the identity of librarians who are professionally trained.

In some cases, budget constraints prevent hiring a professional librarian. In very small libraries, state requirements to hire library directors with master's degrees in library science may impose budgetary demands that jeopardize the library's ability to remain open. Here is an example where the ethical obligation to provide the highest level of service may conflict with the library's ability to provide any service. State certification requirements that set standards according to the population served and specify completion of library science courses rather than the master's degree represent a compromise between service and access. Requirements for additional training for the library director as the library's population base expands reflect the complexity of delivering service to a larger population but also implicitly acknowledge the resulting variations in service. A library board trying to balance staff credentials against hours, collections, and programs must determine what the highest level of service means in a situation of chronic underfunding.

The use of paraprofessionals raises the same questions of professionalism and service. In an opinion piece questioning the ethics of using paraprofessionals at the reference desk, Steve McKinzie, a social science librarian at Dickinson College, argued that the practice violated the standard of the ALA's Code of Ethics calling for the highest level of service and "accurate, unbiased, and courteous responses to all requests." McKinzie asked how librarians could regard their professional reference responsibilities "as something almost anyone can do every bit as well as a librarian."

Librarians, with their innate sense of egalitarianism, their intrinsic parsimoniousness, and their mock modesty, may be reluctant to insist on professional standards and professional responsibilities. They may be unwilling to claim there are some things that librarians can do and no one else. That is understandable, but it is also tragic. It is a mistake for us to undervalue the quality of professional library service, just as it is a dereliction of our responsibilities to underplay our users' needs. It comes down to this: If librarians aren't willing to champion the uniqueness of their calling and the professional dimensions of the profession, then who will?[10]

"As librarians," McKinzie concluded, "we should insist that our professional ethics demand the highest possible quality of traditional library service."

In response, Vickie Salonen, a reference associate in an academic library, rejected the idea that trained paraprofessionals were incapable of delivering high quality reference service and argued that, even in libraries not headed by directors with library degrees, the clientele "receive the same services expected from the 'professional.'" Salonen reported that training at paraprofessional "boot camp," consultation with other staff members, and shared expertise ensured quality service. "Professional ethics, however, need not exclude those who work the frontlines. … Ethical standards need not be elitist."[11]

As we shall see repeatedly, the values declared in statements of professional ethics govern the conduct of all members of a library's staff. Whether professional librarians, trustees, or support staff, all who work in and for the library must be aware of and uphold its ethical obligations. While an ethical code may define a profession, its values must be implemented at all levels. When the Federal Bureau of Investigation launched its Library Awareness Program in the 1980s, looking for possible subversives using unclassified material in academic libraries, agents routinely approached low-level public service staff rather than library managers. While library directors could be expected to know the rules protecting patron confidentiality, circulation staff might be unfamiliar with this obligation and more easily pressured to provide information. An ethical obligation is an institutional as well as a personal one; the protection must be provided regardless of which staffer is in charge.

In the Internet age, professional boundaries are breaking down as new disciplines move into the information field. Schools of library and information science have morphed into iSchools, working with or competing against programs in communications, informatics, and computer science. Associate and bachelor's degrees are adding multiple options for the student interested in information work. Though the MLS degree is the established professional standard, the Internet and the World Wide Web have made information users and information creators of us all. This has generated welcome new interest in library careers among younger students who see libraries as information centers offering the gamut of electronic media. It also has leveled the playing field between librarian and user. Expertise and control no longer apply in the Web 2.0 world.

Among journalists who are experiencing the same effects of ubiquitous information access, the line between professional and amateur and between reporter and blogger becomes less important to users who seek news from sources of greater variety and more questionable authority. While the path to professional journalism less often leads through graduate study than in librarianship, some journalists now reject "professional" status as requiring unwanted obedience to outside standards. Some regard the traditional professional privileges, such as access to government press conferences, as low-level licenses to practice. In such an environment, questions about professional identity and definition abound. Which "journalists" must adhere to standards of professional ethics, and which may benefit from professional standing? In *We Are All Journalists Now*, media lawyer Scott Gant argues that journalists should be defined by the work they do rather than the institutions for which they work. Using such a functional approach allows a journalist to be defined as anyone who gathers information for the purpose of making it available to others. (Under this definition, librarians would qualify as journalists.) It also frees professional status from the requirements of education or experience. The long-sought prize of professional status, Gant suggests, may prove to be a chimera, the end of a misguided quest that undermines the work itself by making those who hold it indebted to those who grant the privileges that make the work possible.[12]

ENFORCEMENT

The lack of a clear line between professionals and all others involved in librarianship also complicates enforcement of the ALA Code of Ethics. Unlike in law and medicine, where the professional status of lawyer and doctor is unambiguous, in librarianship, the title "librarian" does not necessarily connote education, credentials, or experience. When an ethics code is that of a professional organization such as ALA or the American Society for Information Science and Technology (ASIS&T), and the membership is a mix of practitioners, scholars, supporters, board members, and employers, there is no ability to exclude from professional status those who violate the organization's ethical code. In the United Kingdom, membership in the Chartered Institute of Library and Information Professionals (CILIP) is limited to those who qualify on the basis of specific standards, including coursework. Like ALA, CILIP has issued principles of conduct and an ethical code. On its Web site, it provides guidance, through case studies, for compliance with its standards and a hotline for consultation. Further, however, it has empowered a disciplinary panel to hear charges brought against its members and to take action, including punishment and expulsion of proven violators.[13]

The ALA has only briefly, and unsuccessfully, tried to police the conduct of libraries for violation of the Library Bill of Rights. Writing in response to an article by Lee Finks that critiqued the ALA's ethical codes, Richard Stichler proposed the American Association of University Professors (AAUP) as a model. Using local and statewide membership chapters, the AAUP places responsibility for ethical conduct on individual institutions of higher education with violations reported to the AAUP. Censure by the AAUP is believed to put institutions in poor repute, making it more difficult to attract students, recruit faculty, win grants, and solicit outside support.[14]

The situation resembles that faced in journalism where "journalists" may be graduates of journalism programs or may lack formal professional training altogether. The Society of Professional Journalists has its own code of ethics,[15] and most states have enacted shield laws that protect journalists from having to divulge the identity of their sources. The definition of "professional" journalist has been further complicated by the myriad writers, bloggers, and reviewers who are journalists outside of a traditional media environment. The lack of professional definition again raises questions about who is obliged to abide by journalistic ethics and which journalists are protected by shield laws.

CONSISTENCY

The use of professionally trained staff ensures not only a minimum level of quality service but also a degree of consistent service. A uniform standard for professional status makes it more likely that responses to user needs will reflect professional expertise rather than personal values. Paradoxically, it also better equips librarians to make exceptions in a consistent, principled way, since shared training and values will influence how exceptions are made.

Library trustees, who are largely responsible for hiring the directors of public libraries, have their own organization within the ALA and their own code of ethics. The first Ethics Statement for Public Library Trustees, adopted by the boards of directors of the American Library Trustees Association (ALTA) and the Public Library Association (PLA) on June 5, 1985, made library service an integral part of trustee obligations, stating in its first provision, "Trustees must promote a high level of library service while observing ethical standards." In 1988, this mention of service was removed, however, and the emphasis put on the ethical conduct of the trustees rather than on their duty to ensure library service. The modified version, approved by the PLA, reads, "Trustees, in the capacity of trust upon them, shall observe ethical standards with absolute truth, integrity, and honor."[16]

The selection of a library's director is among the chief responsibilities of library trustees. In setting the requirements for this position, board members are determining the level and quality of the library's service. Do library boards make ethical decisions about the level of service the library can provide when they set the hiring standards for its director and determine support for professional development? If the director is not required to have professional training, then services provided by nonprofessionals, including reference, collection development, and programming, will not receive professional guidance or oversight.

Without a requirement for minimal levels of professional preparation, disparities in staffing create the possibility of discrepancies in levels of service and inconsistencies in the delivery of service. In 1981, the ALA undertook a publicity campaign to promote its newly adopted Statement on Professional Ethics. Using *Ethical Sin Lists* proposing possible ethical issues and a feature in *American Libraries*, the ALA invited librarians to consider how they would respond to ethical dilemmas. The very first hypothetical posed by "Is It Ethical?" involved the meaning of service in what appeared to be a straightforward situation. "A patron requests an auto repair manual, then asks the librarian to name a good mechanic. The librarian knows one; but is it proper to offer a name?"[17] The inclination to be helpful and provide service suggests that the librarian should share the mechanic's name; professionalism suggests not. Since a personal recommendation would depend upon the identity and experience of the person behind the desk, rather than on consumer information sources in print and online, it would be no better than the patron asking a stranger at a bus stop. The expertise that librarians bring to their positions from training and experience is what differentiates the highest level of service from information provided by neighbors. Knowledge of the "best reading" was part of the profession's earliest statement on service; transformed in the digital era to "best information," it remains the essence of the profession's contribution to service. Unlike a bartender's recommendation of a good restaurant, information provided at the reference desk does not constitute an endorsement, but information the patron can use to make an independent judgment.

Making, implementing, and enforcing rules require an understanding of professional service, sensitivity to the various roles and users of a library, and sufficient judgment to make principled exceptions. While rules in libraries should be understood and enforced by all staff members, library professionals bear responsibility for setting ethical standards and assisting staff in their development of ethical awareness. To do this requires a professionally trained staff. Following the presumption in favor of service, only a high degree of evidence to the contrary, such as severe financial exigencies that might necessitate closing a library altogether, might overcome this presumption.

QUESTIONS

- When the code of ethics declares that librarians offer the highest level of service, what does that mean in terms of professional preparation?
- How must a library be staffed and its employees trained in order to deliver the highest quality service?
- How does a library ensure consistency in responding to patron information needs?

COMPETENCE

In addition to the formulation of ethical standards, professional associations have adopted statements of competencies which can help library educators prepare future professionals and employers in hiring and training staff. Such competency statements help ensure consistency and add to the promise of the highest level of service. In 1903, Mary Plummer identified four essential areas of preparation needed to preserve material and make it available: knowledge of bibliography, technique, administration, and personal preparation, which she linked to ethics.[18] Writing about the ethics of librarianship in 1946, Helen Haines declared that librarians must know books and people.[19] Many contemporary competencies recall the early ethical codes that emphasized skills, courtesy, and customer orientation, and the canons of Charles Knowles Bolton and writings of Arthur Bostwick that prized efficiency and promptness.

The Special Libraries Association (SLA), which has not adopted its own code of ethics, was a leader in formulating statements of professional competencies. Published first in 1997 and revised in 2003, the SLA competencies are divided into professional and personal competencies. Professional competencies include skills involved in managing information organizations, resources, and services, along with applying information tools and technologies. Each competency area begins with a description of the function and ends with applied scenarios. Personal competencies are described as that set of attitudes, skills, and values that enable practitioners to work effectively and contribute positively to their organizations, clients, and the profession. Anchoring both professional and personal competencies are two core competencies deemed paramount to the values and viability of the profession. One is an appreciation of the merits of developing and sharing knowledge at conferences and through publication and collaboration. The other is a commitment to ethical practices. "Information professionals commit to professional excellence and ethics, and to the values and principles of the profession."[20]

In its statement of Competencies of Law Librarianship, approved by its executive board in March 2001, the American Association of Law Libraries (AALL) identified core competencies applicable to all law librarians. These would be acquired early in a professional career and encompass specialized competencies in areas of practice including library management, information technology, collection care and management, teaching, and reference, research, and client services. A law librarian in a small library might be expected to be proficient in more than one or all of these areas. The AALL envisioned practitioners using these competencies to identify areas for professional growth and employers using them for hiring, evaluation, and promotion decisions. Among the personal competencies, three seem most closely related to ethics: a strong, demonstrated commitment to excellent client service, adherence to the Ethical Principles of the AALL, and active pursuit of personal and professional growth through continuing education.[21]

The competency statements of three units of the ALA similarly combine personal and professional qualities and a commitment to service, but not all include an ethical component. "Competencies for Librarians Serving Young Adults" was first adopted by the Young Adult Library Services Association's (YALSA) board of directors in 1981 and was revised in 1998 and 2003. Its numerous competency indicators are grouped into seven areas, beginning with leadership/professionalism, and moving through a combination of personal and professional traits covering communication, administration planning/managing, and knowledge of materials, and ending with access to information and services, two core ethical values. The area of leadership/professionalism specifically includes three ethical competencies.

A commitment to professionalism is demonstrated by adherence to the ALA's Code of Ethics, promotion of a nonjudgmental attitude, and the preservation of confidentiality.[22]

A statement of Intellectual Freedom Core Competencies, adopted by the Intellectual Freedom Round Table at the 2002 ALA conference, separated competencies for students from competencies for professional librarians, and for each further separated content knowledge from communication skills. While focused on knowledge of First Amendment issues and the ability to explain and defend them, the competencies included a familiarity with the ALA's own positions on intellectual freedom, a central component of library ethics.[23]

The Competencies for Reference and User Services Librarians, approved by the Reference and User Services Association's (RUSA) board of directors in 2003, represents another constituent part of the ALA adopting competency standards, this time in a particular area of service rather than in a certain kind of library or for a particular clientele or user group.[24] Under broad areas of practice, including access, knowledge base, marketing, collaboration, evaluation, and assessment, the competencies point to a high level of service without specifically mentioning adherence to ethical values. In an interesting parallel to the ALA code of 1938, competencies related to collaboration are organized in terms of relationships with various library constituencies: users, colleagues, the profession, and beyond the library and the institution.

CURRENCY

Implicit in the ethical obligation to provide the highest level of service is the need for librarians to remain current in their field. While continued professional development seems embedded in the concept of professionalism itself, current codes and competency statements make this obligation explicit. Many of the personal and professional competencies enumerated across the specialty areas can be acquired, enhanced, and updated by continuing education. The acquisition and development of those skills is a shared responsibility of professionals, employers, and professional associations. The 1995 ALA code, in language incorporated into the AALL code for law librarians, calls for continuous striving for professional excellence in its concluding provision.

We strive for excellence in the profession by maintaining and enhancing our own knowledge and skills, by encouraging the professional development of co-workers, and by fostering the aspirations of potential members of the profession.[25]

But as early as Mary Plummer's proposed code in 1903, the only specific mention of professional development was linked with the librarian's service attitude and the obligation to keep up-to-date.

And suppose that I hear that my methods are antiquated, that I prefer ruts and my own comfort to the service of the public; it is plainly my duty not to resent this without self-examination, and if I find it true, either to infuse more energy and self-denial into my character, or to yield my place to someone who can fill it worthily.[26]

In Plummer's view, the failure of a librarian to remain current threatened to undermine the reputation of the profession itself.

The codes officially adopted by the ALA and other library associations reiterate currency as an ethical obligation. In the section governing the relation of the library to his profession in the ALA's 1938 code, the librarian was called on to recognize librarianship as an educational profession and to "realize that the growing effectiveness of their service is dependent upon their own development." Librarians were expected to have membership in library organizations and be ready to attend library meetings and conferences. The introduction to the 1981 statement declared that "Librarians are dependent upon one another for the bibliographical resources that enable us to provide information services, and have obligations for maintaining the highest level of personal integrity and competence." In the Medical Library Association Code of Ethics for Health Sciences Librarianship, the duty for professional development must be assumed by the librarian and is owed to oneself. "The health sciences librarian assumes personal responsibility for developing and maintaining professional excellence."[27]

Medical librarians, like librarians in fields such as law and engineering, work alongside professionals whose status is linked to their compliance with continuing-education requirements. Though voluntary, continued professional development for these librarians is imperative and facilitated by their membership in organizations such as the Special Libraries Association (SLA), the Medical Library Association (MLA), and the American Association of Law Libraries (AALL) which offer abundant continuing-education opportunities. In librarianship, where practitioners are not licensed, and there are no universal and often no state-mandated requirements for continuing education, librarians must assume responsibility for maintaining their professional skills.

In the present, dynamic information environment, the obligation for librarians to remain current assumes an even greater ethical dimension. As we shall see, librarians have a tradition of readily adding new information formats to their collections. The language of the ALA code is not tied to the book but refers to the free flow of information and ideas. Its revisions have mirrored changes in information formats, from books in 1938 to collections in 1981 and resources in 1996. With new technologies appearing more quickly than codes of ethics can be modified, librarians need to apply ethical standards to new modes of delivery. Interpretations of the Library Bill of Rights, issued more frequently, have provided guidance to librarians in applying accepted principles to non-print materials, videos, and the Internet. The highest level of service requires librarians to master these new technologies, offer them in their libraries, and assist patrons in their use. The ethical obligations of access will be considered in Chapters Four and Five.

COLLEGIALITY

What is noteworthy about the call in the 1995 ALA code for "maintaining and enhancing our own knowledge and skills" is that the obligation extends to "encouraging professional development of co-workers" and "fostering aspirations of potential members of the profession." Various versions of the ALA's codes and their predecessor drafts have all included the relationship between the librarian and staff members. In early codes, this represented a hierarchical relationship between the director and those he (never she) supervised. More recent ethical obligations have included peer relationships among staff members as more work is done in teams and the organizational chart has flattened.

In keeping with her emphasis on professionalism, Mary Plummer in 1903 stressed the need for camaraderie. "We must have esprit de corps," she declared, "and librarianship must be even more than now a sort of freemasonry." Writing from the perspective of library director, Charles Knowles Bolton, in his 1922 draft, included the librarian's duty to advance capable staff to higher levels of responsibility.

A librarian is bound, as opportunity offers, to allow an assistant to prove her ability to do work of a higher character than that usually assigned to her, and to advance those that are capable to more responsible positions in his own library or elsewhere.[28]

The version proposed in 1929 by the ALA's Code of Ethics Committee, chaired by Josephine Rathbone, approached the librarian's duty to staff not in terms of efficient administration but in terms of values.

The relations of the library to the staff within the library should be impersonal and absolutely impartial. The librarian owes to the members of the staff:

Stimulus to growth, to the exercise of the creative impulse, to the development of initiative and of a professional spirit;

Constructive criticism;

Freedom to achieve results and credit for such achievement;

Respect for the authority delegated to the staff;

Friendliness of attitude;

Justice in decision;

Opportunity for professional and economic advancement within that institution or some other;

Encouragement of reasonable suggestions and criticisms for the improvement of service.[29]

The version finally adopted by the ALA in 1938, however, returned the relationship between librarian and staff to the formal, administrative, and procedural viewpoint of Bolton's canons and foreshadowed the more legalistic statement of 1981. As part of relations within the library, the code declared that

13. The chief librarian should delegate authority, encourage a sense of responsibility and initiative on the part of staff members, provide for their professional development and appreciate good work. Staff members should be informed of the duties and problems of the library.

14. Loyalty to fellow workers and a spirit of courteous cooperation, whether between individuals or between departments, are essential to effective library service.[30]

As an obligation to the profession, the librarian, when providing a recommendation for a staff member, was to ensure that it was written in confidence and fair to both the candidate and the prospective employer, presenting an unbiased statement of strong and weak points.

Reflecting a more litigious age, the 1981 statement required that "Librarians must adhere to principles of due process and equality of opportunity in peer relationships and personnel actions." The 1995 version removed the legal phrases and declared instead, "We treat co-workers and other colleagues with respect, fairness, and good faith, and advocate conditions of employment that safeguard the rights and welfare of all employees of our institutions."

What do these ethical standards governing staff relationships mean in practice? Skillful managers recognize their staff as an important library resource, reflected in the consistent place of personnel costs as the largest component of most library budgets. Attracting and retaining high-quality professionals is a key aspect of delivering the highest level of service. Viewed as internal customers, members of the library staff can make or break the library's effort to meet institutional goals. Maintaining staff morale and job satisfaction assumes ethical dimensions if the service is affected by unfair policies or procedures. Management must model ethical conduct in its treatment of staff to establish the right ethical framework for the delivery of services. A boss who plays favorites among the staff should hardly be surprised if employees play favorites among patrons or use unethical means to garner perks not fairly awarded.

A corollary to shared values within the library is the requirement of fair treatment of colleagues and coworkers. Ethical dilemmas can arise in the allocation of professional opportunities, assignment of work hours, and rules regarding attire. We have already seen a professional obligation to advance the profession by encouraging colleagues to pursue continuing education. Access to these opportunities must be made available in an ethical way so that certain staff members are not favored because of personal connections or others denied because of race, age, or personal beliefs. Criteria to determine such matters as support for participation in professional activities, released time for professional writing, and working from home must be public and the process for selection transparent. These might be based on such objective criteria as seniority, job category, or area of expertise, or be awarded on the basis of competition where eligibility requirements and award criteria are grounded in fairness.

QUESTIONS

- In assigning work hours, a supervisor may encounter diverse needs of employees whose schedules are affected by the length of their commute, child care arrangements, outside obligations, or religious observances.

  - When a staff member reports difficulty working nights or on weekends, when that is specified in their position description, on what basis can you take individual needs into account without playing favorites or making decisions on the basis of inappropriate or illegal factors?
  - Can you resolve the matter in a way that meets individual needs and that could be replicated for a worker in the same or an analogous situation?

- Now that differences in work habits and philosophy are appearing between generations of older and younger workers, how can you accommodate preferences about the work environment?
- How may a library formulate an employee dress code that is neutral not only in content but also in matters of age, race, or religion?

DIVERSITY

While current codes do not include respect for racial and ethnic diversity in providing service and supporting staff as a specific ethical obligations, the library profession has affirmed these values while continuing to face challenges in these areas. The 1995 ALA code calls for the highest level of service to all library users without addressing how that service can best be provided in a multiracial and multicultural society. While the code adopts race-neutral language, in practice, librarians have sought to respond to the varying information needs of different peoples, cultures, and languages. What does the highest level of service require in terms of staff to meet these needs? This is an area demonstrating some of the profession's most innovative services to extend the library's reach to new communities of users and also some of the profession's most stubborn resistance to change.

On one side of the ledger, librarians since the end of the nineteenth century have brought library service to immigrant communities. Programs to help newly arrived immigrants adapt to American ways have been followed by programs to help ethnic communities retain and celebrate their cultures. Library service during the generations of segregation following the Civil War often did not exist in African American neighborhoods or was offered in distinctly separate and unequal libraries, usually without the benefit of a professional librarian. The opening of a segregated branch, as in Louisville, Kentucky, or Richmond, Virginia, was viewed as an improvement in library service despite its perpetuation of the race divide. Librarians like Ernestine Rose opened the doors of the New York Public Library to the city's immigrant population and in the 1920s sought to organize within the ALA those interested in library service to African Americans. With support from the Carnegie Corporation, a library school was founded at the Hampton Institute in the 1920s, succeeded by a library school at Atlanta University in 1941. As was then customary, these institutions serving the African American community were initially headed by whites, but had as their goal increasing the numbers of black librarians who would work in often-segregated public libraries, schools, and universities. Even library schools outside the South graduated few African American librarians. Dorothy Porter Wesley, who gathered the Moorland-Spingarn collection of African diaspora materials at Howard University, was the first African American woman to receive a library degree from Columbia, but not until 1935. So the early interest in serving diverse communities was not matched by an interest in training professionals from those communities.

On the other side of the ledger, the ALA and state library associations, particularly in the South, did not treat professional colleagues of color with fairness or respect. In the conduct of their own business, professional associations must make choices with ethical implications, including the selection of meeting sites. At its meeting in Richmond, Virginia, in 1936, however, the ALA agreed to conference arrangements, in keeping with state and local segregation laws, that required the association's African American members to enter through the back door, sit in separate sections during meetings, and be barred from social functions held in public venues. Following this meeting, the ALA adopted a policy that it would not hold its conferences in cities where all of its members could not participate in all conference events.

ALA MEETS IN RICHMOND (1936)

In 1936, the American Library Association held its annual conference in Richmond, Virginia, acting on the recommendation of the ALA Executive Board that it select a meeting site in the South. In making various contracts for conference arrangements, ALA executive secretary Carl Milam agreed to terms that complied with the legal and de facto segregation of the former capital of the Confederacy. Lodging and transportation were segregated by race with conference headquarters located in the major downtown hotels limited to white guests. The ALA agreed that black librarians would not enter through the front doors and that seating in conference sessions would be segregated by race. Black librarians in Richmond were asked to share information about these arrangements with others expected to attend, but many librarians were unaware that they would be asked to comply with these restrictions.

Many black librarians, including Eliza Atkins, refused to attend the meeting. Some whites, to register their protest, crossed the color line to sit on the side of the auditorium designated for blacks. A petition circulated at the conference objecting to the policy. Stanley Kunitz, editor of the *Wilson Library Bulletin*, penned a scathing denunciation of the ALA's acquiescence to segregation as a violation of the association's commitment to democracy. Letters to the editor appeared in the *Wilson Library Bulletin* and *Library Journal* following the conference, most taking issue with the ALA's actions.

In response, the ALA appointed a special committee on race discrimination that recommended that, thereafter, the ALA would not meet in cities where all ALA members could not participate in all conference activities. This policy did not extend to social events associated with the conference, although as *Library Journal* noted, most conference business was conducted at the many dinner meetings and reunions that were a major conference attraction. The ALA did not meet again in the Deep South until 1956, in Miami, after the Supreme Court had found that racial segregation violated the U.S. Constitution.

In 1936, the ALA had not yet adopted a code of ethics. The most recent version proposed by the ethics committee, chaired by Josephine Rathbone, in 1929, contained a clause that library service was not to be denied because of race, creed, or nationality. Bolton's Canons of 1922 did not deal with the race issue but did record the obligations of librarians to their staff, the profession, and society. In 1936, the United States was keenly focused on race issues with the much-heralded performance of African American runner Jesse Owens at the Berlin Olympics. On the other hand, the South represented an area of great potential for the spread of public libraries. Other organizations and foundations, including the Carnegie Corporation and the Rosenwald Fund, were supporting efforts to extend library service to unserved areas largely in the South. Southern librarians were eager to play a greater leadership role in the ALA. The ALA had a policy of not interfering with local public library policy. For the first time, in 1936, the association president was a southerner, Louis Round Wilson, formerly of the University of North Carolina before he became dean of the Graduate Library School at the University of Chicago.

By the mid-1930s, a number of professional organizations had faced the same dilemma and in some cases had been able to negotiate an easing of racial restrictions for conference-related activities. Indeed, Richmond had suspended its segregation ordinance to allow the Organization of Black Elks to meet in the city in the late 1920s.

QUESTIONS

- What values were in play in 1936 when this decision was made?
- What interests were at stake?
- What options might the ALA have had in choosing this site?

SOURCES

"At Richmond," *ALA Bulletin* 30 (June 1936): 511–12.

Carl H. Milam, Memorandum about Negro Delegates to Richmond Conference, May 4, 1936, ALA Circular Letters 1936; Sullivan, Peggy. *Carl H. Milam and the American Library Association*. New York: H. W. Wilson, 1976, 257.

"Editorial Forum: Personal Contacts at Richmond," *Library Journal* 61 (May 1, 1936): 364.

[Kunitz, Stanley J.] "The Spectre at Richmond," *Wilson Bulletin for Librarians* 10 (May1936): 592–93. Reprinted in Ellsworth, Dianne J., and Norman D. Stevens, eds. *Landmarks of Library Literature, 1876–1976*. Metuchen, NJ: Scarecrow Press, 1976, 211–13.

Preer, Jean L. "'This Year-Richmond!' The 1936 Meeting of the American Library Association," *Libraries & Culture* 39 (Spring 2004): 137–60.

"Report of the Committee on Racial Discrimination," *ALA Bulletin* 31 (January 1937):37–38.

"Richmond Conference," *Library Journal* 61 (July 1936): 537.

Van Jackson, Wallace. "Negro Segregation," *Library Journal* 61 (June 15, 1936): 467–68.

Nonetheless, the association allowed state library associations to continue their segregated practices. Claiming to respect local law and custom, the ALA did not object to situations where African American librarians had no professional affiliation or only a separate and unequal one. Nor did the association expand its commitment to racial equality in the professional ranks in the decades following the Supreme Court ruling in *Brown v. Board of Education*. Segregation continued in the state library associations of Louisiana and Alabama long after Jim Crow had been outlawed, and ALA officers continued to attend these segregated state meetings.[31] Not until a 1968 protest led by E. J. Josey did the ALA take action to sever its ties with its segregated chapters and even then did not bar ALA officers from attending the meetings of segregated chapters.[32] Caught between competing values, the ALA ignored the rights of African American professional colleagues and the impact that the system of segregation had on both librarians and communities.

The incorporation of respect for racial and ethnic diversity in the panoply of ethical values of librarianship illustrates the evolutionary process by which experience shapes understanding and values. Having followed an erratic course, modifying its own meeting policy while condoning segregated chapters, the ALA over the last twenty-five years has embraced cultural diversity as a central value of librarianship. The ALA's statement, "Libraries: An American Value," adopted in 1999, declares that "We value our nation's diversity and strive to reflect that diversity by providing a full spectrum of resources and services to the communities we serve."[33]

In policy, library organizations have included respect for racial and cultural differences as part of new formulations of professional competencies. In the area of leadership and professionalism, YALSA competencies state that the young adult librarian "Demonstrates an understanding of and a respect for diverse cultural and ethnic values." In the area of access, reference, and user service, librarians are expected to design "services to meet the special access needs of primary users, including those with disabilities, and those with English as a second language."

END NOTES

1. Wayne A. Wiegand, *Irrepressible Reformer: A Biography of Melvil Dewey.* Chicago: American Library Association, 1996, 61, 62.

2. The modified version was approved at the ALA's 1892 conference in Lakewood, New Jersey, and was carved across the entrance to the model library in the ALA's exhibit at the Columbian Exposition in 1893. See Elizabeth W. Stone, *American Library Development,* New York: H. W. Wilson (1977); John N. Berry III, "Dewey's ALA Motto Still Works Fine," *Library Journal (1876)* 129 (February 15, 2004): 8; and Lillian N. Gerhardt, "That Motto of ALA: On What Occasion Will It Ever Again Be Appropriate?" *School Library Journal* 34 (April 1988): 4. Dewey's own account can be found in Melvil Dewey, "Origin of A.L.A. Motto," *Public Libraries* (1906): 55.

3. Alvin Johnson, *Pioneer's Progress.* New York: Viking Press, 1937, 237.

4. American Library Association Code of Ethics, adopted by the ALA Council, June 28, 1995.

5. Ralph Munn, "The First Step," *ALA Bulletin* 34 (January 1940): 5.

6. John N. Berry III, "'Professional' Is Only a Label," *Library Journal* 120 (July 1995): 6.

7. *Merwine v. Board of Trustees for State Institutions of Higher Learning,* 754 F.2d 636 (5th Cir. 1985).

8. American Library Association Allied Professional Association, http://www. ala-apa.org.

9. "ALA Announces New Head of D.C. Office," *ALA News Releases* 5, no. 4 (September 1999): 1; "Sheketoff Pledges to Raise ALA's Visibility," *ALA Cognotes* [Wrapup] (January 2000): 1, 9.

10. Steve McKinzie, "For Ethical Reference, Pare the Paraprofessionals," *American Libraries* 23 (October 2002): 42.

11. Vickie Salonen, "Para Pro and the Reference Desk," *Library Mosaic* 14, no. 2 (March/April 2003): 10–11.

12. Scott Gant, *We Are All Journalists Now: The Transformation of the Press and Reshaping of the Law in the Age of the Internet.* New York: Free Press, 2007.

13. Chartered Institute of Library and Information Professionals, http://www. cilip.org.uk/policyadvocacy/ethics/introduction.htm; http://www.infoethics.org. uk/CILIP/admin/index.htm.

14. Richard N. Stichler, "On Reforming ALA's Code of Ethics," *American Libraries* 23 (January 1992): 40–44.

15. Society of Professional Journalists Code of Ethics, 1996, http://www.spj. org/ethicscode.asp.

16. Statement for Public Library Trustees [Approved by Public Library Association board of directors and the American Library Trustee Association board of directors, June 8, 1985] in Virginia G. Young, *The Library Trustee: A Practical Guidebook*, 4th ed. Chicago: American Library Association, 1988, 180. In February 1999, the name was changed from American Library Trustee Association to Association for Library Trustees and Advocates. No code of ethics appears in Mary Y. Moore, *The Successful Library Trustee Handbook*, Chicago: American Library Association, 2005, nor on the ALTA Web page, http://www.ala.org/ala/alta/altaorg/ altahistory/altahistory.cfm.

17. "Is It Ethical?" *American Libraries* 14 (February 1983): 79; responses from readers were published in "Reader Forum," *American Libraries* 14 (May 1983): 270.

18. Mary W. Plummer, "The Pros and Cons of Training for Librarianship," *Public Libraries* 8 (May 1903): 208–220.

19. Helen E. Haines, "Ethics of Librarianship," *Library Journal* 71 (June 15, 1946): 848–851.

20. Competencies for Information Professionals of the 21st Century—Special Libraries Association, revised edition June 2003, http://www.sla.org/content/ learn/comp2003/index.cfm.

21. American Association of Law Libraries Competencies of Law Librarianship, approved by the executive board March 2001 http://www.aallnet.org/prodev/ competencies.asp.

22. American Library Association Competencies for Librarians Serving Young Adults, approved by the Young Adult Services Association board of directors, June 1981, revised January 1998 and October 2003, http://www.ala.org/ala/yalsa/ profdev/yacompetencies/competencies.htm.

23. American Library Association Intellectual Freedom Core Competencies, June 2, 2002, http://www.ala.org/ala/ifrt/ifrtinaction/ifcompetencies/ifcompetencies. htm.

24. American Library Association Professional Competencies for Reference and User Services Librarians, approved by RUSA Board of Directors January 26, 2003, http://www.ala.org/ala/rusa/protools/referenceguide/professional.cfm.

25. American Library Association Code of Ethics, adopted by the ALA Council June 28, 1995.

26. Mary W. Plummer, "The Pros and Cons of Training for Librarianship," *Public Libraries* 8 (May 1903): 212.

27. Code of Ethics for Health Sciences Librarianship, Medical Library Association, 1994. http://www.mlanet.org/about/ethics.htm.

28. Charles Knowles Bolton, "The Ethics of Librarianship: A Proposal for a Revised Code," *The Annals of the American Academy of Political and Social Science* 101 (May 1922): 141.

29. "Suggested Code of Ethics," *Library Journal* 55 (February 15, 1930): 165.

30. "Code of Ethics for Librarians [adopted by ALA. Council December 29, 1938]," *ALA Bulletin* 33 (February 1939): 129.

31. For an account of segregation in Alabama public libraries, see Patterson, Toby Graham, *A Right to Read: Segregation and Civil Rights in Alabama in Public Libraries, 1900–1965.* Tuscaloosa: University of Alabama Press, 2002.

32. E.J. Josey has written widely on librarianship and civil rights. See for example, Josey, E. J. "The Civil Rights Movement and American Librarianship: The Opening Round." In *Activism in American Librarianship, 1962–1978*, Mary Lee Bundy and Frederick J. Stielow, eds. Westport, CT: Greenwood Press, 1987, 13–20.

33. "Libraries: An American Value adopted by ALA Council, February 3, 1999," in *Intellectual Freedom Manual*, 7th ed. Chicago: American Library Association, 2006, 266–267.

3

———◆•◆———

SERVICE: FOR WHOM

Basic issues requiring professional judgment concern who is entitled to the library's services and to what services. The second part of the ALA's motto, "The best reading for the largest number at the least cost," suggests an ethical obligation to extend library service to the widest possible audience. Envisioning an ever-growing community of users, library pioneers reached out to new populations and localities and employed innovative means to make books and information available across broader service areas and through new technologies.

But the addition of new patrons brings with it a responsibility to offer new services and fresh ethical dilemmas about how to provide them. And when the quality of library service is affected by economic factors, how are libraries to claim they are providing "equitable service"? The third part of the ALA's motto, "at the least cost," reflected Melvil Dewey's penchant for efficiency but did not address gaps in service between urban and rural areas or between rich and poor communities. When as a nation we still do not have universal library service, the ethic of service to the largest numbers remains unfulfilled.

Even with comparable resources and the wisest stewardship, no two libraries offer equal service either as institutions or to individual patrons. The ethical standard for service calls for "equitable access" and "equitable service policies." The ethical obligation is to provide service that is fair, not equal. How then may librarians ethically, that is fairly, make distinctions between services provided to patrons? The library first sets policy establishing who is entitled to its services. Then, among those eligible library users, what distinctions might it make among different types of services and the levels of service offered? Under what conditions may the library fairly offer service to those outside this group? Before the first patron walks through the door, the library board and the library director face ethical issues: service to whom and what service?

WHICH USERS

The community of actual and potential users varies with each and every library. Even within the same library, it changes over time. So in striving to provide service in an ethical way, the librarian must determine those whom the library is intended to serve. The language of the ALA Code of Ethics and the Library Bill of Rights is inclusive and all-encompassing. The 1995 code declares,

I. We provide the highest level of service to **all library users** through appropriate and usefully organized resources; equitable service policies; equitable access; and accurate, unbiased, and courteous responses to all requests.[1]

The Library Bill of Rights states in its first provision

I. Books and other library resources should be provided for the interest, information, and enlightenment of **all people of the community the library serves.**[2]

What on its face seems rather straightforward proves on examination to be complex and fraught with potential ethical conflicts.

Who Is the Library's Public?

In the days of the subscription library, service was available to those paying a membership fee. Borrowing privileges were defined by the term of the subscription; the rental fee and loan period varied according to the type of material, whether it was a book or magazine and whether it was a new title. The establishment of tax-supported public libraries made residency rather than membership the defining characteristic of those entitled to library service. In theory, when communities support libraries with tax money, service should extend to all those within the taxing jurisdiction, taxpayer or not. Historically, however, public libraries have also limited service on the basis of characteristics such as age and race. As ideas about the role of the public library have evolved, libraries have offered services to different audiences, sometimes making the library irrelevant to large segments of the community.

Academic libraries face many of the same dilemmas as public libraries about whom to serve. As part of institutions of great variation and continuing innovation, they have extended their reach to new communities of students. As public libraries spread across the United States, colleges and universities were expanding opportunities for higher education. While still serving only a small part of the population, post-secondary institutions took on multiple identities as state universities followed private institutions, the Morrill Act provided federal funding for agricultural and mechanical colleges, and undergraduate institutions added graduate research programs on the European model. In the twentieth century, junior and community colleges made higher education accessible to everyone, and normal schools morphed into teachers' colleges and then into state university campuses with missions differentiated by locality and academic concentrations. Infusions of federal aid in the 1950s and 1960s gave higher education, like public libraries, obligations to national as well as to state and local constituencies. So at first the answer seems simple—a college or university library should serve its students and faculty—but immediately becomes more complex.

Ethical issues related to users would seem to arise less frequently in school or special libraries where the identity of those entitled to service is more clearly defined by the nature of the institution. Nonetheless, even school and special libraries with strictly defined constituencies also reflect some of the same variation as public and academic libraries and the potential for ethical dilemmas. Schools, whether public or private, can be organized around different grade-level schemes; school library media services can be organized school-by-school or district wide. Private, independent, religiously affiliated charter schools or those adhering to a unique educational philosophy encircle their community of users in the uniqueness of their missions. Similarly, special libraries take on the identity of the organization they serve. Where user and service policies are not clear, however, the practical pressures of a more closely knit community may lead to requests for favors or special treatment that put the librarian in an uncomfortable ethical position.

Recognition of these institutional differences emerged only as the profession developed and as libraries spread, taking into account local and ethnic differences, community histories, and institutional needs. In every type of library, questions related to users have been complicated by the introduction of information technology that vastly enhances service while posing ethical questions of differentiated levels and kinds of service. Where outsiders might have easily been allowed to consult reference books, magazines, and books, are they similarly entitled to use the library's computers for Internet access and, if so, under what conditions?

These questions are generally answered in practical or political terms, depending on the library's resources or its relationship to outside constituencies or neighboring jurisdictions. Rarely are they addressed as ethical issues, grounding policy in the library's stated commitments to service and access. This is not to say that every library is obliged to provide service to every user. On the contrary, it is because every library is limited in resources and constrained by obligations to its primary users that ethical decision-making is essential to policy choices.

Paradoxically, as our vision of service has become more universal and access to information more global, libraries have become more precise in defining their particular missions and users. A clearly stated mission preempts some of the ethical dilemmas that arise when the guidelines fail to address, in advance, the library's obligations to users or potential users who fall into different categories. Here is an area where effective administration and ethical practice coincide. It is not unethical for a library to offer different services to different users. The ethical dimension arises in defining those categories of users applying appropriate criteria, in making those policies known, and in implementing them in an evenhanded manner.

Categorizing libraries as "public" or "academic," "school" or "special" only starts the process of definition that determines institutional identity and the ethical obligations that flow from it. But librarians would say that their primary duty is service to library patrons and to their community, locality, campus, or parent institution. The basic obligations stated in the ALA Code of Ethics and the Library Bill of Rights provide the touchstone for the whole profession, the starting place from which to interpret values in a variety of contexts, where "service" will have different meanings, shadings, and gradations, chameleon-like, taking on the coloration of its surroundings while retaining its essence.

QUESTIONS

- Is it ethical for a public library to provide different levels of service to those coming from outside its community?
- Is it ethical for a public library to provide some basic service to all for free and charge fees for additional services?
- Now that many public libraries receive private support as well, is it ethical for a library to provide additional services to donors or Friends of the Library?

USERS

Let's examine how ideas about "service to whom?" have evolved in practice. In the late nineteenth century, public libraries circumscribed their own service by a limited view of their role and audience. The ethical obligation to provide service expanded as libraries reached out to new communities of users.

Class

Although Andrew Carnegie envisioned the library as the workingman's gateway to self-education and economic advancement, the public library developed as a middle-class enclave of culture and recreation. Not generally seen as an ethical issue, this initial middle-class orientation constituted a self-fulfilling prophecy which determined the services to be offered and in turn reinforced the exclusion of workers and immigrants. In the first of the ways in which practice shaped an ethical value, practitioners reached out beyond the middle class. At the beginning of the twentieth century, librarians offered both Americanization classes and ethnic materials to attract new immigrant groups to the library. Through the Library War Service during World War I, librarians established libraries in army camps and shipped millions of books to servicemen abroad. Through deposit libraries and county library service, librarians sought to reach farm communities unserved by libraries.

In the 1920s, with support from the Carnegie Corporation, the ALA committed itself to library adult education, seemingly directed at an already educated audience. By reading the best books on various subjects recommended in *Reading with a Purpose* pamphlets and scheduling appointments with a readers' advisor, patrons could tackle books of increasing complexity guided by the library expert. But during the Depression, the pendulum swung toward service to unemployed workers, and libraries became the workingman's club. The increasingly democratic practice of public libraries was echoed in the rhetoric of the ALA's quest for federal funds, begun in 1936, to demonstrate public library service in poor, rural areas, largely in the South. The onset of World War II intensified this linkage of library service and democratic values with an emphasis on the role of libraries in creating an informed citizenry.

In the early postwar years, however, the Public Library Inquiry presented an alternative vision of public libraries suggesting a different service standard with profound ethical implications. Funded by the Carnegie Corporation and conducted by the Social Science Research Council, the studies published by the Inquiry challenged the notion of the public library as a democratic institution with an obligation to universal service. Arguing that, in practice, the public library largely served the segment of the population that already owned books, read newspapers, watched films, and listened to the radio, its authors concluded that the public library's unique and appropriate role was service to this "communications elite."[3] Envisioning a basis for library service at odds with the democratic underpinnings of the ALA's quest for federal support, these findings were largely rejected by the library community. They are of continuing importance, nonetheless, as an alternative mission of the public library generally, and as a possible gauge of how a particular library sees its role and measures its service to its community. Even if the library in fact largely serves a middle-class audience, its role in making information accessible to everyone underscores its fundamentally democratic role.

Location

The democratization of the public library movement was embodied in the library extension efforts undertaken with Carnegie Corporation support in the 1920s and given impetus during the Depression. In 1936, the ALA published a small illustrated booklet, *An Equal Chance*, that documented the disparities in library service available in urban areas, largely in northern states, and in rural communities, largely in the South. Aimed at reducing this disparity by the use of federal funds, the ALA began a process of redefining the "community" served by libraries. In Andrew Carnegie's vision, library service was local and dependent on the initiative and continuing support of the residents of the community served. The movement for library extension was based on larger units of service, often county systems that could rest on a broader financial base and offer better services to larger numbers of people. The Library Services Act, finally passed in 1956, added state participation and federal support to this multitiered system of library service, with states expected to devise plans for library service and contribute matching funds. Despite the regular reauthorization and continuous reinterpretation of the act, there is no national mandate for public library service, and many rural communities remain unserved or underserved by public libraries.

Extended into the Internet era, this same disparity persists between the different levels of Internet connectivity that divide rural and urban areas. The economic barriers that impeded the development of library service in the 1930s keep rural communities from full access to electronic resources. The gap is no longer expressed in terms of libraries, per capita spending, or volumes circulated, but in terms of bandwidth. Supporters of the Telecommunications Act of 1996 sought to address this "digital divide" by providing discounted connectivity fees for rural areas, using arguments echoing from the 1930s about unequal and unfair distribution of support.

QUESTIONS

- Should a state that receives federal funds for libraries require that all communities provide public library service?
- What obligation does a public library have to provide service to schoolchildren who live in nearby communities that have no public libraries?
- Should all public libraries within a state have to meet certain standards regarding budget, staffing, and Internet connectivity in order to guarantee minimum levels of service to all state residents?

Age

How should the age of the library patron affect the service provided? While we can readily imagine ethical issues arising in decisions about library services and materials based on a patron's age, considerations of age do not appear in any of the versions of the ALA's codes of ethics. Age does not figure either in the early ethical drafts of Plummer and Bolton, or in the code adopted by the ALA in 1938 or in its 1995 code. They have referred instead to "all library users" or to "all users entitled to use the library," which can, in fact, be used as a basis for exclusion as well as inclusion of certain categories of users.

Just as nineteenth-century libraries were designed for a literate, middle–class population, they were also intended for adult members of the community. At a time when only a small proportion of the population went to high school, children were not within the orbit of early public libraries. Here again, the pioneering work of individual librarians opened the door to young people and altered the perception of age as a factor in the ethical equation. In the 1890s, John Cotton Dana expanded library service to children at the Denver Public Library, as did Herbert Putnam in Minneapolis. Pioneering children's librarians Anne Carroll Moore and Frances Clark Sayers established children's rooms as the center of multidimensional service to children that featured storytelling, arts, music, and drama. In his ALA presidential speech in 1915, Hiller Wellman actually wondered whether library service to children had gone too far when weighed against its cost.[4]

The obligation to serve patrons of all ages emerged not from revisions of the code of ethics but in an amendment to the Library Bill of Rights when it was added in 1967 almost as an afterthought following a preconference on "Intellectual Freedom and the Teenager." The provision was specifically reaffirmed in 1996.[5] Nonetheless, age has posed some of the thorniest ethical dilemmas faced by librarians in determining whom the library is to serve and, as we shall see later, with what material. There is a dichotomy in the way in which age figures in library service. On one hand, youngsters and seniors are among the groups that can benefit most greatly from services and materials tailored to their particular physical and informational needs. On the other, age is specifically not to be a factor in determining *policies* for library access and usage.

Once public libraries opened their doors to children, the issue of age took on other dimensions. How old must a child be to have a library card? If children develop at their own pace, how are libraries to determine at what age a child is eligible for library privileges? Believing that reading and library usage are promoted by early exposure to books, libraries have instituted programs for the very young. Friends groups deliver books and library information to mothers and newborns still in the hospital. Libraries offer story times for caregivers and children during the day and for parents and their children in bedclothes at night. Stops at daycare centers are an established part of bookmobile routes. Libraries at least since the 1930s have offered parenting education classes as part of their service to families.

If the librarian's professional role is based on knowing books and people, service to children, as for all others, requires the expertise of librarians to build collections and to create opportunities to match book and reader. In the matter of children, however, the ALA has determined that parents are the appropriate arbiter of children's reading. This means that libraries do not circumscribe their collections because of individual taste or objections. One family's concerns cannot limit access to other families with a different point of view. Nonetheless, libraries have devised policies in ways intended to honor both the library's ethical obligation to make material available without reference to age and the parents' responsibility to make decisions about their own children's reading. Family cards that allow parental control over borrowing and access to children's records represent one example in which deference is given to an ethical value while accommodation is made only for those with a different priority. The presumption is in favor of providing service without regard to age; this is overcome only with the explicit written authorization of parents or guardians.

Unattended Children

Economic and technological changes have posed new ethical issues for librarians in providing service to young people. As women returned to the workforce, many libraries faced the question of unattended children spending long hours in the library. In the matter of materials, the ALA had generally taken the position that a child's reading was a family matter to be determined between parents and their youngsters. When a child is left unsupervised in the library, however, the child's safety and well-being become a matter of concern to the library. Formulating a policy on unattended children in the library involves issues of ethics in determining which children are allowed to use the library and what services the library will provide. May the library set an age at which children may be left unattended or is that a matter for families to decide? How old must a person accompanying a child be? What happens when a child is unattended at the time of a library's closing?

These determinations vary from community to community. The ethical obligation is to set a standard based on objective criteria that can be easily determined and equitably enforced. Such factors as whether the child or its parents are known to the librarians should not exempt them from rules stating a minimum age for unaccompanied visits to the library. Evenhanded enforcement is essential to the acceptance and operation of such a policy. Professionalism requires that librarians provide service within the realm of their expertise and decline to render assistance more appropriately offered by parents, siblings, or babysitters. To formulate such policies, libraries should work with community and parent organizations and social service and law enforcement agencies and publicize such policies as broadly as possible.

A further perceived danger to children in the library has arisen with the introduction of computer access. In pre-Internet days, the issue for young people revolved around their access to print and the possibility of exposure to "adult" materials. With the World Wide Web, the potential for access to inappropriate material not specifically selected by the library seems to pose a threat of an entirely different dimension. We will address these issues in Chapter Four.

Some libraries, honoring the ethical obligation in the Library Bill of Rights not to circumscribe library access by age, do not specify ages at which children may come to the library on their own, preferring to regulate behavior. Rules governing noise and unruly conduct should apply to all patrons. Likewise, the care of all persons left unattended and in need of assistance at the close of business should be handled according to a policy based on need or circumstance, not age.

Race and Ethnicity

The codes of ethics of the ALA have manifested various interpretations of the meaning of service to different populations. Bolton's canons and the 1938 code define service and the community served in a narrow and bureaucratic way. The process of deciding which groups or patrons are entitled to service can be used both to deny and expand library service. Certain categories have been identified by law as illegal and unconstitutional bases for this purpose, race foremost among them. But until the Supreme Court declared racial segregation in public education unconstitutional in the 1954 case of *Brown v. Board of Education*, race matters involved a large element of ethical choice.

In its stand on racial issues, the ALA's position was influenced by both the respect and the autonomy it accorded individual libraries and local laws and by its own rhetoric about the democratic role of the public library. The ALA was founded in 1876 at the height of southern reconstruction, the backlash against freed slaves, and the glorification of the Ku Klux Klan, followed by the imposition of segregation in public facilities extending even to federal government agencies. Mary Plummer and Charles Knowles Bolton drafted their early codes of library ethics at the height of the Jim Crow era, following the 1896 Supreme Court decision upholding separate-but-equal facilities in the case of *Plessy v. Ferguson*.

Unusual for its day, the draft proposed by the ALA's code of ethics committee in 1929 provided that library service was not be limited by race or nationality. The committee's chair, Josephine Rathbone, had worked with Mary Plummer at the Pratt Institute and had advised Charles Knowles Bolton on his original draft in 1909, when race would certainly not have been considered a factor in ethical library service. But by the late 1920s, the country's interest in race issues had intensified. The Carnegie Corporation had supported the establishment of a library school at Hampton Institute, and some other library schools were admitting African American students. So it was in keeping with these efforts that the draft declared:

The staff owes impartial, courteous service to all persons using the library. Among the patrons entitled to use the library no distinctions of race, color, creed or condition should influence the attitude of the staff, and no favoritism should be tolerated.[6]

This was followed by language that called for a welcoming attitude rather than cold officialdom.

Though considered, this draft was not adopted. Instead, the language in the approved 1938 code declared that libraries were to provide service "to all entitled to service," language that allowed libraries in segregated communities to deny service to African Americans who by law were barred from using the public library. In practice, public libraries contrived a variety of devices to either offer or deny library service to African American users. Libraries as in Louisville, Kentucky, and in Richmond, Virginia, opened separate branches in African American neighborhoods. These could be, and were, viewed as a progressive measure because they offered service to the African American residents, in contrast to the many communities which offered no library service. On the other hand, rather than breaking down racial barriers by allowing black persons to use all public library facilities, these segregated libraries, which never received equal or even proportional appropriations, further perpetuated segregation.

Despite the stand taken by the ALA after its 1936 conference in Richmond, refusing to meet in cities where meetings would be governed by segregation laws, the association did little more until the 1960s, when Eric Moon, in a series of editorials in *Library Journal*, called on the profession's conscience and demanded an end to complicity in racial discrimination. Like Stanley Kunitz, editor of the *Wilson Library Bulletin* in the 1930s, Moon was keenly aware of the disjunction between professed values and professional practice on matters having to do with race.[7]

Immigrants

Public libraries in big cities have been eager to open their doors to newly arrived immigrants. As successive waves of newcomers have accepted the invitation of public libraries to use their resources, attend their programs, and use library meeting rooms, librarians have developed standards to assure high levels of service to those who do not speak English or know U.S. customs. In 1988, the board of the Reference and Adult Services Division of the ALA adopted guidelines for providing library services to Spanish-speaking library users. Written in consultation with REFORMA, the National Association to Promote Library and Information Services to Latinos and the Spanish-Speaking, the guidelines were revised and approved in 2007 by the board of the Reference and Users Services Association.

Although focused on one language group, the guidelines emphasize the national, regional, and cultural differences within this community. In their essence, they provide guidance for librarians working with any group for whom English is not their first language. These guidelines reflect a great degree of ethical sensitivity in seeking to provide the highest level of service within the limitations imposed by financial constraints. Covering all aspects of library service, the guidelines emphasize relevancy, attention to cultural diversity, the use of local vendors, the recruitment of Spanish-speaking personnel, and engagement in community activities. At the same time, they specify that materials are to be selected and evaluated using standard criteria.[8]

In the late 1990s, questions of service to racial and ethnic minorities arose in the larger debate over immigration policy and whether public services should be provided to undocumented workers. Some jurisdictions proposed to ban the children of undocumented residents from public schools even if they were citizens of the United States. Barring these children from the public library would seem contrary to the tradition of the public library as free and open to the public, with library cards available on proof of residency, not citizenship. Further, since undocumented workers also are taxpaying members of the community, a denial of service based on their immigration status, like barring African Americans on the basis of their race, raises questions about the provision of equitable service. In keeping with other ethical presumptions, service should be provided unless an overwhelming case can be made to the contrary.

QUESTIONS

- What is a librarian's ethical obligation when community sentiment favors a library policy that is contrary to what the profession stands for? Can you think of some examples?
- In the current debate over public services for undocumented workers, what ethical values are in play that might affect the position of the public library?

People with Disabilities

Recognition of the library's responsibility to serve people with disabilities has been slow to develop. Special services for the blind and hearing impaired have been provided since 1931 through the Library of Congress Library Services for the Blind and Physically Handicapped working through state libraries. Here is an area where legislation has overtaken an ethical obligation to provide library services to those with disabilities. The Americans with Disabilities Act of 1990 has compelled libraries to do what an ethical approach to library service would have required and should have produced. Because of the cost of providing special equipment and services, many libraries in the past ignored the needs of those with disabilities or sought private funding rather than use library funds for this purpose. The common design of Carnegie libraries, with the main entrance at the top of a flight of stairs, is emblematic of the physical barriers to the library that impeded access to materials and services. Interior, as well as exterior, inaccessibility in many areas has characterized library design.

The new awareness of the needs of library users with disabilities should have awakened the profession to the special needs of its various users. The provision of services to people with disabilities has enhanced service for all, with standards of accessibility extending to all aspects of library service, including Web sites.

QUESTION

- When not obligated by law, how far you will go in providing service to users with special needs? How will you decide?

PATRON CONDUCT

The promise of service to all users of the library requires that libraries set, promulgate, and implement clear guidelines on acceptable and unacceptable behavior. Rules should be based on objective criteria that can be easily determined and fairly enforced. Age poses a dilemma in terms of conduct in the library, arising both in the formulation of rules and their enforcement. An ethical approach requires that rules focus on conduct rather than on age, status, or condition. Since young people are more likely to test the limits, boundaries determining acceptable conduct should be clearly set. A general statement about unruly behavior leaves too much to the imagination and too much scope for discriminatory application of a rule. On the other hand, rules that are too specific may seem aimed at youngsters rather than at their conduct.

The librarian must navigate among the conduct of various users in setting and enforcing standards applicable to all. For example, limits on noise should be judged on an absolute objective scale (decibels, distance) rather than on patron reaction (annoyance). Teen talk may be a bother to some while the chatter of adults may blend into the background unnoticed. Golden oldies coming out of an MP3 player may be OK, but not heavy metal. Remembering that the library welcomes all points of view, rules must be content neutral (loud classical music is subject to the rules the same as loud rap music). This is especially true since complaints about ethnic music may reflect racial or ethnic prejudice.

Public libraries have encountered difficulty with teen conduct in after-school hours. Lacking a better place to congregate and let off their pent-up energy, teens head to the public library where, in some communities, they have disrupted the routine and unsettled the nerves of librarians and other library users. The varied approaches that libraries have taken to deal with unruly teens suggest various ethical issues. In Joliet, Illinois, for example, the librarian limited access to the library during after-school hours, requiring teens to go through a registration process, showing an ID and library card, in order to be admitted.[9] No other patrons were required to do this. The Wickliffe, Ohio, Public Library required that students under the age of fourteen be accompanied in the library between 2:30 and 5:30 pm or enroll in a library program.[10]

In late 2006, teen behavior in the Maplewood, New Jersey, Memorial Library was so out of control that the library threatened to close during after-school hours between 2:45 and 5:00 pm. On an ethical accounting sheet, this remedy seems to deny service in the name of improving service and demonstrates the need to protect a core value, here, service, while addressing the immediate problem, unruly conduct, in an ethical way. Shutting down the library to all in order to address the bad behavior of a few negates the library's claim to serve the whole community and undermines its reputation for competence and equitable service. In early 2007, the trustees of the Maplewood Memorial Library rescinded their decision, two days short of its implementation, upon receiving additional funding from the township to help the library develop new after-school programs.[11] Consultation with community organizations to address the larger issue of where teens can go after school, in advance of a crisis, might provide a positive resolution and save the library bad publicity.

Issues raised by young people in the library have overlapped with concerns about other groups of what some librarians dubbed "problem patrons." Such a label focuses on the status of the patron rather than the objectionable conduct and is at odds with the librarian's obligation to meet patron needs in a non-judgmental fashion. Just as problems that arise most often among a certain age group (cracking gum, making out, or listening to MP3 players), others are commonly associated with economic condition and are not intrinsic to personal identity. Whenever economic hard times bring homeless people to the sheltering warmth of public libraries, librarians must separate conduct from status and make rules that apply to behavior, not to specific users.

As with any library rules, those that apply to people living on the streets or in shelters often grow out of experience. Indeed, many policies that govern patron conduct seem to catalog recent mischief that is now specifically outlawed pending further revision for misdeeds beyond the imagination of rule writers. And as with policies that seem to have been inspired by the after-school crowd, regulations dealing with matters such as sleeping in the library, offensive body odor, personal effects brought into the library, and conduct toward other patrons must be drafted and enforced in a generally applicable, content neutral, easily enforceable way. The Seattle Public Library, for example, limited personal goods that could be brought into the library to the size of what could fit under a library chair, and then revised the limit to exact dimensions. Like the rule for luggage that may be carried onto an airplane, this can be enforced consistently by all members of the library staff and applied to anybody bringing in a backpack, bedroll, or shopping bags.

Consistency of staff response is essential to ethical rule enforcement. As in the provision of service, whether and how a rule is enforced should not depend either on the identity of the staff member in charge or the identity of the patron whose conduct is at issue. If the library bans sleeping, and calls for sleepers to be awakened and then asked to leave for a repeat offense on the same day, all sleepers must be awakened, and, on dozing again, shown to the door, dowagers and homeless alike. Otherwise, the library loses its credibility and its reputation for fairness. If too many people must be awakened and ejected, the problem may be with the rule and not with the conduct.

KREIMER v. MORRISTOWN, NJ (1989)

In May 1989, after a series of incidents in which patrons and staff were bothered by the behavior, dress, and bodily odors of homeless people in the library, the board of the Joint Free Public Library of Morristown and Morris Township, New Jersey, enacted a "Patron Policy" to define standards of conduct and hygiene for those using the library. The policy was directed in particular at Richard R. Kreimer, a lifelong resident of Morristown who was then about forty years of age and living on the streets. While spending long hours at the library, Kreimer annoyed other patrons by staring at them and following them around. Since life on the street meant that Kreimer bathed infrequently, patrons and staff also objected to his mere presence in the library. The library had not previously had a policy to deal with such problems, but on numerous occasions had asked Kreimer to leave the library when patrons complained or staff found his conduct objectionable.

When, in the summer of 1989, Kreimer was asked to leave the library under the new rules, he objected to the policy and to the practice of singling him out. On his behalf, an ACLU attorney negotiated with the library and secured some "clarification" of the rules. These modifications were approved by the board in July 1989. Kreimer was not satisfied, however, and filed suit in federal district court against the Morristown library, police, and local government officials challenging the constitutionality of three particular provisions of the patron policy:

[1] Patrons shall be engaged in activities associated with the use of a public library while in the building. Patrons not engaged in reading, studying, or using library materials shall be asked to leave the building.

[5] Patrons shall respect the rights of other patrons and shall not harass or annoy others through noisy or boisterous activities, by unnecessary staring at another with the intent to annoy that person, by following another person through the building with the intent to annoy that person, by playing

Walkmans or other audio equipment so that others can hear it, by singing or talking to oneself or any other behavior which may reasonably result in the disturbance of other persons.

[9] Patrons shall not be permitted to enter the building without a shirt or other covering of their upper bodies or without shoes or other footwear. Patrons whose bodily hygiene is so offensive as to constitute a nuisance to other patrons shall be required to leave the building.

In May 1991, District Judge H. Lee Sarokin issued a summary judgment in favor of Kreimer. While upholding the shirts-and-shoes requirement, he found the rest of the above-mentioned provisions to be unconstitutionally vague and overbroad. He declared them null and void on their face and enjoined the library from enforcing them. Sarokin based his decision on a finding that a public library is a public forum that provides free access to receiving information. As such, its conduct is subject to a test of strict scrutiny and its regulations limited to reasonable time, place, and manner restrictions.

Under other circumstances, the library community might have welcomed Judge Sarokin's decision. He extolled the virtues of the public library as a quintessentially democratic institution. "The public library," he wrote, "is one of our great symbols of democracy. It is a living embodiment of the First Amendment because it includes voices of dissent. It tolerates that which is offensive." In a much-quoted passage, he continued,

Society has survived not banning books which it finds offensive from libraries; it will survive not banning persons whom it likewise finds offensive from its libraries. The greatness of our country lies in tolerating speech with which we do not agree; that same toleration must extend to people, particularly where the cause of revulsion may be of our own making. If we wish to shield our eyes and nose from the homeless, we should revoke their condition, not their library cards.

While acknowledging that some patron conduct might exceed the bounds of the acceptable, he ruled that the provisions at issue might lead to a discriminatory enforcement based on "the whim or personal vagaries of the persons in charge."

Board members and staff of the Joint Free Library of Morristown and Morris Township found that Sarokin's ruling left them without the ability to impose or enforce rules related to patron conduct and appealed to the Third Circuit Court of Appeals. The appellate court decided in their favor and lifted the injunction. It found that the library was a limited public forum, that is, open to the public only for the "specified purposes of exercising their First Amendment rights to read and receive information from library materials." As a limited public forum, a library could restrict conduct that interfered with its normal operations. In the court's view, "A library is a place dedicated to quiet, to knowledge and to beauty.... Its very purpose is to aid in the acquisition of knowledge through reading, writing, and quiet contemplation."

The court specifically upheld the three rules that Sarokin had found impermissibly vague and overbroad: that the library could require patrons to use the library for library purposes, prohibit noisy and boisterous activities, and remove patrons whose offensive bodily hygiene was a nuisance to others. In addition to the ruling itself, the library community took satisfaction in the court's finding that the First Amendment not only prohibits laws that censor information but additionally "encompasses the positive right of public access of access to information and ideas." Speaking on behalf of the Freedom to Read Foundation, which had filed an amicus brief in the case, its president C. James Schmidt declared the decision a win-win for libraries and library users.

Restrictions on the right to receive information in the library should usually be rejected, but regulation of other non-First Amendment conduct and content neutral regulations tailored to minimize interference with the use of the library for access to information may be upheld if they serve the library's important goals.

Balancing its obligations to libraries and patrons, the ALA formulated both a statement reiterating its commitment to library service to the poor and guidelines outlining appropriate policies to deal with offensive user behavior.

At the Joint Free Library of Morristown and Morris Township, librarians, trustees, and donors held a party to celebrate the conclusion of their long legal ordeal. Heralding their victory in a case that defined patron access and the role of the library in enabling patrons to receive information, they closed the library to the public.

QUESTIONS

- What ethical values were in play in this situation?
- Do you see any ways this situation might have been resolved without going to trial?
- What are the risks of going without a policy on patron behavior? Of formulating a policy in response to the conduct of one patron?
- Do you agree with the court's depiction of the role of a public library as a place to "aid in the acquisition of knowledge through reading, writing, and quiet contemplation"?
- How does a library reconcile its obligations to diverse populations when their needs conflict?

SOURCES

"ALA/Freedom to Read Foundation Responds to Latest Morristown Ruling," [ALA press release] March 26, 1992.

Farmer, Leslie S. J. "The Homeless, What's a Library to Do?" *WLW Journal* 15 (Summer 1992): 7–8.

Gaughan, Tom. "A Long Distance Call from a Homeless Man," *American Libraries* 21 (February 1990): 92.

Gaughan, Tom. "Stakes Rise in Lawsuit against N.J. Public Library," *American Libraries* 21 (November 1990): 940–941.

Hanley, Robert. "Homeless Man Has Deal in 2nd Suit in Morristown; Insurer Settles Despite Library's Objection," *New York Times*, March 3, 1992, B7.

Hanley, Robert. "Library Wins in Homeless-Man Case; Panel Says Offending Others Is Grounds to Evict Morristown Man," *New York Times*, March 25, 1992, B8.

Hanley, Robert. "Ruling Bars Libraries from Banning the Homeless as Offensive," *New York Times*, May 23, 1991, B1, B10.

"Homeless Crisis Hits Home at Suburban Library," *American Libraries* 20 (November 1989): 950–951.

Kreimer v. Bureau of Police for the Town of Morristown, 765 F. Supp 187 (DNJ May 22, 1991).

Kreimer v. Bureau of Police for the Town of Morristown, 958 F2d 1242 (3rd Cir. 1992).

"Libraries and License," *Wall Street Journal*, June 12, 1991.

"Library Hygiene in Morristown," [Editorial] *New York Times*, March 28, 1992, 22.

"Seeking a Balance: Patrons & Policies," *New Jersey Libraries* 25 (Fall 1992): 2–24. Including Hammeke, Nancy Byouk, "*Kreimer v. Morristown*: We Lived Through It and Won!" 12–15; "June 20, 1992 Proposed Guidelines for the Development of Policies Regarding User Behavior and Library Usage from the American Library Association," 22–24.

"The Little Library That Could," [Review & Outlook] *Wall Street Journal*, March 26, 1992.

Making exceptions for patron conduct in a principled way is a hallmark of ethical practice. Here is an example. If an out-of-town visitor stops at the public library on the way to the airport, with luggage far exceeding the allowable size, how might the library make it possible to accommodate the visitor while honoring the rule? Might an exception say that all those falling into the category of out-of-town travelers visiting the library on their way to or from their transportation may use the library, checking with library staff for an appropriate place to store their bags? If the library is visited by members of a family whose ancestor's portrait hangs on the library's wall, might a principled exception be made to allow them to take its picture despite a general ban on photographs? In determining a principled exception, staff might ask whether, if faced with the same or a similar situation, they could respond in the same way. For example, ethical decision making would require that the rule about baggage apply to travelers who were going by bus or train as well as by plane. It might even prompt the library to consider the installation of lockers that would benefit local users and visitors alike. Similarly, the rule about photographs might be waived in the case of a donor wishing to take a picture of his family's gift to the library.

GROUPS

Defining groups that may use a public library's meeting rooms, exhibit spaces, and bulletin boards requires the kind of content-neutral differentiation demanded by a standard of equitable service policies. While the ALA Code of Ethics does not provide specific guidance, the Library Bill of Rights makes clear that the allocation of these library resources is to be determined by objective criteria governing the type of groups or the proposed usage of the facilities, not the ideas or points of view to be expressed.

Through economic hard times of the Depression and the spirited political and social controversies of the New Deal, public libraries in the 1930s opened their doors to groups wishing to debate the topics of the day. Turning from a cultural to a democratic mission, libraries sought a role in creating an informed citizenry. Providing meeting space for group discussion extended the work libraries had already done in organizing programs on current events. In Des Moines, Iowa, the library, led by librarian Forrest Spaulding, had organized a program of citywide public forums with support from the Carnegie Corporation and then federal emergency funds. The meeting room in the Des Moines Public Library was used by political groups, including local communists and socialists on alternate Sundays.

The provision of the Library's Bill of Rights adopted by the Board of Trustees of the Des Moines Public Library in November 1938 included the kind of content-neutral criteria that should characterize an ethical policy determining what groups may use a library meeting room and under what conditions.

4. Library meeting rooms shall be available on equal terms to all organized non-profit groups for open meetings to which no admission fee is charged and from which no one is excluded.[12]

By limiting usage to not-for-profit groups that held meetings open to all without charge, Des Moines established criteria that could be readily and consistently applied. In adopting its own Library Bill of Rights in 1939, the ALA took a different approach. Emphasizing the democratic function of library meeting space, it called for availability on equal terms without regard to group beliefs or affiliations and without the more specific limits applicable in Des Moines.

3. The library as an institution to educate for democratic living should especially welcome the use of its meeting rooms for socially useful and cultural activities and the discussion of current public questions. Library meeting rooms should be available on equal terms to all groups in the community regardless of their beliefs or affiliations.[13]

The Library Bill of Rights revised and adopted by the ALA in June 1948 modified this version only slightly to apply on "equal terms to all groups in the community regardless of the beliefs and affiliations *of their members.*"[14]

The current clause of the Library Bill of Rights applying to meeting rooms and exhibit spaces, adopted on January 23, 1980, and affirmed on January 23, 1996, substitutes a standard of equity for one of equality but retains a content-neutral basis for the use of library rooms and bulletin boards.

VI. Libraries which make exhibit spaces and meeting rooms available to the public they serve should make such facilities available on an equitable basis, regardless of the beliefs or affiliations of individuals or groups requesting their use.[15]

The ALA's current Library Bill of Rights leaves it up to each library to determine what is an "equitable basis" for determining what groups may take advantage of this library service. Interpretations of the Library Bill of Rights have sought to clarify how libraries may make choices among the various groups that might seek to use the library's rooms or bulletin boards. Following an incident involving a fracas over an exhibit by the Ku Klux Klan in the public library in Winston-Salem, North Carolina, in the spring of 1979, the ALA Council approved its first interpretation on exhibit spaces and meeting rooms. Emphasizing the need to develop and publish policies governing the use of library spaces, it reiterated that eligibility requirements could not pertain to the content of the meeting or exhibit or the beliefs or affiliations of the sponsors.[16]

KKK EXHIBIT IN WINSTON-SALEM (1979)

Following its policy on the use of library meeting space, the Forsyth County Public Library in Winston-Salem, North Carolina, granted permission to the Knights of the Ku Klux Klan to hold an evening program in the library auditorium in February of 1979. Under the policy, public groups were allowed to use the auditorium for a single event that was free, open to all, and of public interest. The library board had endorsed the Library Bill of Rights in 1974 and reviewed it again in deciding to approve the Klan's request. As the library director, William Roberts III, explained, "This is the South. We do have Klanspeople in the United States, and they have just as much right to use our auditorium as any other organization." The county attorney agreed with the board's decision, but outraged citizens registered their complaints.

Instead of presenting a program in the auditorium, the Klan displayed a collection of KKK paraphernalia, including robes, hoods, insignia, and crosses. Before the exhibit opened, the library trustees viewed the exhibit, and when a trustee objected to one of the pamphlets on display, it was removed. Outside the library, demonstrators representing the National Association for the Advancement of Colored People and B'nai B'rith picketed in protest, charging that the library in effect had endorsed the KKK. In the library's view, it was endorsing not the Klan but free expression. When the exhibit opened, a large crowd, including news reporters, Klansmen, uniformed American Nazis shouting "Sieg Heil," and members of the leftist National United Workers Organization surged into the library. According to one report, black picketers who tried to enter the library were barred by the police. When a fight broke out inside, police quelled the disruption and cleared the hall. The exhibit closed early.

Looking back, the library and board believed they had acted correctly. According to the librarian, "You can't pick and choose among the groups that want to use the library, as long as they obey the rules. If we have to err, let's err on the side of freedom." The library's board reaffirmed its policy.

As a public institution dedicated to free expression and free access to ideas presenting all points of view concerning the problems and issues of our times, all meeting rooms and exhibit space ... are available on equal terms for the lawful activities of all groups and persons, regardless of their beliefs or affiliations.

The library's defense of free access attracted favorable press attention. An editorial in the *Winston-Salem Journal* praised the library's policy for its "reasonable guidelines" and concluded "as one board member said, '... the library's open to all.' That is as it should be." In its coverage, *American Libraries* noted what had gone unremarked, that at the same time the Klan displayed its paraphernalia in the auditorium, the library had an exhibit upstairs observing Black History Month.

QUESTIONS

- How did the library view of allowing the KKK to use the library auditorium differ from those who objected to the library's decision?

- What other steps might the library have taken to prepare for a possible disruption?
- What can be done to assure that library board members as well as the library director affirm the ethical values of the profession?

SOURCES

Berman, Sanford. "Comment," *Wilson Library Bulletin* 54 (September 1979): 5.

"Free Access in Forsyth Co." *Wilson Library Bulletin* 53 (June 1979): 683.

"KKK Clash Prompts Change in Meeting Room Policy," *Library Journal* 104 (July 1979): 1,403.

"KKK Library Exhibit Causes Melee in N.C." *Library Journal* 104 (April 1, 1979): 776.

Pearson, L. R. "KKK—and NBC—Spotlight Winston-Salem Library," *American Libraries* 10 (April 1979): 164.

Rosenfeld. H. E. "Klan Fracas at Forsyth Co. PL." *Wilson Library Bulletin* 53 (March 1979): 488, 490.

The most recent interpretation of the Library Bill of Rights on Meeting Spaces incorporates the standards set in the opinion of the federal circuit court of appeals in the case of *Concerned Women of America v. Lafayette County/Oxford, Mississippi*.[17]

Following a federal circuit court of appeals decision in the suit brought by Concerned Women of America against the Lafayette County/Oxford Public Library in Oxford, Mississippi, the ALA Council separated the interpretations for meeting rooms and exhibits and offered more specific guidance on meeting rooms that reflected the court's decision in that case.

CONCERNED WOMEN OF AMERICA AND THE LAFAYETTE COUNTY/OXFORD, MISSISSIPPI PUBLIC LIBRARY (1988)

In response to a phone request, the librarian of the Oxford, Mississippi Public Library denied permission to Concerned Women of America (CWA) to use the library auditorium to discuss and pray about current political issues. The library's refusal was based on its policy that limited use of the meeting space to

... groups or organizations of civic, cultural, or educational character, but not for social gatherings, entertaining, dramatic productions, money-raising or commercial purposes. It is also not available for meetings for social, political, partisan or religious purposes, or when in the judgment of the Director or Branch Librarian any disorder is likely to occur.

In response, Concerned Women for America, represented by the American Civil Liberties Union, sought an injunction that would require the library to allow use of the auditorium by CWA and other religious and political groups and for social gatherings and dramatic productions. The plaintiffs argued that since the library had allowed a variety of groups to hold meetings at the library, including Navy recruiters (closed meeting to discuss recruiting strategies), Oxford swim club (general meeting, rules policies for pool), AAUW (panel discussion on women in nontraditional occupations), American Legion (regular post meeting), and National Association of Retired Federal Workers (potluck luncheon, lecture on Alzheimer's disease), the library had become a public forum. Thus its denial of access to CWA was an infringement of the First Amendment right to free speech in a public forum and a violation of the Constitution.

The library unsuccessfully argued that as a limited public forum it could restrict the use of its meeting rooms. The library claimed that it had not discriminated on the content of speech, but had denied use by all religious or political groups. A federal judge issued a preliminary injunction against the library in September, 1988; a year later, a federal circuit court affirmed this decision. It found that the library's practice of allowing diverse groups to use the auditorium for purposes unrelated to the library opened this forum to the general public and that its refusal of access to Concerned Women of America constituted discrimination based on the content of speech and an infringement of the First Amendment.

According to its librarian, James Anderson, writing in *Public Libraries*, the library lacked funds to appeal. He foresaw two options for the library-closing its meeting space to all but library-sponsored activities or allowing unrestricted access.

We are advised that if the second option is selected the library could only impose reasonable restrictions governing the time, place, and manner or use of the facility. No groups could be excluded because of the religious, political, commercial, or social content of their proposed meetings. Under this option, events from political rallies to flee markets could be conducted in the auditorium.

In 1991, the American Library Association modified its interpretation of the Library Bill of Rights provision on meeting rooms to accord with this legal decision. But in 2006, a federal appeals court reached an opposite decision in a similar case, *Faith Center Church Evangelistic Ministries v. Glover*, reversing the issuance of a preliminary injunction against the Contra Costa County Public Library. In that case, the Antioch, California, branch had granted permission to the Faith Center

Church to hold meetings in the library but then rescinded its permission on finding that a planned program included an afternoon religious service following a morning workshop and discussion.

By making its meeting room available, the library sought "to encourage the use of the library meeting rooms for education, cultural and community related meetings, programs, and activities" and provided that non-profit and civic organizations, schools, for-profit, and government organizations could hold "meetings, programs, or activities of educational, cultural or community interest" on a first-come, first-served basis, during library hours. The policy, modified over the course of the litigation, prohibited use of library space for religious services. In July 30, 2004, Faith Center sought an injunction to prevent the library from excluding its program on the basis of its religious purpose policy. It argued that even language barring religious services constituted viewpoint discrimination.

In contrast to the decision in Concerned Women for America, the 9th Circuit found that a public library is a limited public forum. This means that the library is allowed to impose restrictions on the use of its space if they are viewpoint neutral and reasonable in light of library purposes. The county's decision to disallow the use of library space for religious worship met these tests of viewpoint neutrality and reasonableness.

As in the case involving Concerned Women for America, the court found that diverse groups had used the library's meeting space, including the Sierra Club, Narcotics Anonymous, and the East Contra Costa Democratic Club. It noted that the library had applied its policy restrictions consistently. Unlike the court in *Concerned Women*, it distinguished between a group discussing a religious topic and one conducting a worship service. The part of the Faith Church's program that involved religious discussion would be a permissible use of library space; the part devoted to religious worship would not.

What is clear in either case, if a library allows religious or political groups to use library space for the discussion of religious or political issues, it may not make distinctions on the basis of the views of particular groups. Rules may differentiate between types of organizations and categories of use, but they may not bar discussion based on religious or political affiliations or beliefs.

QUESTIONS

- Here are two cases related to the use of library space for religious purposes. What similarities and differences do you see in these cases?
- In the Faith Center case, the court declared that the library could restrict use of its meeting space for a function that might undermine the library's

primary function "as a venue for reading, writing, and quiet contemplation." Do you agree with this characterization?

- Libraries have the option of limiting the use of library space to library purposes. How would you define a library's purpose? What activities might it justifiably exclude on this basis?
- Some library meeting room policies require that all meetings held in the library by outside groups be open to the public. What are the pros and cons of such a requirement?

SOURCES

Anderson, James F., "As If We Didn't Have Enough to Do": A Report on the Case of the Concerned Women of America versus Lafayette County/Oxford Public Library. *Public Libraries* 29 (May/June 1990): 172–174.

Concerned Women for America v. Lafayette County/Oxford Public Library (Mississippi) 699 F. Supp. 95 (N.D. Mississippi 1988); 883 F2d 32 (5th Cir. 1989).

"Federal Court Ruling Affects Library Meeting Rule Policies," *The Unabashed Librarian*, no. 75: 26.

Faith Center Church Evangelistic Ministries v. Glover, 05-16132 9th Cir.

DC No. CV-04-03111-JSW OPINION appeal from US Dist Ct for the Northern District of California, Jeffrey S. White, District Judge, Presiding, argued 2/2006, filed Sept. 20, 2006.

The text of Article VI remained the same. So did the advice that libraries develop and publish policies governing use of library meeting space, and define the time, place, and manner of use. As before libraries were to avoid reference to the content of meeting, beliefs, or affiliations of sponsors. But the example closely follows the court's decision.

If meeting rooms in libraries supported by public funds are made available to the general public for non-library sponsored events, the library may not exclude any group based on the subject matter to be discussed or based on the ideas that the group advocates. For example, if a library allows charities and sports clubs to discuss their activities in library meetings rooms, then the library should not exclude partisan political or religious groups from discussing their activities in the same facilities. If a library opens its meeting rooms to a wide variety of civic organizations, then the library may not deny access to a religious organization. Libraries may wish to post a permanent notice near the meeting room stating that the library does not advocate or endorse the viewpoints of meetings or meeting room users.[18]

To avoid situations where group affiliation might cause controversy, libraries have the option of limiting the use of meeting rooms for library-related purposes only.

More recently, the 9th Circuit Court has reached a contrary conclusion in the case of Faith Center Church, which allows libraries to devise policies that preclude religious or political organizations from using library meeting rooms for some purposes. Such a ruling is actually more in keeping with library tradition in which policies may exclude certain types of organizations (for-profit groups) or activities (worship services) as long as the rule applies to all organizations of that type without distinctions made on the basis of their point of view. Since the law in this area is unsettled, libraries need to consult counsel but also make clear the tradition of libraries in making meeting space available in an equitable and content-neutral way.

ACADEMIC LIBRARIES

Academic libraries face many of the same issues in determining who may access their collections and use their facilities. As higher education has become more universal and its institutions more diverse and differentiated, college and university libraries have honed their access policies and stepped up enforcement of patron conduct. As with the public library, questions about who may come through the door have increasingly been separated from the matter of what information resources they may use once they get there. With databases and journals available online, the visitor to the library has access in print to just a fraction of the library's resources.

While differentiating levels of service within an academic library is not unethical, it must be done in such a way that all patrons falling within a given category receive the same general access privileges. That is, levels of service must be defined in objective, content-neutral ways. So, for example, if the library provides service to visiting scholars, eligibility for such privileges might be conditioned on degrees earned or faculty status at another institution. Privileges must not be denied because of the subject of the research topic or granted because of the lustrous reputation of the visitor's home institution. Undergraduates might be barred from a law library as a general rule, with an exception made on the basis of a demonstrated research need, vouched for by a faculty member. Alumni might be granted free borrowing privileges not available to the general public, but access to databases might require payment of a fee and conditioned on compliance with licensing agreements.

Rules governing patron conduct in an academic setting also reflect the changes in the mission of the college or university library from a repository of research materials to the center of community conversation. Trying to attract students to the library in an age when information can be easily accessed from dorm room or coffee house, academic libraries have employed a variety of techniques to make their environment more appealing and their atmosphere more relaxed, going so far as to merge library and student center, install library cafes, and allow drinking in the stacks and at computer terminals. Where drinking and eating in the library were once forbidden in the interest of protecting library materials, they are now encouraged in hope of attracting students. Regulations concerning the type of food and beverage, the kinds of permitted containers, or the places where students may eat and drink must be characterized by clear guidance, widespread publicity, and evenhanded enforcement. Where group work is encouraged, it may be easier to limit the size of the group than its noise level. It should also be clear which library staff members are responsible for rule enforcement. And of course, any rule governing student conduct should govern staff and faculty conduct as well, including cell phone conversations, use of library elevators, and sleeping on library couches.

QUESTIONS

- How much service should academic libraries provide to alumni? Circulation privileges? Interlibrary loan? Access to databases? Free? For a fee?
- Which alumni are entitled to service—all alums, dues-paying members of the alumni association, or Friends of the University Library?
- At a publicly supported institution, what services may be offered to members of the public? Which members of the public? What services?
- Does a library at a community college have a different obligation to the public than the library at a state university? Does geography matter? Does the library at a land-grant institution in a remote rural area have a different obligation than the library in an urban research institution in a city well-served by its public library?

Having focused on the ethical aspects of service, we will now turn our attention to the ethical dimensions of access, the core value of librarianship which infuses service and defines the central mission of all librarianship.

END NOTES

1. American Library Association Code of Ethics, adopted by the ALA Council June 28, 1995.

2. American Library Association Library Bill of Rights, adopted June 18, 1948; amended February 2, 1961, June 27, 1967, and January 23, 1980, reaffirmed January 23, 1996, by the ALA Council, in *Intellectual Freedom Manual*, 7th ed. Chicago: American Library Association, 2006, 56–57, http://www.ala.org/ala/oif/statementspols/statementsif/librarybillrights.htm.

3. For a summary of the study's findings, see Robert D. Leigh, *The Public Library in the United States: The General Report of the Public Library Inquiry.* New York: Columbia University Press, 1950. See also Douglas Raber, *Librarianship and Legitimacy: The Ideology of the Public Library Inquiry.* Westport, CT: Greenwood, 1997.

4. Hiller C. Wellman, "The Library's Primary Duty," [President's Address] Berkeley Conference, June 3–9, 1915, 89–93.

5. Judith F. Krug and James A. Harvey, "The History of the Library Bill of Rights, Part One," *American Libraries* 3 (January 1972): 80–82; "The History of the Library Bill of Rights, Part Two," *American Libraries* 3 (February 1972): 183–184, at 184. Other sources: Ervin J. Gaines, "The Library Bill of Rights: The ALA Intellectual Freedom Committee Proposes a Revision," *Library Journal* 92 (March 1, 1967): 984–985, with side-by-side comparisons of present text, adopted 1948, revised 1961, and text proposed for 1967 adoption. "San Francisco Conference [Council]," *ALA Bulletin* 61 (July/August 1967): 822-824; "San Francisco Conference: Preconferences ["Intellectual Freedom and the Teenager"], *ALA Bulletin* 61 (July/August 1967): 833. For a retrospective, see Lillian N. Gerhardt, "Been There, Done That," *School Library Journal* 41 (December 1995): 4. Gerhardt was the *SLJ* editor-in-chief. This was the first in a series on the freedom of access.

6. "Suggested Code of Library Ethics," *Library Journal* 55 (February 15, 1930): 165.

7. For editorials on race discrimination, see Eric Moon and Karl Nyren, eds., *Library Issues: The Sixties.* New York: R. R. Bowker, 1970, 117–151.

8. "Guidelines for Library Services to Spanish-Speaking Library Users Approved by the Board of Directors of the Reference and User Services Association, January 2007," *Reference & User Services Quarterly* 47, no. 2 (2007).

9. "Rowdy Teens Get Carded at Library," *School Library Journal* 50 (January 2004): 16.

10. "Ohio Bars Unchaperoned After-Schoolers," *American Libraries* 37 (March 2006): 18–19.

11. "Maplewood Stays Open, Will Offer More Programming," *American Libraries* 38 (February 2007): 14.

12. "The Library's Bill of Rights," *ALA Bulletin* 33 (January 1939) [inside back cover], adopted by the Des Moines [Public Library] Board of Trustees, November 21, 1938.

13. "Library Bill of Rights, 1939," *Intellectual Freedom Manual*, 7th ed. Chicago: American Library Association, 2006, 59.

14. "Library Bill of Rights," *ALA Bulletin* 42 (1948) [Adopted by the ALA Council in Atlantic City on June 18, 1948].

15. Library Bill of Rights, adopted June 18, 1948. Amended February 2, 1961, June 27, 1967, and January 23, 1980, by the ALA Council. *Intellectual Freedom Manual*, 7th ed., 55–56, http://www.ala.org/ala/oif/statementspols/statementsif/librarybillofrights.pdf.

16. Exhibit Spaces and Meeting Rooms: An Interpretation of the Library Bill of Rights. [Adopted by the ALA Council, midwinter, 1981; edited version prepared by Frances C. Dean, chair, Intellectual Freedom Committee], *Newsletter on Intellectual Freedom* 30 (March 1981): 31, 34.

17. *Concerned Women for America v. Lafayette County/Oxford Public Library* (Mississippi) 699 F. Supp. 95 (N.D. Mississippi 1988); 883 F2d 32 (5th Cir. 1989).

18. Meeting Rooms: An Interpretation of the Library Bill of Rights. Adopted by the ALA Council, July 2, 1991.

4

ACCESS: WHAT INFORMATION

Selection, then, begins with a presumption in favor of liberty of thought; censorship, with a presumption in favor of thought control. Selection's approach to the book is positive, seeking its values in the book as a book, and in the book as a whole. Censorship's approach is negative, seeking vulnerable characteristics wherever they can be found—anywhere within the book, or even outside it. Selection seeks to protect the right of the reader to read; censorship seeks to protect—not the right—but the reader from himself from the fancied effects of his reading. The selector has faith in the intelligence of the reader; the censor has faith only in his own.

—Lester Asheim[1]

In 1976, Robert Hauptman, then a library school student, reported "an experiment in ethics" inspired by a series of fatal bombings. Describing himself as young, bearded, and deferential, he approached librarians in six public and seven academic libraries, confirming first that they were the reference librarian and then asking for information on how to construct a small explosive device, particularly the chemical properties of cordite, and then inquiring about its potency, "whether a small amount will blow up, say, a normal suburban house." Hauptman's hypothetical perfectly demonstrates the intersecting values of service and access. (As we shall see, it also raises concerns about patron privacy and philosophical conflicts of interest.) Although it is not certain that those identifying themselves as reference librarians actually held professional degrees, the query did raise the issue of service by whom, since Hauptman was gauging their adherence to the ALA Code of Ethics. It also suggested the possibility that the identity of the requester would affect the response, raising the question of service for whom. In fact, one librarian refused service to Hauptman, not because he might be a potential anarchist, but because he was not a student at the college. And because of the potentially harmful uses of the information requested, the example also presents the question of access to what information. Hauptman expressed astonishment that, "Of the thirteen librarians queried, not one refused to supply the information on ethical grounds."[2] In fact, the responses seem firmly grounded in the ethical values of service and access. Hauptman does not address what factors, such as erratic behavior or an explicit threat, other than the nature of the requested information that would justify a refusal to provide assistance. Taking our cue from Lester Asheim, we will argue that a commitment to both service and access requires a presumption in favor of the library user unless compelling circumstances suggest otherwise.

As the core ethical value of librarianship, providing access to information is what distinguishes librarians from other professionals and defines the professional identity of practitioners. Having seen the interconnection between service and access in the many ways that service policies can foster or impede access, we will now concentrate on the content of information itself. We are especially interested in how librarians have viewed their role not just in making information available but in deciding *what* information libraries will make available. In this, the decisions of librarians have reflected the intellectual currents of their day as well as the legal standards that set the outer boundaries of the permissible. Within that realm, however, librarians have vast scope for choice. What they choose to make available reveals how they see the role of libraries and their own duty as information professionals. In this chapter, we will see that ideas about this have evolved as our legal framework and society have changed. In the next chapter, we will see how these ideas have changed with the development of new technologies to deliver information.

PRINCIPLES

Early Codes of Ethics

As with the ethical dimensions of service, the ethical definition of access derives from the role of librarians and libraries, but early draft codes did little to address the *type* of material librarians were to provide. Accepting the role of the library as a cultural and educational institution and the role of the librarian in selecting books to further this purpose, Mary Wright Plummer and Charles Knowles Bolton paid little attention in their codes to the content of library collections. Instead, they focused on the needs of patrons and the obligation of the librarian to library users. Speaking in 1903, Plummer expected the professional librarian to know the history of books and have a mastery of administration and technique, but cautioned against a mechanical librarianship. Instead, she sought library service where "the borrower's real wishes and grievances can be heard and intelligently attended to."[3]

In the canon on book selection, Bolton's 1922 draft stated, "Purchases of books should reflect the needs of the community rather than the personal taste or interest of the librarian. His selection of books should be catholic, and his power to guide be exercised with discretion." Then in a comment, he added: "A library is not a collection of books made after a fixed pattern. Each community has its bookish needs unlike those of any other community under the sun. It is this infinite variety that gives the profession which collects and makes books useful its attraction." Commenting on "A Librarian's Province," Bolton raised the specter of censorship. Note that his concern was not that patrons would be denied access to information but that they might be harmed by exposure to potentially harmful or offensive material.

Censorship of reading is a perilous No Man's Land on the boundary of a librarian's province. How far an executive should go in exposing books which are in his opinion destructive of morals and society, and those issued frankly as propaganda, is a serious question.[4]

For Bolton, however, determining the boundaries of the permissible in a library collection was the responsibility of the board of trustees, and not the librarian.

The 1929 draft presented by the Committee on the Code of Ethics, chaired by Josephine Rathbone, regarded the content of the collection as part of the relationship between the librarian and the library's constituency. The librarian was to win favor for the library by assuming an active role in the life of the community and taking care not to offend against community standards of decorum.

The librarian, representing the governing body, should see that the library serves impartially all individuals, groups and elements that make up it[s] constituency. In the case of the public library as a non-partisan institution the books purchased should represent all phases of opinion and interest rather than the personal tastes of the librarian or board members. In an official capacity, the librarian and members of the staff should not express personal, religious, or economic issues, especially those of a local nature.[5]

The Code of Ethics finally adopted by the ALA in December 1938 similarly lodged responsibility for the content of the collection in the librarian's obligation to the library's constituency.

The chief librarian, aided by staff members in touch with the constituency, should study the present and future needs of the library, and should acquire materials on the basis of those needs. Provision should be made for as wide a range of publications and as varied a representation of viewpoints as is consistent with the policies of the library and with the funds available.[6]

Thus, the first official ethical pronouncement on access to information suggested that the library both meet community information needs and make diverse points of view available. The possibility that these might be at odds was not addressed.

Library Bill of Rights

The adoption of the Library Bill of Rights by the ALA in 1939 provided the ethical underpinnings of access that the association's Code of Ethics, adopted just six months earlier, lacked. Emerging from a political setting, the Library Bill of Rights focused on the politically controversial rather than the morally offensive. This was understandable in a society then facing threats of fascism abroad and fears of Communism at home and for a profession seeking to define a new concept of itself. Aimed at public libraries, the Library Bill of Rights simultaneously called for collections based on community interest:

1. Books and other reading matter selected for purchase from the public funds should be chosen because of value and interest to people of the community

But without regard to the identity or philosophy of the author:

and in no case should the selection be influenced by the race or nationality or the political or the religious views of the writers.

And reflecting diverse points of view:

2. As far as available material permits, all sides of questions on which differences of opinion exist should be represented fairly and adequately in the books and other reading matter purchased for public use.[7]

Although said to have been prompted by the controversy over John Steinbeck's novel, *The Grapes of Wrath*, published in 1939, the Library Bill of Rights did not address the inherent contradiction in these standards which was demonstrated by the refusal of the library in Steinbeck's hometown to carry the novel.[8]

The 1948 revision of the Library Bill of Rights incorporated a harsher view of would-be censors, in both moral and political spheres, and a stronger statement of the librarian's duty to fight them.

3. Censorship of books, urged or practiced by volunteer arbiters of morals or political opinion or by organizations that would establish a coercive concept of

Americanism, must be challenged by libraries in maintenance of their responsibility to provide public information and enlightenment through the printed word.

At the same time, it retained language inserted in October 1944 that incorporated the standard of "factually correct" in selection considerations. In language that would remain until 1967, provision of diverse viewpoints was to be limited to those of sound factual authority.

2. There should be the fullest practicable provision of material representing all points of view concerning the problems and issues of our times, international, national, and local; and books or other reading matter of sound factual authority should not be proscribed or removed from library shelves because of partisan or doctrinal disapproval.[9]

Responding to Cold War witch hunts, librarians amended the Library Bill of Rights in 1951 to proscribe labeling and applied its provisions to all information formats. But for almost four decades of war, political upheaval, civil rights agitation, and ongoing censorship battles, the ALA did not modify its Code of Ethics. When the concise 1975 Statement on Professional Ethics and the 1981 Code of Ethics finally replaced the lengthy and interpretive 1938 code, they provided only the most general guidance on what materials libraries were ethically obliged to make available. The introduction of the 1981 code declared:

In a political system grounded in an informed citizenry, librarians are members of a profession explicitly committed to intellectual freedom and the freedom of access to information. We have a special obligation to ensure the free flow of information and ideas to present and future generations.[10]

Making Choices

We saw in earlier chapters that librarians moved from service to access as their primary value. Beginning in 1975, statements of library ethics emphasized access to diverse ideas, no single definition of truth, but a commitment to the marketplace of ideas, and an acceptance of controversy as part of the democratic process. Though codes of library ethics and the Library Bill of Rights make clear the overarching concept of access, ethical dilemmas arise in practical situations where the presence of material in a collection prompts patron or community objections. The most difficult issues that librarians face today about the content of their collections are the same as in earlier generations: sexually explicit text or images, controversial political ideas, and suspect or offensive religious beliefs.

To provide access ethically, librarians must understand the difference between what is obscene and what is offensive, negotiate the differences between selection and censorship, and find a balance between quality and demand. In fulfilling the responsibility of the library to society in providing access to information, they must also heed the concerns of patrons who wish to protect the most vulnerable members of society from harm. In providing access, librarians must help patrons understand not only the role that all libraries play in making information available but the different roles and responsibilities of individual libraries. The more material there is from which to choose, and the broader the legal protections of the First Amendment, the more contentious will be the debates over the proper boundaries of library access.

Concerns about access at the start of twenty-first century are much the same as they were at the close of the nineteenth century. At about the time library pioneers founded the ALA in 1876, courts established the legal standard for obscenity that reflected society's fear of dangerous ideas and their potential impact on the young and vulnerable. And while the ethical obligations of twenty-first-century librarians differ from those of their nineteenth-century forebears, the nature of the controversial material, and often the material itself, remains the same. From *Huckleberry Finn* to *Harry Potter*, evolution to global warming, *Fanny Hill* to *The Higher Power of Lucky*, sexual equality to sexual orientation, legal standards, social change, and library practice have met on the contested turf of information access.

This is an area where language matters. Librarians, board members, and library users need to understand three crucial differences:

- between **obscene**, a legal term, and **offensive**, a societal term of disapprobation
- between **censorship**, the purposeful exclusion of otherwise appropriate material, and **selection**, the exercise of professional judgment based on institutional and user requirements
- between a professional standard of **quality** and a democratic standard of **demand**

We will look at each of these in turn and then at the tools librarians have developed to help them make these choices in an ethical way.

Since the 1939 Library Bill of Rights and the 1975 Statement of Ethics, the library profession has opposed censorship and urged librarians to provide access to diverse points of view. But how can librarians make ethical choices about the information they provide?

OBSCENE VERSUS OFFENSIVE

Obscenity Defined

As librarians formulate criteria for choosing materials to add to their collections, legislatures and courts formulate standards for the limits of free expression under the First Amendment. Laws and judicial decisions establish the boundaries of the permissible, framing the universe of information from which librarians may select. Shaped by the same societal currents, legal standards defining access and library ideas governing collections demonstrate a similar expanding tolerance. Basic questions about the standards to be applied in obscenity cases and in book selection have shared concerns about the potential harm that explicit sexuality, political ideology, or religious unorthodoxy might have on society's most vulnerable members. The First Amendment of the U.S. Constitution, adopted in 1791, provided that:

Congress shall make no law respecting an establishment of religion, or prohibiting the free exercise thereof; or abridging the freedom of speech, or of the press; or the right of the people peaceably to assemble, and to petition the Government for a redress of grievances.

The First Amendment protected freedoms of the press and speech from acts of Congress, but left states free to enact their own obscenity statutes. The legal definition of obscenity adopted widely in the United States derived from the standard set in an 1868 case in England that involved not pornography but blasphemy; but the crucial determinant was the effect of such material on society's most vulnerable members. In the case of *Regina v. Hicklin*, the court held,

I think the test of obscenity is this, whether the tendency of the matter charged as obscenity is to deprave and corrupt those whose minds are open to such immoral influences, and into whose hands a publication of this sort may fall.[11]

In 1908, when ALA president Arthur Bostwick articulated the standard of "the good, the true, and the beautiful" for public library circulating collections, he expressed a widely shared belief that society needed to shield its members from potentially harmful information. Writing in 1923 about the need to collect more modern fiction, Mary Rothrock specifically excluded readers who were immature and books that were beyond the pale. Library restrictions based on age, the exclusion of works by political radicals and novels on sexually explicit themes, and myriad other measures to control "objectionable" books all sought to protect the reader from exposure to whatever society at large or the local community deemed dangerous.[12]

In advocating the addition of modern fiction to public library collections, Mary Rothrock and Helen Haines considered an average adult as the potential reader, thus anticipating in a library setting the standard formulated in the 1933 *Ulysses* case. Imported into the United States by publishers at the Modern Library to test the legal standard of obscenity, James Joyce's masterpiece was tried in a customs proceeding in which the book itself was the defendant. Judge John Woolsey's decision allowing importation overturned decades of legal precedent by judging the work according to the reaction of an average, normal adult (*l'homme moyen sensual*) and by looking at the work as a whole, rather than at salacious excerpts or offensive words.[13] Applied to a library setting, this standard of access suggested that librarians should no longer look for the one unacceptable flaw that would bar the admission to a collection, as Bostwick had proposed in 1908, but should consider the merits of the work as a whole.

Subsequent court rulings further established these principles. In the 1950s, the Supreme Court ruled that obscenity was not protected by the First Amendment but also established a test for obscenity that did not include erotic classics like *Fanny Hill: Memoirs of a Woman of Pleasure* if such works were found to have some redeeming social value.[14] In 1973, the Supreme Court formulated the current three-part test for obscenity:

(1) whether the average person applying contemporary community standards would find that the work, taken as a whole, appeals to the prurient interest; (2) whether the work depicts or describes in a patently offensive way, sexual conduct specifically defined by state law; and (3) whether the work, taken as a whole, lacks serious literary, artistic, political, or scientific value.[15]

Most states have adopted obscenity standards incorporating this, though some have no obscenity laws at all. In 1956, the Supreme Court held that the equal protection and due-process clauses of the Fourteenth Amendment require states to abide by First Amendment standards. They may not give less protection to free speech and free press than is guaranteed by the First Amendment. They may, however, establish a broader interpretation and allow greater freedom than defined by the Supreme Court.

Libraries and courts are both concerned about community standards. In obscenity cases, the question remained: by what community's standards was material to be measured? In the case of *Pope v. Illinois*, decided in 1987, the Supreme Court interpreted the "third prong" of its obscenity test to mean that the value of a work was to be determined by objective standards, not by the standards of a particular community.

The proper inquiry is not whether an ordinary member of a given community would find [some] value in the allegedly obscene material, but whether a reasonable person would find such value in the material taken as a whole.[16]

In an obscenity prosecution, this means that both the prosecution and the defense may offer expert testimony on the value of the material. The tastes of a local community cannot be the gauge of that worth; rather, a reasonable person determines its value based on the evidence presented. In thinking about library collections in an analogous way, "expert testimony" as to the worth of a work is presented through book reviews and the opinions of literary and cultural commentators. Exclusion of a controversial but worthy work from a collection merely because it is offensive to the local community is by this standard unethical.

QUESTION

- Kathleen Molz argued in "The Public Custody of High Pornography"[17] that even material that is protected by the First Amendment may not be suitable for a public library, which as a public trust must be a responsible steward of a community's resources. Debate the pros and cons of her position.

The Social Context

Since obscene material is not protected by the First Amendment, the production, possession, or sale of such material is illegal. Further, material is not obscene until a court of law has determined that it meets the legal standard for obscenity. Note, also, that the obscenity standard applies only to material that is sexually explicit, not excessively violent or racially or ethnically repugnant. It is in this vast borderland of offensive materials that librarians face challenges to their collections. Dorothy Broderick, founding editor of *Voice of Youth Advocates*, maintained that a library needs to have something in the collection to offend everyone.[18] With changes in societal values and taste, over time the same work may be offensive to different groups and for different reasons.

In 1885, less than a decade after the founding of the ALA, the Committee of the Public Library of Concord, Massachusetts, removed Mark Twain's recently published *Adventures of Huckleberry Finn* from its shelves.[19] Committee members feared that Huck's rascally example would exert a dangerous moral influence on the young, the same concerns that often prompt citizens today to demand the removal of material from library collections—apprehension that a dangerous idea, sexually explicit content, or unacceptable religious views will harm the young, uneducated, or impressionable. In more than a century since *Huckleberry Finn* was published, its presence on library shelves and on school reading lists has been challenged for its racist language, the relationship between a white boy and a black man, and the possible homoerotic themes in the story. In the 1950s, the National Association for the Advancement of Colored People and author Ralph Ellison sought to have it removed from the reading lists of New York City public schools for depicting an inappropriate relationship between a black man and a white youth. The catalog of charges against the novel document changing societal values and concerns about youth, race, and homosexuality. Like *Ulysses, The Adventures of Huckleberry Finn* appears on lists of literary masterpieces and most challenged works. Similarly, John Steinbeck's *The Grapes of Wrath*, published in 1939, incurred the opposition of farm organizations, California businesses, Oklahoma natives, political conservatives, and disapproving clergy, and remains, like *Huckleberry Finn* and *Ulysses*, among the masterworks perennially targeted by concerned citizens.

The *Pico* Decision

While the Supreme Court's First Amendment cases have dealt largely with the definition of obscenity, its sole case involving a school library collection dealt with books that were offensive, and potentially harmful, because of their political, sexual, and racial content. The Supreme Court handed down its decision in *Board of Education, Island Trees Free School District No. 26 v. Pico* in 1982, but the case had begun in 1975, when the library's collection reflected the country's recent civil rights struggles and the war in Vietnam. In *Pico*, members of a Long Island school board used a list compiled by Parents of New York United (PONYU) to direct the removal of "objectionable" books that they described as "just plain filthy" from the high school and junior high school library. The board subsequently appointed a committee of staff and parents to decide on the disposition of the books but rejected its recommendation that most of the books be retained. A lower court dismissed a suit brought by students, finding no constitutional violation, but a court of appeals reversed and the Supreme Court upheld this judgment, remanding the case for a determination of whether the books had been removed for political or doctrinal reasons.

The court's plurality opinion by Justice William Brennan remains the Supreme Court's only ruling that defines the right of students to access potentially controversial ideas or offensive material in a school library.

... [J]ust as access to ideas makes it possible for citizens generally to exercise their rights of free speech and press in a meaningful manner, such access prepares students for active and effective participation in the pluralistic, often contentious society in which they will soon be adult members ...

For Brennan, the motive of those who would remove books from the shelf was crucial.

Our Constitution does not permit the official suppression of <u>ideas</u>. Thus whether petitioners' removal of books from their school libraries denied respondents their First Amendment rights depends upon the motivation behind petitioners' actions. If petitioners [the school board] <u>intended</u> by their removal decision to deny respondents access to ideas with which petitioners disagreed, and if this intent was the decisive factor in petitioners' decision, then petitioners have exercised their discretion in violation of the Constitution ...[20]

The decision concluded, "Local school boards may not remove books from school libraries simply because they dislike ideas contained in those books and seek by their removal to prescribe what shall be orthodox in politics, nationalism, religion, and other matters of opinion."[21]

In an appendix to his dissent, Justice Lewis Powell included excerpts from the allegedly objectionable works by Langston Hughes, Eldridge

Cleaver, Bernard Malamud, Kurt Vonnegut, and Alice Childress, and the anonymous author of *Go Ask Alice*. The presence of minority writers and political dissidents and works with explicit language exemplified the kind of materials most frequently challenged in public as well as school libraries. With page numbers for offensive passages and italicized expletives, the appendix ran counter to both legal and library standards for considering a work as a whole and determining its merits apart from the identity of the author.[22] Materials that were politically radical, sexually explicit, and potentially harmful to young people remained central concerns for those seeking to impede access to information.

In 1986, the ALA first adopted an interpretation of the Library Bill of Rights defining access in a school library setting. Most recently modified in 2005, Access to Resources and Services in the School Library Media Program states that

The school library media program plays a unique role in promoting intellectual freedom. It serves as a point of voluntary access to information and ideas and as a learning laboratory for students as they acquire critical thinking and problem-solving skills needed in a pluralistic society.[23]

The school library media specialist is to promote principles of intellectual freedom while working with teachers and building collections to support the mission of the school district. The interpretation echoes the *Pico* decision in calling for collections that are "free of constraints resulting from personal, partisan, or doctrinal disapproval." School boards are to adopt "policies that guarantee students access to a broad range of ideas."

SELECTION VERSUS CENSORSHIP

In their quest for professionalism, librarians endlessly explored the terrain between censorship and selection. Before the ALA adopted the Library Bill of Rights in 1939, the value of service was ascendant. Librarians saw selection decisions as a central aspect of the service they provided, applying their expertise to make informed choices about materials in their collections and judicious recommendations to readers seeking advice. *Pico* raised questions of access in the context of a school library, with the court finding that the First Amendment rights of students must be protected in order to ensure the long-term health of democracy. It reminds us that questions of appropriate access to material are answered in the context of the particular identity of the library, its institutional mission, and its clientele. The universe of material is so broad and the information output so enormous that libraries must define their individual roles and identify the extent to which they will collect in various subject areas. Ethical standards governing individual selection decisions must be seen in a similar institutional context.

"The Good, the True, and the Beautiful"

In 1908, Arthur Bostwick, then head of circulation at the New York Public Library, titled his presidential address to the ALA, "The Librarian as Censor." Bostwick was careful to define the limits of the censor's role, making clear that he was not speaking of research libraries but of those for the free use of the general public. Indeed, he began,

Let us admit at the outset that there is absolutely no book that may not find its place on the shelves of some library and perform there its appointed function. From this point of view every printed page is a *document*, a record of something, material, as the French say, *pour server*, from a mass of such material neither falsity, immorality, nor indecency can exclude it.

Thus, a research library such as the Kinsey Institute for Formal Research at Indiana University may lawfully collect materials to support studies that document changing sexual mores. A research library may maintain collections of racial ephemera or states' rights pamphlets that would be highly inappropriate in a public library.

For public library circulating collections, though, Bostwick argued that the librarian as censor was obliged to select "the Good, the True, and the Beautiful."

Those books that we desire, we want because they fall under one or more of these three heads—they must be morally beneficial, contain accurate information or satisfy the esthetic sense in its broadest meaning. Conversely we may exclude a book because it lacks goodness, truth or beauty. We may thus reject it on one or more of the three following grounds: badness—that is undesirable moral teaching or effect; falsity—that is, mistakes, errors or misstatements of fact; and ugliness—matter of manner offensive to our sense of beauty, fitness or decency.[24]

The librarian, as censor, would be a "sifter," filtering material and protecting patrons from the bad, the false, and the ugly. Much like an exclusive club barring an otherwise eligible member, Bostwick said, the librarian would look for the one disqualifying aspect that would cause a book to be censored rather than selected. Interestingly, it was the matter of truth that most perplexed Bostwick, especially in nonfiction works meant for a popular audience.

WILSON LIBRARY BULLETIN AND THE SEX QUESTIONNAIRE (1992)

For his June 1992 column in the *Wilson Library Bulletin*, librarian and humorist Will Manley offered a tongue-in-cheek questionnaire, "Librarians and Sex." Librarians were invited to answer questions ranging from the professional ("Should libraries carry *Playboy, Playgirl,* and *Playguy?* Should circulating videotapes be labeled with MPAA ratings?") to the personal (Check all the places where you have had sex: sleazy motel room, kitchen floor, car, airplane, library ....). As Manley later described it, he received a phone call on June 17 from Leo Weins, president of the H. W. Wilson Company. Weins, with whom Manley had worked amicably for twelve years, expressed his unhappiness with the survey, reported receiving an objection to the column from a subscriber, and dismissed Manley from the *Bulletin*. In a later statement, Weins declared that the offending survey "contained inappropriate language and was completely inconsistent with either the publishing standards of the Wilson Company or the *Bulletin*'s editorial responsibility." Further, Weins ordered the destruction of any copies of the issue not already mailed to subscribers along with all the copies that would have been distributed at the ALA conference to be held later in June in San Francisco.

Outrage at the dismissal of Manley and the destruction of the journal was immediate, vocal, and widespread. H. W. Wilson editor Mary Jo Godwin and five columnists resigned in protest. Members of the Social Responsibilities Round Table picketed the H. W. Wilson booth in the conference exhibit hall. SRRT member Sanford Berman introduced a resolution censuring the conduct of H. W. Wilson at the first ALA Membership Meeting on June 29:

WHEREAS Will Manley was last week summarily dismissed as a *Wilson Library Bulletin* contributor because his June 1992 column, which included a "Librarians and Sex" questionnaire, displeased the H. W. Wilson Company President; and

WHEREAS the H. W. Wilson Company President has order that all remaining copies of the June 1992 issue be discarded; and

WHEREAS Mary Jo Godwin, WLB Editor, has resigned in protest;

THEREFORE BE IT RESOLVED that the American Library Association censure the H. W. Wilson Company for this flagrant act of censorship; commend Mary Jo Godwin for her personal integrity and outstanding commitment to intellectual freedom; demand the immediate reinstatement of Manley and Godwin, together with public apologies by the Wilson Company to both persons; encourage all libraries and individuals to immediately cancel their WLB subscriptions and urge all other WLB contributors to boycott the magazine unless and until Manley and Godwin are reinstated with apologies; and

BE IT FURTHER RESOLVED that copies of this resolution be sent to the H. W. Wilson Company and library press.

In an editorial in the July issue of *Library Journal*, John Berry and Francine Fialkoff noted that the *Wilson Library Bulletin* had published some of the profession's most eloquent defenses of the freedom to read, including Lester Asheim's classic, "Not Censorship, But Selection." They expressed dismay that this censorship had been at the hand of a respected member of the library community and lamented the damage done to one of fundamental credos of librarianship.

Will Manley landed on his feet. Retaining his sense of humor, he observed that the H. W. Wilson president "apparently doesn't know that SEX is a subject heading in RGPL. But there is one thing that Mr. Weins does not need to worry about. *Readers' Guide* still does not index *Playboy.*" Manley's column was soon appearing in *American Libraries*, where in 1997 he published a follow-up sex questionnaire. Fired editor Mary Jo Godwin won the 1992 Robert B. Downs Intellectual Freedom Award. The *Wilson Library Bulletin* did not fare so well. Although it denied any connection between the two events, in 1995 the H. W. Wilson Company ceased publication of the bulletin for librarians that had served the profession since 1914.

QUESTIONS

- In what ways is a professional publication bound by the profession's ethical values?
- Under what circumstances might it be appropriate for a librarian or other staff member to resign in protest?

SOURCES

American Library Association, Annual Conference 1992, Resolution on Wilson Library Bulletin 1991–92 MD#3.

Berry, John N. III, and Fialkoff, Francine. "Censorship at H. W. Wilson: Librarians Will Not Forget Those Tragic Days in June," [Editorial] *Library Journal* 117 (July 1992): 6.

Flagg, Gordon. "Wilson Editor Mary Jo Godwin Resigns over Will Manley Column," *American Libraries* 23 (July/August 1992): 543.

Manley, Will. "Facing the Public: Of Spoons and Spooning," *Wilson Library Bulletin* 66 (June 1992): 85. "Librarians and Sex," [questionnaire] *Wilson Library Bulletin* 66 (June 1992): 86.

Manley, Will. "Librarians and Sex: Round 2 of the Survey," *American Libraries* 28 (August 1997): 120.

Manley, Will. "The 'S' Word," *American Libraries* 23 (September 1992): 645.

Respecting the Adult Reader

In the early 1920s, Mary Rothrock and Helen Haines urged librarians to consider collecting more explicit fictional works. Writing in *Library Journal* in 1923, Rothrock took explicit exception to Bostwick's idea of the librarian as censor and invited both discussion and disagreement.

I venture to express a conviction that the librarian is not a censor for adult readers. That is, the librarian is not concerned primarily with the exclusion of books from the library on the ground of their possible moral effect on mature readers.

She described an environment of changing tastes which were reflected in the publication of books on topics that previously had been outside public discourse.

The theory that the librarian should act as a censor implies that there are certain fixed, unchanging standards by which the morality or immorality of a book can be determined.

A novel was not truth, she noted, but a means to see the world through another's eyes. Its effect would vary with each reader. For a reading public that was larger and more diverse, Rothrock proposed restoring the motto, "The function of the library is to bring to all the people the books that belong to them." Honoring this varied public, Rothrock argued that censorship was contrary to the principles of a democratic community.

For a long time we have regarded as our American ideal the development of individual intelligence and responsibility and we have considered the free public library one of the means essential to reaching this ideal. If the library is to allow its policy of book selection to be shaped by the capacities and limitations of the immature, inexperienced, and irresponsible, it surrenders one of its noblest responsibilities—that of receptivity to various opinions—and it faces the perilous certainly of losing its contact and its influence with the mature, thoughtful, responsible public. The idea that the librarian is a censor seems to me to be based on the misconception that it is the function of the library to teach man morality. On the contrary, the library is but one means of his teaching himself.[25]

The following year, Helen Haines proposed that Bostwick's formulation be abandoned all together. The rightful role of the librarian, she wrote, was not as censor but as selector.

In its consideration of modern fiction the public library, I think, should first of all hold to the principle that censorship is not the province; selection is. The public library, supported by public funds, must use its money for the best advantage of its public. It must select from the mass of current literature in every field. Selection may be defined as the choice of what is adjudged the best, from standards of literature and from practical standards of usefulness or timeliness or legitimate demand. Censorship may be defined as restriction for exclusion for reasons of orthodoxy or moral disapproval. The public library should disclaim censorship and practice selection.

According to Haines, books did not so much shape life as reflect it.

Our present-day leveling of former barriers, our disregard of former standards, our analyzing, experimenting, working out all kinds of theories, are all reflected in fiction.... Psychoanalysis is studied and discussed in women's clubs all over the country; beautifully transmuted into fiction in *Anne Severn and the Fieldings*, it is viewed with suspicion by many librarians and becomes a "questionable" book.[26]

Reflecting changes in society's values and understanding, the best fiction experimented with new, and often controversial, themes and treatments. Thus, concluded Haines, "Selection should be representative of types and tendencies in fiction ... and in this the larger public library should especially be tolerant and inclusive." By necessity, she noted, a smaller library's collection would be more narrow.

Not Censorship, but Selection

The ethical dimensions of access were wonderfully elaborated in a series of works in the early 1950s that restated the duty of librarians to provide information reflecting diverse points of view, reexamined the differences between selection and censorship, and reemphasized that providing access to information does not constitute an endorsement of it.

In 1950, Columbia University Press published the second edition of Helen Haines's by-then classic work, *Living with Books*, on the art of book selection. Haines, who had played a crucial behind-the-scenes role in the revision of the Library Bill of Rights in 1948, had in fact authored a powerful section relating to political freedom and civil rights that not been included in the final version. In *Living with Books*, she recommended that public libraries include works about Karl Marx and Communism in their collections though some might have argued for their exclusion for want of factual authority.[27] Haines herself was attacked by Oliver Carlson[28] as a Communist sympathizer, an episode suggesting that librarians of less stature and fewer defenses might jeopardize their positions by following her advice.

In 1953, in the chilly years of the early Cold War, Lester Asheim revisited the censorship/selection dichotomy in the context of politically controversial works. His article in the *Wilson Library Bulletin*, "The Librarian's Responsibility: Not Censorship, But Selection," explored the abstract concept of intellectual freedom in the practical world of book selection. Using *Ulysses* as his example, he approached book selection much like Judge Woolsey had explored the legal standard for obscenity. According to Asheim, the selector considered the whole work and its major themes; the censor focused on isolated parts and unrelated passages taken out of context. The selector considered the reaction to the work of a rational, intelligent adult; the censor feared for its impact on the weak, warped, or irrational. The selector found reasons to keep a book, its strengths and values overshadowing minor objections; the censor sought reasons to reject it, its weaknesses and potential for misinterpretation causing its exclusion. Overall, the selector's approach was positive, the censor's negative.

In Asheim's view, selectors and censors took a different view of readers as well. The selector had faith in the intelligence of the reader; the censor had faith in his own intelligence. The selector sought to protect the right of the reader to read; the censor sought to protect the reader from the possible effect of reading. Most importantly, Asheim declared that the selector begins with a presumption in favor of liberty of thought, the censor with a presumption in favor of thought control.

The aim of the selector is to promote reading, not to inhibit it; to multiply the points of view which will find expression, not to limit them; to be a channel of communication, not a bar against it. In a sense, it could be said, perhaps, that the librarian is interfering with the freedom to read whenever he fails to make some book available. But viewed realistically, the librarian is promoting the freedom to read by making as accessible as possible as many things as he can. And I think it is typical of his selection that it is more likely to be in the direction of stimulating controversy and introducing innovation than in suppressing the new and perpetuating the stereotype. That is why he so often selects the works which shock some people. For the books which have something new to say are the ones most likely to shock.[29]

The librarian who yielded to anticipated pressures and sought to avoid controversy by rejecting a book was, concluded Asheim, a censor. Asheim's presumption in favor of liberty of thought honored the right of citizens to reject opinions with which they disagreed but not to interfere with the expression of those opinions. "So long as the opposing point of view may be expressed, the reader has the right to reject it, to take issue with it, and even to try to convince others of its falsity."

The Freedom to Read

In June 1953, the American Association of Publishers and the ALA jointly issued the Freedom to Read Statement, a bold declaration of professional identity and values. Sharing a common interest in making the best books available to the most people, publishers and librarians declared that in making ideas available, they were serving the broadest and most basic interests of a democracy. Many of the propositions of the Freedom to Read Statement reiterated the values stated in the Library Bill of Rights and its interpretation. Publishers and librarians were to make available the widest diversity of views, including those considered unorthodox or dangerous. These choices were not to be based on the personal history or affiliations of the author. Nor was a work to be prejudged by a label characterizing its contents. Providing access to ideas did not constitute an endorsement of them.

The Freedom to Read Statement proclaimed that no group, not publishers, librarians, government, or church, has the right to coerce taste, limit reading, or suppress the efforts of writers. As guardians of the people's freedom to read, publishers and librarians had a responsibility to challenge the efforts of those who sought to impose their own standards or tastes. By providing books that enrich the quality and diversity of thought and expression, librarians and publishers "demonstrate that the answer to a 'bad' book is a good one, the answer to a 'bad' idea is a good one."

We state these propositions neither lightly nor as easy generalizations. We here stake out a lofty claim for the value of books. We do so because we believe that they are good, possessed of enormous variety and usefulness, worthy of cherishing and keeping free. We realize that the application of these propositions may mean the dissemination of ideas and manners of expression that are repugnant to many persons. We do not state these propositions in the comfortable belief that what people read is unimportant. We believe rather that what people read is deeply important; that ideas can be dangerous; but that the suppression of ideas is fatal to a democratic society. Freedom itself is a dangerous way of life, but it is ours.[30]

Endorsed by a wide array of civic and educational groups, the Freedom to Read Statement, with only minor modifications over the years, stands as one of the most powerful explications of the ethics of access.

Self-Censorship

In 1956, researcher Marjorie Fiske undertook a study of California public and school libraries to determine the effect of well-publicized bookbanning efforts on library book selection. Proposed by the Intellectual Freedom Committee of the California Library Association, sponsored by the School of Librarianship of the University of California at Berkeley, and supported by the Fund for the Republic, *Book Selection and Censorship*, issued in 1959, revealed the extent to which librarians sought to avoid controversy over books in their collections. Using information on approximately two dozen communities of different sizes and drawing from more than 200 interviews, researchers found that librarians more often responded to perceived threats rather than to actual ones. Reports of the efforts of crusading parents seeking the removal of books from library collections were more effective than the crusaders themselves in keeping books off library shelves. They found that when librarians stood up to would-be book banners, censorship efforts were more likely to fail. Despite its relatively limited nature, the Fiske Report, as it came to be known, became synonymous with self-censorship, wherein books never reach the shelves or are silently removed for fear of disapproval or controversy.[31]

Truth Versus Balance

Since Arthur Bostwick called on librarians to collect material that was truthful, or factually correct, librarians have debated about their obligation to present "the truth." In her own presidential address to the ALA in 1916, Mary Plummer questioned the need to protect people from dangerous ideas and deemed the presentation of various points of view as the best means to ascertain "truth." In this, she placed libraries squarely within the free marketplace of ideas. No book could permanently damage truth, Plummer argued. Rather, it evoked objections and thus produced a forum for discussion. She was hopeful that, because hers was the first generation to "face facts however disconcerting," the library could, in fact, be "truth's handmaid."[32]

As we have seen, however, the 1939 Library Bill of Rights was amended to limit library materials to those "of sound factual authority," language retained in the 1948 revision and not removed until 1967. Debates over controversial materials continue to pit one group's "truth" against another's. But how much of each side's point of view must a librarian add to a collection? Do ethical standards of access require an equal representation of opposing ideas? Recall that the 1995 code of ethics requires equitable access policies, and that libraries may collect materials at different depths to satisfy their institutional missions. Putting together the ethical standard and best collection development practice, a public library might decide on a small number of works that are current and accurate, while a research library might collect at a comprehensive level with works that document the evolution of a topic, including disproven theories, invalid evidence, and discredited thinkers.

Librarians, like journalists and lawyers, serve a higher professional calling. Journalists, whose professional code calls on them to strive for the truth, are challenged by the extent to which they must report on ideas held by only a small portion of the community. Do they create a misleading impression if they give equal coverage to the two opposing points of view? Lawyers represent clients of dubious repute in the interest of a system of justice that allows due process for all. Librarians make available material of a controversial nature to protect the interest of a society in free access to information. Like hearsay evidence, which a court may not admit in order to prove the truth of its content, the presence of a book on a library shelf does not vouch for its accuracy. Rather, it serves as evidence that at some time and place, the creator of the work believed it to be true.

Librarians have faced controversy over collecting material that denies that the Holocaust happened. Although this point of view is elaborated in books, journals, and conferences, adherents constitute only a small proportion of those who have knowledge of the matter. Collections including works on this topic might reflect this disparity and might vary further according to institutional mission. In *The Freedom to Lie*, John Swan and Noel Peattie debated whether libraries should include the writings of the Holocaust deniers at all. Swan argued that it was part of the librarian's duty to allow representation of even repugnant ideas, while Peattie maintained that some ideas were too dangerous to be included. A classification number gathering material on the denial of the Holocaust, while not constituting a label, does give the reader information about the point of view presented.

THE CALIFORNIA LIBRARY ASSOCIATION AND THE HOLOCAUST DENIER (1983)

Planning its Banned Books Week observance in 1983, the Torrance, California, public library refused a request by David McCalden to exhibit materials that claimed the Holocaust never happened, noting that works such as *Anne Frank's Diary—A Hoax* offered one-sided points of view by obscure authors. Truth Missions publisher and former director of the Institute for Historical Review, a Holocaust-denial organization, McCalden then approached the Intellectual Freedom Committee of the California Library Association (CLA). Following the suggestion of a committee member, he applied for exhibit space at the association's eighty-sixth annual conference to be held in Los Angeles and for a meeting room to present a one-hour program on "Free Speech and the Holocaust" about the suppression of Holocaust deniers' point of view. With some opposition, the application was approved by the Conference Program Planning Committee. Upon being informed of this by the president of the Friends of California Libraries, the American Jewish Congress telegraphed its strong objections to the executive director of the CLA, Stefan Moses, who was himself a Jewish refugee from the Nazis. After a meeting between the two organizations, the CLA cancelled its exhibit contract with McCalden and Truth Missions. When McCalden threatened to sue, the CLA, acting on advice of counsel, rescinded its cancellation.

Local politicians, including Mayor Tom Bradley, then exerted pressure on the CLA. In a resolution that expressed the right of Americans to convey their views, the Los Angeles City Council called on the CLA to deny a platform to voices of hatred and threatened to withdraw the city's participation in CLA activities. The Los Angeles Public Library Board of Commissioners threatened to withdraw from the CLA, a move that would have cost the association an estimated $13,000 in dues. The Los Angeles Police Department advised the CLA of death threats, possible violence, and its inability to provide adequate police protection. When the CLA again cancelled

McCalden's contract, the city council rescinded its resolution. The ACLU of Southern California observed, "If ideas that are pernicious, that are offensive to people, can't be presented to a library association, then where can they be heard?"

In response to the controversy, the CLA adopted a policy requiring that all conference programs be sponsored by an association chapter, committee, or constituent organization, and be approved by the Conference Program Planning Committee. On his part, McCalden sued the CLA, the Simon Weisenthal Center for Holocaust Studies, the American Jewish Congress, and the Los Angeles City Council, claiming a deprivation of his First Amendment rights. In 1992, the U.S. Supreme Court upheld a ruling by the Ninth Circuit Court of Appeals that would have allowed the trial to proceed. By then, McCalden had died, or by some accounts, staged his death and disappeared, followed by his widow, who had carried on the suit.

QUESTIONS

- Is the fact that a book presents a one-sided point of view or is written by an obscure author sufficient to exclude it from a banned books exhibit or a collection?
- Is a library association exhibit hall different from a library collection? Do different ethical standards apply?
- How might the CLA have explained its decision to allow the Truth Mission material to be displayed?
- What steps can library associations take in advance to educate politicians and civic and religious groups about the meaning of intellectual freedom?

SOURCES

"California Library Association Bars, Then Admits Anti-Holocaust Exhibitor," *LibraryHotline*, November 19, 1984.

"CLA Cancels 'Holocaust Hoax' Publisher," *Newsletter on Intellectual Freedom XXXIV* (January 1985): 1, 30–31. [taken from the *LA Times*, November 13, 17].

"CLA Sets New Policies after 'Truth Missions,'" *Library Journal* 110 (May 1, 1985): 21.

Elliott, Mark, and Michael McClintock. "Holocaust 'Revisionists' and the California Library Association," *MidstreamMagazine* 32 (April 1986): 36–38.

Kamm, Susan. "In the News: 'Holocaust Hoax' Publisher Barred from Annual Convention of California LA after Controversy Spreads through State; Association Reexamines Its Policies on Exhibits and Programs," *American Libraries* 16 (January 1985): 5–7.

> *Simon Wiesenthal Center for Holocaust Studies, et al. v. McCalden, Viviana,*
> *Administrator of the Estate of David McCalden,* 504 U.S. 957 (1992).
> "Speech and the Holocaust," *Washington Post,* June 8, 1992, A18.
> Swan, John, and Noel Peattie. *The Freedom to Lie: A Debate about Democracy.*
> Jefferson, NC: McFarland, 1989, 5–7 and *passim.*

On a topic such as global warming, where there is a disproportionate scientific consensus on one side of the question, how does a library provide access to information that reflects the nature of the debate over the scope and cause of the problem?

The Best Books

The ethical obligations involved in choosing the content of library collections have developed as the profession itself has evolved in practice and in its own conception of itself. We have seen how, in its formative years, and without any code of ethics or statement of values, the ALA adopted as its motto, "The best reading for the largest number at the least cost." We know that Melvil Dewey envisioned a dynamic librarian, actively engaging readers and improving popular taste. Discussing what was "best," he wrote in "The Profession,"

> He [the librarian] must see that his library contains, as far as possible, the best books on the best subjects, regarding carefully the wants of his special community. Then, having the best books, he must create among his people, his pupils, a desire to read these books. He must put every facility in the way of readers, so that they shall be led on from good to better. He must each teach them how, after studying their own wants, they may themselves select their reading wisely. Such a librarian will find enough who are ready to put themselves under his influence and direction, and, if competent and enthusiastic, he may soon largely shape the reading, and through it the thought, of his whole community.[33]

Note that even in this proclamation of quality, Dewey was careful to include the librarian's obligation to his or her particular community. But what if the reading interests and information needs of the library's users do not coincide with the librarian's notion of "best"?

Despite their rhetoric, early librarians were often unable or unwilling to fulfill this part of Dewey's formulation. Since Carnegie had provided support for library buildings but not for staff or collections, many public libraries depended on donations to build their collections and on the provision of popular fiction to attract users. Nonetheless, in asserting their professional status, librarians claimed authority for making choices about what material was to be accessible in library collections. To accomplish this, library pioneers developed tools and devices to aid in the process of book selection. Used in common, these catalogs, bibliographies, and reviews served as guides to quality mainstream publications within a safe middle ground of taste and opinion. Helping to raise the standards in small, newly established libraries, they also defined access within a narrow spectrum of political discourse and literary expression.

Expertise

This first generation of bibliographic tools included *Library Journal*, founded in 1876 by Melvil Dewey, Frederick Leypoldt, and R. R. Bowker; *Publishers' Weekly*, published by R. R. Bowker; and *Booklist*, an ALA journal of book reviews, begun in 1907. The addition of library service to children and the resulting demand for children's books led to specialized journals like *The Horn Book* and *School Library Journal*. A reviewing service outside the library/publishing world was offered by Virginia Kirkus, who added a warning sign to reviews of books that might prove controversial. Decisions about whether a book was to reviewed could affect sales and how long it stayed in print.

Strengthening the bibliographic arsenal, classified catalogs constituted a professional judgment about the standard, basic, and essential works for library collections, particularly in smaller libraries that lacked a professionally trained librarian. The publication of early catalogs by the ALA coincided with notable civic occasions and celebrations: the 1893 edition, published with the U.S. Bureau of Education, appeared in time for the World's Columbian Exposition in Chicago, and the 1904 edition, a joint endeavor of the ALA, the Bureau of Education, the Library of Congress, and the Government Printing Office, and edited by Melvil Dewey, debuted for the St. Louis Exposition. Classed by the Dewey Decimal System, it included annotations of 8,000 volumes and a subject index. These catalogs demonstrate the paradox of access and selection. While setting a standard of works suitable for a library collection and expanding the range of choices, they did so within the narrow confines of cultural orthodoxy.

Each successive catalog mirrored changes in taste and interests. Helen Haines noted that the 1926 *ALA Catalog*, published on the association's fiftieth anniversary, showed a growing interest in information itself, bibliographies, conspectuses, outlines, and yearbooks, which she described as "all part of the modern consolidation, condensation, and popularization of knowledge."[34] The 1926 edition, she noted, in contrast to the 1904 version, included more works on philosophy, social and applied science, and fine arts, but fewer on religion, natural science, and history. It also manifested generally conservative political ideas and middle-class tastes, omitting American author F. Scott Fitzgerald, European writers Marcel Proust and James Joyce, and Felix Frankfurter's book on the radicals Sacco and Vanzetti.[35]

The H. W. Wilson Company and the R. R. Bowker Company have continued to publish the bibliographic tools that librarians need to build collections. Many rural libraries are not yet staffed by professional librarians. Selecting small numbers of volumes from within a narrow range, they turn to authoritative sources of mainstream material. At the same time, new tools from within and outside the profession give librarians access to a broader range of viewpoints. The Alternative Press Index and a host of Web sites, for example, allow librarians who are so inclined to tap into unorthodox, unfamiliar, and unpopular ideas.

But even tools like the H. W. Wilson indexes can reflect biases and narrow the range of possibilities. Like the choice of which books to review, decisions about which magazines and journals to index affect subscription decisions by libraries. In the late 1980s, the publisher and editor of *Mother Jones* urged librarians to demand that H. W. Wilson index their magazine in the *Readers' Guide to Periodical Literature*, something sure to increase its base of users. Although H. W. Wilson disclaimed a connection, the magazine was soon included in the RGPL coverage.[36] The choice of subject headings can also facilitate or impede access to materials. Sanford Berman, cataloging librarian at the Hennepin County Public Library in Minnesota, led a decades-long crusade to persuade the Library of Congress to adopt subject headings more reflective of the subject matter and common usage and less offensive to members of ethnic and racial minorities.[37]

Similarly, library users rely on the advice of experts to guide their reading. In another step toward the professionalization of library work, libraries in the 1920s appointed readers' advisors who were available by appointment to plan a course of systematic reading for individual readers. The ALA published its *Reading with a Purpose Series*, with well-known experts recommending books in their field. With the distribution of millions of these booklists, librarians noted an increase in circulation and publishers saw an increase in sales of the featured titles. Established also in the 1920s, the Book-of-the-Month Club relied on an editorial board to choose the best literature for middle-class readers but again within a narrow range. In the following chapter, we will see how new technologies have greatly expanded access to alternative material and to the advice of experts, both professional and amateur.

Control

While library associations, publishers, and reviewers provide expertise to help build collections, local librarians exercise control that determines access to them. To ensure the proper educational purpose and prevent works from falling into the wrong hands, early librarians adopted a variety of stratagems. Collecting literature rather than popular fiction, librarians upheld the high cultural mission of the library. Closed stacks kept patrons from the serendipitous discoveries of browsing and required that they divulge their reading interests in order to have the desired book fetched from the shelf.[38] Some libraries made popular fiction available only in branches, reserving the main library for more scholarly pursuits, or required that patrons check out a work of nonfiction along with each novel they borrowed. Some libraries made popular fiction available for a rental fee, while "literature" could be borrowed for free from the library's collection. Early public libraries served adults only, lent some books only on presentation of a letter of permission, or established age limits.

These control devices were not seen as an inappropriate limit on access but as an aspect of professional judgment in determining which books were suitable for which readers. In 1922, Louis Feipel completed a survey of major public libraries to determine how they handled "questionable fiction" and reported his findings in the same year that Bolton published his revised canons in the *Annals*. Many libraries reported staff reading such books before putting them on the shelves, placing them only in the main library, or in a locked case, closed stack, restricted shelf, or separate collection, listing books that had been acquired but might be objectionable, giving reasons for rejecting a title, and withdrawing or moving a book upon receiving complaints.[39]

Quality Revisited

In fact, it was just this "questionable fiction" that readers were demanding. In 1933, Lyman Bryson, a leader of the adult education movement, urged librarians to read *True Crime* and see what their readers really wanted. Striking a balance between quality and demand, Helen Haines, in 1935, published the summation of her advice in *Living with Books: The Art of Book Selection*. Squarely with Melvil Dewey in her belief that the librarian's obligation was to provide the best reading to the largest numbers, Haines emphasized that selection was to be based on a work's positive attributes and its appeal to a broad audience. But the selection of the best works did not preclude meeting the community's particular needs and tastes. In an article "The Ethics of Librarianship," Haines argued that librarians needed to know both books and people. A knowledgeable librarian could provide access to quality works while meeting popular demand. Moreover, according to Haines, a collection should include works on topics that might prove controversial. Before the adoption of either the ALA Code of Ethics in 1938 or its Library Bill of Rights in 1939, Haines articulated an ethic of access that honored the reader's ability to tackle serious or unpopular ideas and the librarian's obligation to meet the community's information tastes and preferences.

As we have seen, the studies of the Public Library Inquiry in the years immediately following World War II recommended that libraries acknowledge that they served only a small portion of the population, those members of the middle class who were affluent, well educated, and already consumers of information. Further, the researchers recommended that libraries continue to focus their service on this "communications elite." They also offered advice on the appropriate content of public library collections. Believing that libraries would be unable to compete with the emerging mass media, radio, film, and television, the studies urged that public libraries collect serious works of long-lasting value, or of a controversial nature, and leave the distribution of popular fare to newsstands, drug stores, and rental collections. Again, access to material would be segmented by class.

Demand

The debate about quality versus demand and the type of material that public libraries should make available arose again in the 1970s, with Charles Robinson and the Baltimore County Public Library (BCPL) at the epicenter of a movement to "Give 'em What They Want."[40] According to Robinson and Nora Rawlinson, later editor of *Library Journal*, the public library as a tax-supported institution is obliged to provide what the public wants to read, not what librarians think they should read. To respond to demand, the BCPL, along with many libraries adopting this model, buys large numbers of current bestsellers, thus reducing wait-lists and waiting times, turns over material in its collection, jettisoning items that do not circulate, and applies a retail approach to book displays.

Critics of this approach accuse librarians of pandering to the lowest common denominator in taste, turning librarians into order clerks and libraries into bibliographic McDonald's. Other critics suggest that it gives librarians grounds to exclude materials that would be offensive or controversial in a particular community because of lack of demand or interest. Even academic libraries have been criticized for adopting this approach and dumbing down their collections in the face of student demand.[41] Proponents of a quality, or a literature-centered, policy argue that librarians can help shape demand by public programming, displays, and pathfinders, all traditional methods employing the expertise of librarians to promote the "best" books. While proponents of both demand and quality hope that the public will demand what is "best," librarians such as Murray Bob and Nancy Pearl actively inform readers of possibilities beyond the best-seller list.[42] Where information on virtually everything is available, the librarian still has a significant role to play in determining access to the best information in a print environment.

QUESTIONS

- What if library users want materials that are antithetical to institutional goals or offensive to a segment of the community?

- Is apparent lack of interest always an appropriate ground to exclude materials from a collection?
- What do you say to a librarian who declares that, "There are no Muslims in my community. Why should the library have books on Islam or by Muslim authors?"

Coda

At the turn of the twenty-first century, the response to a trio of books for children replayed all the access issues librarians had struggled to resolve. In 2002, Linda de Haan and Stern Nijland's *King and King*[43] told the story of a prince who, urged by his mother to find a suitable princess to marry, found her brother instead and lived with him happily ever after. In 2005, Peter Parnell and Justin Richardson's *And Tango Makes Three*[44] told the true story of two male penguins who adopted an egg and raised it when it hatched. Parents concerned about the potentially harmful effects of these picture books about gay relationships demanded removal of the books from school and public libraries. In 2006, the reaction of some school librarians to Susan Patron's young-adult novel, *The Higher Power of Lucky*,[45] showed how far librarians have to go in honoring the ethic of access. Garnering enthusiastic reviews, and ultimately the Newbery Award, the book raised the concerns by the author's use of the word "scrotum" on the first page.

THE HIGHER POWER OF LUCKY (2007)

On January 22, 2007, at a press conference at the ALA's midwinter meeting in Seattle, *The Higher Power of Lucky* was declared the winner of the prestigious Newbery Medal honoring the year's best work in children's literature. The novel, intended for readers in grades four through six, was the second by Susan Patron, a collection development librarian for children's materials at the Los Angeles Public Library. It tells the story of Lucky Trimble, a ten-year-old girl living in a tiny desert town with her father's ex-wife after her mother was killed by a bolt of lightning. Fearing abandonment, Lucky draws on what she has learned, while eavesdropping on various self-help groups, about a higher power. Published in a run of 10,000 copies in the fall of 2006 by Atheneum/Richard Jackson, a Simon & Schuster imprint, the book garnered favorable reviews in *School Library Journal*, *Horn Book Magazine*, *Kirkus Reviews*, *Booklist*, and the *Bulletin of the Center for Children's Literature*. In a review for the online *Common Sense Media*, Matt Berman observed,

This kind of book is catnip to Newbery committees: the lack of plot, the eccentric characters in a small community, the combination of humor and pathos, the sad but plucky protagonist in dire straits, the unhurried and media-free lives the characters lead—it's all here. And author Susan Patron does a lovely job of it.

None of the reviews warned about potential problems.

Until it won the Newbery Medal, *The Higher Power of Lucky* was heading for respectable if not overwhelming sales. Since many librarians automatically purchase copies of Newbery and Caldecott winners, *Lucky*'s prize gave school librarians a second selection opportunity, and some did not like what they saw. In mid-February, *Children's Bookshelf*, an electronic newsletter of *Publishers Weekly*, reported "Listservs Buzzing over Newbery Winner." Dana Nilsson, a teacher/librarian at the Sunnyside Elementary School in Durango, Colorado, had posted objections to the book on LM_Net, a listserv for school library media specialists. She objected to Patron's use of the word scrotum on the first page in describing a dog being bitten by a rattlesnake:

Part of my job is to introduce students to quality, age-appropriate literature. I would not be doing my job if I booktalked or recommended this book to young audiences. This book has some great qualities—it shows a girl in an insecure situation wanting stability in her life. The inclusion of genitalia does not add to the story one bit and that is my objection. Because of that one word, I would not be able to read that book aloud. There are so many other options that the author could have used instead.

Nilsson claimed to have received twenty-five off-list replies supporting her position.

The ensuing controversy spilled over from library lists onto the front page of the *New York Times* and reports on the evening news, cable television, and public radio and in international media as well. Stories recounted that the book had been banned from school libraries in some places and removed from the shelves in others. Young-adult author Jordan Sonnenblick of Authors Supporting Intellectual Freedom (ASIF) expressed concern that school librarians had not strongly defended the book. In an editorial, the *New York Times* described "a few queasy librarians" choosing not to order the book because of "one troublesome word" and, in response, librarians all over flinching at the furor that seemed to confirm the priggish librarian stereotype.

Librarians did speak out, however. In a letter published in the *Times* on February 25, Kathleen Horning, president of the Association for Library Service to Children, and Cyndi Phillips, president of the American Association of School Librarians, defended the right of parents and children to have access to books:

Libraries are about inclusion rather than exclusion. Part of living in a democracy means respecting each other's differences and the right of all people to choose for themselves what they and their families read.

Pat Scales, former chair of the Newbery Award committee, declared that refusing to stock the book was nothing short of censorship. "The people who are reacting to that word are not reading the book as a whole. That's what censors do—they pick out words and don't look at the total merit of the book." Nilsson claimed that the media had misrepresented the professional judgment of those with reservations about the book and noted that many of them had ordered it nonetheless.

The controversy seemed to give the book an even bigger boost in sales than might have been expected of a Newbery winner. After the prize was announced, the publisher ordered an additional 100,000 copies. Following press coverage of Dana Nilsson's comments, *The Higher Power of Lucky* soared from the high 600 thousands in sales on Amazon.com into the top forty overall and the top ten among children's books.

QUESTIONS

- Can you think of an example where the presence of one word might justify the exclusion of a book from a school library collection?
- How can school librarians prepare to explain to the principal, parents, the public, and the press how they select materials for the school library media center?

SOURCES

Bosman, Julie. "Debate Fuels Book Sales," *New York Times*, February 24, 2007, B8.

Bosman, Julie. "With One Word, Children's Book Sets Off Uproar," *New York Times*, February 18, 2007.

Goldberg, Beverly. "Newbery-Winner's 'Scrotum' Reference Raises Ruckus," *American Libraries* 38 (April 2007): 16.

Horning, Kathleen, and Cyndi Phillips. "A Book for Kids," [Letter to the Editor] *New York Times*, February 25, 2007, WK13.

"Librarians Debate Award-Winning Novel," *New York Times*, February 23, 2007. [Associated Press story]

Maughan, Shannon. "Controversy over Newbery Winner: A Follow-Up," *Publishers Weekly Children's Bookshelf*, February 22, 2007.

Maughan, Shannon. "Listservs Buzzing over Newbery Winner," *Publishers Weekly Children's Bookshelf*, February 15, 2007.

Oleck, Joan. "The Higher Power of Patron," *School Library Journal* 53 (March 2007): 42–45.

"One Troublesome Word," [Editorial] *New York Times*, February 21, 2008.

Reviews:

Berman, Matt, *Common Sense Review,* http://www.commonsensemedia.org [n.d.]; http://www.commonsensemedia.org/book-reviews/Higher-Power-Lucky.html.

The Bulletin of the Center for Children's Books (January 2007); Furness, Adrienne, *School Library Journal* 52 (December 2006); Gershowitz, Elissa R., *Horn Book Magazine* (January/February 2007); Goldsmith, Francisca, *Booklist* (December 1, 2007); *Kirkus Reviews* 74, issue 20, October 15, 2006, issue 23, December 1, 2006.

These episodes violated nearly every stricture concerning access in library codes of ethics and the Library Bill of Rights. School library media specialists worried about the impact of these books on youngsters or feared parental objections to exposing children to words or ideas they considered offensive. A number of school librarians reported that they would not purchase these books, a chilling reprise of Marjorie Fiske's findings of self-censorship in the 1950s. Forgotten, too, were strictures that parents and not librarians should make decisions about children's reading, and that works should be judged as a whole, not on the basis of one word.

Parents continue to fear for the safety of their children as they explore a world of books where popular and well-written stories often reflect issues that are roiling society. While claiming professional expertise in book selection, librarians remain vulnerable to pressure and the anticipation of controversy. If librarians have not yet embraced and internalized the differences between selection and censorship or acknowledged their primary responsibility in making materials and ideas accessible, how well equipped are they to apply these ethical standards in a digital environment? We will discuss this in the next chapter.

END NOTES

1. Lester Asheim, "The Librarian's Responsibility: Not Censorship, But Selection," *Wilson Library Bulletin* 28 (September 1953): 67.

2. Robert Hauptman, "Professionalism or Culpability? An Experiment in Ethics," *Wilson Library Bulletin* 50 (April 1976): 626. Reporting on his own experiment requesting information on how to freebase cocaine, Robert Dowd encountered a similar willingness among librarians to provide the information and approved this response as an appropriate exercise of professional service. See Robert C. Dowd, "I Want to Find Out How to Freebase Cocaine or Yet Another Unobtrusive Test of Reference Performance," *The Reference Librarian* no. 25–26 (1989): 483–493. Hauptman responded in Robert Hauptman, "Professional Responsibility Reconsidered," *RQ* 35 (Spring 1996): 327–329.

3. Mary W. Plummer, "The Pros and Cons of Training for Librarianship," *Public Libraries* 8 (May 1903): 211–212.

4. Charles Knowles Bolton, "The Ethics of Librarianship: A Proposal for a Revised Code," *Annals of the American Academy* 101 (May 1922): 145–146.

5. "Suggested Code of Ethics," *Library Journal* 55 (February 15, 1930): 165.

6. Code of Ethics for Librarians, Adopted by the ALA Council, December 19, 1938. *ALA Bulletin* 33 (February 1939): 129.

7. "The Library Bill of Rights Adopted June 1939 by the Council of the American Library Association," *Intellectual Freedom Manual*, 7th ed. Chicago: American Library Association, 2006, 59.

8. Marci Lingo, "Forbidden Fruit: The Banning of *The Grapes of Wrath* in the Kern County Free Library," *Libraries & Culture* 38 (Fall 2003): 351–377.

9. Judith F. Krug and James A. Harvey, "The History of the Library Bill of Rights, Part One," *American Libraries* 3 (January 1972): 81.

10. "Statement on Professional Ethics, 1981, adopted June 30, 1981, by the ALA Council," *American Libraries* 12 (June 1981): 335; *Intellectual Freedom Manual*, 7th ed. Chicago: American Library Association, 2006, 262.

11. *Reg. v. Hicklin* (1868 L.R.3 Q.8. 360).

12. Evelyn Geller, *Forbidden Books in American Public Libraries, 1876–1939: A Study in Cultural Change*. Westport, CT: Greenwood Press, 1984.

13. *U.S. v. One Book Entitled "Ulysses,"* 5 F. Supp. 182 (S.D. N.Y. 1933), 72 F.2d 705 (2d Cir. 1934).

14. *A Book Named John Cleland's "Memoirs of a Woman of Pleasure," et al. v. Attorney General of Massachusetts*, 383 U.S. 413 (1966).

15. *Miller v. California*, 413 U.S. 15 (1973).

16. *Pope v. Illinois*, 481 U.S. 497 (1987).

17. Kathleen Molz, "The Public Custody of High Pornography," *American Scholar* 36 (Winter 1966–1967): 93–103.

18. "A Dorothy Broderick Scrapbook," *Voice of Youth Advocates* 20 (June 1997): 97–107.

19. Justin Kaplan, *Born to Trouble: One Hundred Years of Huckleberry Finn*. Washington, D.C.: Library of Congress, 1985.

20. *Board of Education, Island Trees Free School District No. 26 v. Pico*, 457 U.S. 853 (1952) at 871.

21. Ibid., at 872.

22. Ibid., at 897.

23. Access to Resources and Services in the School Library Media Program, an Interpretation of the Library Bill of Rights, adopted July 2, 1986; amended January 10, 1990, July 12, 2000, and January 19, 2005. *Intellectual Freedom Manual*, 7th ed. Chicago: American Library Association, 2006, 102–104, http://www.ala.org/ala/oif/statementspols/statementsif/interpretations/accessresources.htm.

24. Arthur Bostwick, "The Librarian as Censor: Address of the President, American Library Association, Lake Minnetonka Conference, 1908," *Library Journal* 33 (July 1908): 257.

25. Mary U. Rothrock, "Censorship of Fiction in the Public Library," *Library Journal* 48 (May 15, 1923): 456.

26. Helen E. Haines, "Modern Fiction and the Public Library." *Library Journal* 49 (May 15, 1924): 460.

27. Helen E. Haines, *Living with Books*, 2nd ed. New York: Columbia University Press, 1950, 361, 402.

28. Oliver Carlson. "A Slanted Guide to Library Selection," *The Freeman* 2 (January 14, 1952): 239–242.

29. Lester Asheim, "The Librarian's Responsibility," 67.

30. Freedom to Read: A Joint Statement by the American Library Association and the Association of American Publishers, adopted June 25, 1953; revised January 28, 1972, January 16, 1991, July 12, 2000, and June 30, 2004. *Intellectual Freedom Manual*, 7th ed. Chicago: American Library Association, 2006, 215–220, http://www.ala.org/ala/oif/statementspols/ftrstatement/freedomreadstatement.htm.

31. Marjorie Fiske, *Book Selection and Censorship: A Study of School and Public Libraries in California*. Berkeley: University of California Press, 1959.

32. Mary Wright Plummer, "The Public Library and the Pursuit of Truth," *ALA Bulletin* 10 (July 1916): 113–115.

33. Melvil Dewey, "The Profession," *Library Journal* 1 (September 30, 1876); reprinted in Dianne J. Ellsworth and Norman D. Stevens, *Landmarks of Library Literature, 1876–1976*. Metuchen, NJ: Scarecrow Press, 1976, 21–23.

34. Haines, *Living with Books*, 2nd ed., 67–68.

35. Herbert B. Ehrman, *The Case of Sacco and Vanzetti: A Critical Analysis for Lawyers and Laymen*. Boston, MA: Little Brown, 1962.

36. Adam Hochschild, "Of Indexes and Editors," *Mother Jones* (June/July 1987): 8.

37. For a sampling of Berman's writings, see Sanford Berman, *Worth Noting: Editorials, Letters, Essays, an Interview, and Bibliography.* Jefferson, NC: McFarland, 1988. See also http://www.sanfordberman.org.

38. Evelyn Geller, *Forbidden Books in American Public Libraries, 1876–1939.*

39. Louis N. Feipel, "Questionable Books in Public Libraries—I," *Library Journal* 47 (October 15, 1922): 857–861; "Questionable Books in Public Libraries—II," *Library Journal* 47 (November 1, 1922): 907–911.

40. Nora Rawlinson, "'Give 'em what they want!'" *Library Journal* 106 (November 15, 1981): 2,188–2,195; For an interview on Charles Robinson's retirement, see Nancy Pearl, "Gave 'em what they wanted," *Library Journal* 121 (September 1, 1996): 136–38.

41. Brian Quinn, "McDonaldization of Academic Libraries?" *College & Research Libraries* 61 (May 2000): 248–261.

42. Murray L. Bob, "The Case for Quality Book Selection," *Library Journal* 107 (September 15, 1982): 1,707–1,710; Nancy Pearl and Craig Buthod, "Upgrading the McLibrary," *Library Journal* 117 (October 15, 1992): 37-41. See also Nancy Pearl, *Book Lust: Recommended Reading for Every Mood, Moment, and Reason.* Seattle: Sasquatch Books, 2003, and follow-up volumes.

43. Linda de Haan and Stern Nijland, *King and King*. Berkeley, CA: Tricycle Press, 2002.

44. Justin Richardson and Peter Parnell, *And Tango Makes Three*. New York: Simon & Schuster, 2005.

45. Susan Patron, *The Higher Power of Lucky*. New York: Atheneum, 2006.

5

◆·━━◆━━·◆

ACCESS: WHICH FORMAT

In 1994, at the dawn of the age of the Internet, a reader in New Zealand found *Fanny Hill: Memoirs of a Woman of Pleasure* available on the computer of Indiana University and requested that it be removed lest children access this classic of erotica.[1] *Fanny Hill*, written by John Cleland in about 1750, had been declared obscene under state law in the United States as early as 1821, but as we have seen, the Supreme Court in 1966 found that it was not obscene under the court's new definition. At the time of the complaint about the electronic version of *Fanny Hill*, it was noted that the Indiana University library contained a number of copies of the work.

Do new ethical issues related to access arise when content appears in new formats? When a book is read on the radio or available on the Internet must the librarian add additional factors to the ethical equation? In dealing with visual media such as films, photographs, or digital content on the World Wide Web, librarians encounter many of the same concerns that they face in a world of print about possible harm to youngsters or others who are somehow vulnerable. These fears are reflected in Supreme Court cases that established the constitutional standard for access to films, radio, television broadcasts, and the Internet. Librarians in a visual, nonprint, digital age have had to learn a new vocabulary of legal permissibility and establish a new outlook on access. Where information is instantly and globally available, librarians are experiencing both a loss of control and an increasing need for expertise.

We have seen how the courts expanded the protection of the printed word by redefining obscenity, with the 1933 decision of Judge Woolsey in the *Ulysses* case and the ruling of the Supreme Court in *Miller v. California*. We know that material deemed by a court to be obscene is not protected by the First Amendment. Under the current obscenity standard, it is unlikely that a library would come close to collecting the kind of hard-core print materials for which it might face an obscenity charge. But in the transition from text to visual images and from print to electronic access, librarians may make available not only the offensive but the impermissible.

The criminal obscenity prosecution of the owner of a Cincinnati, Ohio, art gallery in 1990, for displaying photographs by Robert Mapplethorpe, offers a recent example. Responding to citizen complaints about the suggestive, homoerotic themes of Mapplethorpe's black-and-white still-lifes and portraits, the district attorney brought charges under a local obscenity ordinance. As is recommended for a library that is reviewing a challenge to material in its col-lection, the exhibit remained open during the trial. After hearing expert wit-nesses for the prosecution and defense testify on the artistic worth of the photographs, a jury found the gallery owner not guilty. Might fear of prose-cution keep a library from acquiring a book of Mapplethorpe photographs?

ROBERT MAPPLETHORPE PHOTOGRAPHS (1990)

In April 1990, a retrospective exhibit of Robert Mapplethorpe photo-graphs opened at the Cincinnati Contemporary Arts Center amid contro-versy, threats, record crowds, long lines, and the possibility of criminal obscenity prosecution. An exhibition of Mapplethorpe's photographs at the Corcoran Gallery in Washington, D.C., the previous year was can-celled when its homoerotic and sadomasochistic themes prompted objec-tions to the images themselves and to public funding of the arts.

The retrospective exhibit was funded in part by the National Endow-ment for the Arts, raising questions about public funding of sexually explicit art, but the same exhibit was displayed in another venue in Washington and in other cities with little objection. The director of the Corcoran later resigned. The city of Cincinnati, headquarters of the National Coalition against Pornography, was known for its strict enforcement of obscenity standards, most notably a successful prosecu-tion of Larry Flynt, publisher of *Hustler* magazine. Nonetheless, the de-cision of the Arts Center to host the Mapplethorpe exhibit garnered public support evidenced by a large number of new memberships and a public demonstration on behalf of the show. Business leaders and potential donors also indicated their support of the gallery.

Almost as soon as the show opened, a county grand jury indicted the Cincinnati Contemporary Arts Center and its director, Dennis Barrie, on state obscenity charges involving seven of 175 photographs. Mem-bers of the grand jury viewed the show anonymously. A federal judge issued a temporary restraining order that kept police from removing any photographs, shutting down the exhibit, or intimidating the public to keep them from viewing it. At trial, the prosecutor had to prove that the photographs met the three-part obscenity test formulated by the Supreme Court in *Miller v. California*: that they lacked serious literary, artistic, political, or scientific values, that they appealed to prurient interests as measured by an average person applying contemporary community standards, and that they depicted in a patently offensive way conduct specifically set forth in state law.

A jury of four men and four women heard the first obscenity case brought against an art gallery in U.S. history. The prosecution offered few witnesses to prove the lack of artistic values of the photographs. In contrast, the defense called to testify art critics from both Cincinnati newspapers and the directors of four art museums, including the curator of the show at the Institute of Contemporary Art in Philadelphia and the director of the University Art Museum in Berkeley, California, where it was exhibited. After deliberating for less than two hours, the jury found the Cincinnati Contemporary Arts Center and its director not guilty of obscenity charges for displaying the Mapplethorpe photographs.

QUESTIONS

- What similarities do you see in the roles of libraries and museums in making material available to the public?
- What ethical values do libraries and museums have in common?
- Might a library have been prosecuted for having a book or DVD showing Robert Mapplethorpe's photographs?
- Should librarians have come to the defense of the director of the art gallery?
- How might a museum or library minimize the potential controversy over images in their collections or exhibits?
- Might the American Library Association have taken this obscenity prosecution into account when deciding whether to hold its midwinter meeting in Cincinnati in 1995?

SOURCES

Mansnerus, Laura. "The Cincinnati Case: What Are the Issues and the Stakes," *New York Times*, April 24, 1990, C15.

Masters, Kim. "Art Gallery Not Guilty of Obscenity," *Washington Post*, October 6, 1990, A1, A14, A15.

Masters, Kim. "Jury Chosen for Obscenity Case; Opening Arguments Begin Today in Cincinnati Gallery Trial," *Washington Post*, September 28, 1990, C1, C4.

Masters, Kim. "Obscenity Trial Asks: 'Is It Art?' Jurors Examine Mapplethorpe Works," *Washington Post*, October 2, 1990, E1, E3.

Wilkerson, Isabel. "Cincinnati Center Indicted for Mapplethorpe Show," *New York Times*, April 8, 1990, 1, 26.

Wilkerson, Isabel. "Judge Bars Action against Exhibition; Rules Mapplethorpe Show in Cincinnati Cannot Be Shut before Obscenity Trial," *New York Times*, April 17, 1990, A10.

Yardley, Jonathan. "In Cincinnati, Experts as Witnesses," *Washington Post*, October 15, 1990, B2.

NEW FORMATS ARE NOT A NEW PHENOMENON

New information formats are not a new phenomenon in libraries. At the fiftieth anniversary celebration of the ALA in 1926, Melvil Dewey warned of the increasing competition libraries faced from the new media of motion pictures and radio. Dewey declared that "the book is not sacred" and urged librarians to "give to the public in the quickest and cheapest way information and recreation in the highest plane," in whatever medium was most efficient.[2] By the mid-1920s, county libraries were already circulating not only books but phonographs, films, lantern slides, sheet music, stereographs, and globes. Adult education librarians at the Cleveland Public Library were working with local movie theaters to promote motion pictures based on books, and Judson T. Jennings of the Seattle Public Library was complaining that his staff's enthusiasm for music, dramatics, and exhibits threatened its primary function— the promotion of reading. The ALA Committee on Library Extension used a slide presentation on a "pictoral" to promote rural library service.[3] With funding from the Carnegie Corporation, librarians in the 1940s promoted films and other audiovisual material as a complementary means to provide access. The Louisville Free Public Library made available information through books, microcards, film, radio transcriptions, and framed artwork reproductions. In addition, the main library was able to broadcast music, performances, and educational programs through a network connection to its branches and local schools. In 1950, *Newsweek* magazine reported that the library was the first in the country to start its own FM radio station.

WPFL will be on the air a minimum of five hours daily. A typical menu would include dramatic sketches, science chats, documentaries … biographical sketches, and recorded music. These features will be transmitted from noon to 3 P.M., and there will also be an evening show. Announcers will read fifteen minute selections from some famous book—usually two in an evening. It might be possible to hear fifteen minutes of Charlotte Bronte's "Jane Eyre," three quarters of an hour of classical music, then a quarter-hour of Stephen Crane's "The Red Badge of Courage.[4]

The Louisville library was also a television pioneer. Installing two sets in its main building and one in each branch, it allowed library users to see this new educational and entertainment medium at a time when few households owned or could afford one. A generation later, libraries played the same role by installing computers before the public could afford them and introducing the possibilities of this new technology to make available material not historically part of library collections.

Each one of these new information formats brings with it new capabilities and also new legal and ethical dilemmas.

QUESTIONS

- Do new media pose new or different threats to young, uneducated, or vulnerable listeners or viewers?
- When dealing with new information formats, how do we know what ethical standards to apply?
- Is it unethical *not* to provide access in variety of formats?
- Is filtering a form of censorship or selection?
- In a global information environment, are standards of quality and professional expertise still relevant?
- Does the introduction of new information technologies introduce a new tension between service and access?

We will explore these questions by looking at new technologies in turn, but first we will see how codes of ethics have dealt with the implications of information appearing in a variety of known and unknowable formats.

WHAT CODES OF ETHICS TELL US (OR DON'T TELL US) ABOUT FORMATS

As we have seen, librarians were collecting, making available, and promoting material in a variety of formats long before the ALA adopted its first code of ethics in 1938. Early librarians were enthusiastic about the possibility of reaching new users through radio and film, though some were concerned about using library funds for new formats and activities at expense of the library's primary commitment to reading. Others saw the use of multiple formats as a fulfillment of this mission. In this area, we see again how practice preceded the codification of ethical standards. Early library codes of ethics and the Library Bill of Rights did not reflect the multimedia nature of existing library collections.

As in the words "library" and "bibliography," the concept of "book" was embedded in the early codes of ethics. The foundation of library work, emblazoned in the ALA motto, was to provide the best reading. Although Mary Plummer's draft code called for professional knowledge of all recorded knowledge, it was bibliographic expertise that made librarianship a profession and not a craft. In his canons, Charles Knowles Bolton saw the librarian as bookman. Carl Roden

declared that bringing books and men together was the profession's great contribution to humanity. Helen Haines, in "The Ethics of Librarianship," declared
that the librarian must know both books and people.

The Library's Bill of Rights, adopted in 1938 by the board of trustees of
the Des Moines Public Library, referred to books, reading matter, and publications. The ALA Library Bill of Rights, adopted in 1939 and revised in
1948, used the same language of books and reading matter, though the 1948
version included the protection of intangible ideas as well as tangible books
and referred to the responsibility of libraries "to provide information and
enlightenment through the printed word."[5] The 1975 Statement of Professional Ethics and subsequent codes incorporated the concept of the free flow
of information but continued to refer to books and library materials.

Thus, though librarians had for decades been using films and making radio
broadcasts, the ALA did not specifically address the ethical dimension of access
to information in nonbook formats until 1951. Then, in a footnote, it applied
the Library Bill of Rights, adopted just three years before, to all information
media. Nonetheless, despite changes in society and technology, the association's 1938 Code of Ethics remained unchanged. Since librarians could not
turn to the ethical statement of their own profession for guidance, what could
they learn from law and experience? As we will see, many of the fundamental
tensions that played out in a print environment reappeared in debates about
standards of access to film, the radio, and the Internet.

EDUCATION VERSUS ENTERTAINMENT

Film

The introduction of the motion picture in the late nineteenth century
stirred all the nascent fears that accompanied the mass distribution of popular fiction made possible by cheap pulp paper and machine-sewn bindings.
With more immediacy than print, stories told on film delivered a powerful
message and evoked an emotional response. Even the silent, short films of
the era seemed to convey dangerous ideas, potentially harmful to minors
and hazardous for the working classes. Efforts to censor films came from
many of the reform and religious groups that earlier had organized purity
crusades such as Anthony Comstock's New York Society for the Suppression of Vice,[6] and in 1910, Congress considered legislation to create a film
censorship board that would do on the national level what review boards
were doing in the states.

We have seen the measures used by libraries to deal with "objectionable"
popular fiction. Objectionable films were also handled in various ways. The
movie industry itself, eager to forestall creation of a national censorship board,
established an internal office to set and police standards of acceptable film content. Named the Hays Office for Will Hays who headed it in the 1920s and

1930s, this effort at self-censorship denied broadcast distribution rights to films that did not adhere to strictures on language and conduct. The fact that a film was distributed in the nation's theater chains demonstrated that it had met these standards, an assurance of mainstream values if not cinematic quality.

In contrast to this control mechanism, educators and civic activists pooled their efforts to produce *The Green Sheet*, a newsletter that provided information about films and the recommendations of the participating groups. The ALA participated in this effort to inform moviegoers about what they might expect to see at the theater. Religious organizations, such as the National Organization for Decency in Literature, developed their own rating schemes to guide their members while they sought to remove offending material from circulation altogether. In 1935, the H. W. Wilson Company introduced the *Movie Review Digest* to provide librarians the same information about films that its *Book Review Digest* did about books.

As we have seen, librarians promoted early public libraries as educational and cultural institutions, though the popular fiction they often circulated belied this higher purpose. In the first case to determine the constitutional standard to be applied to film, the Supreme Court similarly wrestled with the question of whether the motion picture provided a new means of education or a striking advance in entertainment. The case of *Mutual Film Corporation v. Industrial Commission of Ohio*, decided in 1915, pitted filmmaker D. W. Griffith against the state board in Ohio that previewed films and determined their suitability for distribution. The film at issue was *The Birth of a Nation*, based on two novels by Thomas Dixon, *The Clansman* and *The Leopard's Spots*. With their offensive depiction of freed slaves during the Reconstruction period and their glorification of the Ku Klux Klan, these works in print had roused the opposition of the National Association for the Advancement of Colored People (NAACP), founded in 1909. Their appearance in a dramatic film portrayal sparked further protest by civil rights and other organizations. At the same time, with the nation segregated along racial lines, Dixon's novels had a large following.

In print, these novels were controversial and offensive, but even under the existing obscenity statutes, there was no claim that these books were not protected by the First Amendment. In the *Mutual Film Corporation* case, the court had to decide whether the film version was also protected by the First Amendment. Judges, like librarians confronted with a new information medium, often seek analogies with existing media and ask whether existing standards for access or selection may be applied. Analyzing the medium of film in 1915, the Supreme Court asked whether movies were like a newspaper, an information medium protected by the First Amendment, or like a circus, a mere commercial entertainment that did not require constitutional protection. The court held that the First Amendment did not apply to film and specifically mentioned that the potentially harmful effects of film required government regulation.

It cannot be put out of view that the exhibition of moving pictures is a business pure and simple, originated and conducted for profit, like other spectacles, not to be regarded, nor intended to be regarded by the Ohio constitution ... , as part of the press of the country or as organs of public opinion. They are mere representations of events, of ideas and sentiments published and known, vivid, useful and entertaining no doubt, but ... capable of evil, having power for it, the greater because of their attractiveness and manner of exhibition. It was this capability and power, and it may be in experience of them, that induced the State of Ohio ... to require censorship before exhibition ... We cannot regard this as beyond the power of government.[7]

In outspoken remarks to a meeting of booksellers in 1924, author Thomas Dixon called film censorship a violation of freedom of the press, condemned censorship of either movies or books, and likened the two media.

Now ladies and gentlemen, there is absolutely no difference between the censorship of a picture and the censorship of a book, because the motion picture is a new form of printing in which Edison taught us that we could use rays of the sun to etch characters on yellow parchment, instead of black printer's ink—that is all. There is the identical print, involved in both cases.

Recalling his opposition to the proposed national film censorship board fifteen years earlier, Dixon declared that the censorship of films would be followed by demands for censorship of books and newspapers. Attributing the ban on *The Birth of a Nation* to "peanut-politicians," Dixon took issue with those who wanted to censor in order to protect children from what is immoral, filthy, and indecent, and recounted the difficulties posed by a quest for truth in a work of art. To Dixon, a true account of American history showed the "criminal paranoic" John Brown against the poised, intellectual, and patriotic Robert E. Lee. Censorship, he claimed, threatened his ability to communicate his understanding of "truth."[8]

In 1952, at about the time that the ALA applied the Library Bill of Rights to films, the Supreme Court reversed its decision in the *Mutual Film Corporation* case. Now an accepted medium, film no longer required the court to explain the new technology. The case of *Joseph Burstyn, Inc. v. Wilson* involved the decision by the New York Board of Regents to deny an exhibiting license to Roberto Rossellini's film *The Miracle* for its alleged sacrilege. Despite the controversial and, to some, offensive nature of the story, the court found that the film represented a significant work of art on a serious theme. It held that movies were "a significant medium for the communication of ideas" and thus protected by the First Amendment.[9] Interestingly, neither of the Supreme Court's landmark decisions on film involved sexually explicit material.

LIBRARY BILL OF RIGHTS UPDATED

Age

Like the courts, librarians struggle with the appropriate standards to apply to nonprint materials. As we have seen, Library Bill of Rights expanded to include nonprint formats in 1951, and in 1967 proscribed limits on access based on age. In 1989, these two concepts merged in a new interpretation that asserted the right of children and young adults to information in all formats. Originally written to apply to videotapes and other audiovisual materials and equipment, it was revised in 2004 using broad language to encompass emerging technologies.

Policies that set minimum age limits for access to any nonprint materials or information technology, with or without parental permission, abridge library use for minors.... Librarians, when dealing with minors, should apply the same standards to circulation of nonprint materials as are applied to books and other print materials except when directly and specifically prohibited by law....

The interests of young people, like those of adults, are not limited by subject, theme, or level of sophistication. Librarians have a responsibility to ensure young people's access to materials and services that reflect diversity of content and format sufficient to meet their needs.[10]

As it does with print materials, the ALA acknowledges and supports parents in exercising their responsibility to guide their own children's reading and viewing. Librarians can assist parents in this effort by making available reference tools and reviews that provide information about content, subject matter, and recommended audiences for nonprint materials.

Labels

About the same time the ALA revised its Library Bill of Rights to include age, changes made by the movie industry in handling controversial film content forced the ALA to reconsider its stand on labeling. Breaking away from strictures on language and conduct, the Motion Picture Producers Association introduced a ratings system that assigns a letter designation based on language, violence, and sexual content. Further, by assigning a PG-13 rating, the industry sought to indicate material inappropriate for viewing without parental guidance, and an R rating to identify material inappropriate for any viewer under age eighteen. Rather than controlling content, the new system sought to influence the distribution of films and the decisions of patrons about what films their children might attend.

The ALA had opposed labeling since 1951; religious and civic organizations devised their own movie rating schemes and, in some cases, urged their members to boycott certain films altogether. But ratings assigned by the industry and included in film packaging pose a different problem. As with the content of a work itself, the ALA could not endorse a particular rating scheme, but neither could it remove or obscure information about a film's rating.

With the music and gaming industries adding their own ratings to CDs and computer games, the ALA in 2005 renamed its statement "Labels and Rating Systems: An Interpretation of the Library Bill of Rights." It reiterates the basic principle that presence in a library collection of a piece of music or a game does not constitute an endorsement of content by the library. It condemns as censorship any labels that warn, discourage, or prohibit users from accessing material while it affirms viewpoint-neutral directional aids as a means to facilitate access. With respect to ratings, the interpretation declares,

A variety of organizations promulgate ratings systems as a means of advising either their members or the general public concerning their opinions of the contents and suitability or appropriate age for the use of certain books, films, recordings, Web sites, or other materials. The adoption, enforcement, or endorsement of any of these ratings systems by the library violates the Library Bill of Rights.

Librarians are not to remove industry ratings that appear on film, music, or game containers nor are they to add their own labels about the content.

Publishers, industry groups, and distributors sometimes add ratings to material or include them as part of their packaging. Librarians should not endorse such practices. However, removing or destroying such ratings if placed there by, or with the permission of, the copyright holder—could constitute expurgation.[11]

Although some libraries make available additional information on the meaning of the industry ratings at a location near film and music displays, the interpretation deems such practice unacceptable and a form of censorship. Here we see the fine line between service, where additional information is provided to guide patron choices, and access, where such information may be seen as prejudicial labeling.

The Freedom to View

Since the powerful Freedom to Read Statement adopted in 1953 applied to printed works, the ALA adopted a parallel Freedom to View Statement in 1990. It declared that

The FREEDOM TO VIEW, along with the freedom to speak, to hear, and to read, is protected by the First Amendment to the Constitution of the United States. In a free society, there is no place for censorship of any medium of expression.

The same basic principles of access formulated in a print environment apply in a nonprint environment:

that audiovisual materials communicated ideas essential to the constitutional guarantees of free expression,

that such materials needed to represent diverse ideas and means of expression,

that selection of a work did not constitute approval or imply agreement with its contents,

that labeling was an impermissible means of prejudging such materials,

that a work could not be excluded because of the moral, religious or political beliefs of its creator,

and that efforts to censor such materials had to be vigorously resisted.[12]

Ethical dilemmas that involve controversial and offensive works frequently recur, posing challenges to librarians who may fear unpleasant publicity or funding repercussions. As new technologies give added life to works that originally appeared in print, they prolong exposure to negative stereotypes and distasteful subjects. Despite its racist and offensive portrayals of freed slaves, *The Birth of a Nation* is considered a landmark cinematic achievement and has been praised by film critics for its innovative direction and cinematography. Had D. W. Griffith been a less talented filmmaker, it would have gone the way of the novels on which it was based. In an interesting reprise of earlier controversies, when the Library of Congress organized a showing of significant American films, it omitted *Birth of a Nation* allegedly because of its racist content. After a public outcry, the movie was shown in the series along with a panel discussion that provided social and filmmaking context.

THE LIBRARY OF CONGRESS AND *THE BIRTH OF A NATION* (1993)

In the fall of 1993, when the Library of Congress announced a yearlong celebration of the first century of American cinema, its opening series on early films did not include D. W. Griffith's *The Birth of a Nation*. Based on *The Clansman*, a novel by Thomas Dixon that was set in the South during Reconstruction, the motion picture glorified the Ku Klux Klan and caricatured freed slaves. On the film's release in 1915, the recently organized National Association for the Advancement of Colored People (NAACP) called for a boycott and staged demonstrations at theaters showing the film. When Griffith challenged the power of Ohio's censorship board, the U.S. Supreme Court ruled that films, as commercial entertainment, were not protected by the First Amendment. *The Birth of a Nation* became a cinematic landmark. Almost three hours long, it employed new techniques that were to become filmmaking standards: close-ups, flashbacks, multiple camera angles, and the simultaneous telling of parallel stories. Highly successful and continuously shown through the 1920s, the film was used by the KKK as a recruiting tool.

When, in 1992, the Library of Congress added *The Birth of a Nation* to the National Film Registry of films to be preserved for their cultural, historical, or aesthetic significance, the NAACP again protested. Its chair, William F. Gibson, wrote to the *Los Angeles Times* that the film was an insult to more than 30 million African Americans. "To honor this film and its filmmaker is to pay tribute to America's shameful racial history and to encourage a repeat of that history." Jill Brett, responding on behalf of the Library of Congress, observed that the registry was a means to preserve films as documents for researchers of American history. Brett noted that John Singleton, director of *Boyz N the Hood* and a member of the Library of Congress film board, had nominated the film as a "history lesson." John Hope Franklin, renowned historian of the African American experience, agreed. Calling the subject dastardly and accusing the film of libeling a whole race of people, he nonetheless acknowledged Griffith's filmmaking talents and the movie's landmark status.

When in the following year, *The Birth of a Nation* was glaringly absent from the Library of Congress's own film retrospective, *Washington Post* reporter Ken Ringle observed, "In a development that says something about the touchy current state of free speech, race relations and intellectual history in the nation, the Library of Congress today begins a yearlong commemoration of 100 years of motion pictures by shunning the controversial classic with which, in a very real sense, all American cinema began." After rumors circulated that the decision had been made under pressure from the LC Affirmative Action Office, Patrick Loughney, curator of the library's film programs, took responsibility: "Quite candidly, it is a sensitive subject. I decided it wouldn't be fair to just put the film out there where people might be caught unaware by it and where controversy over the social issues might drown out any discussion of the historical or the aesthetic." He expressed the hope that the film might be shown in a setting that permitted discussion of its historical context, technical aspects, and African American points of view.

Part III of the film retrospective did feature a special symposium on "Cinema and the Misrepresentation of History." The panel, moderated by Librarian of Congress James Billington, included John Hope Franklin, Thomas Cripps, author of *Slow Fade to Black*, a study of African American filmmaking, and William Greaves, actor and producer of a documentary on African American journalist, Ida B. Wells. Opening the discussion, Billington stated that, "Bigoted and racist as its treatment is of African Americans, 'The Birth of a Nation' is an inescapable part of our history." He explained that its inclusion on the National Film Registry did not imply "some kind of national honor." As part of the symposium, the film itself was shown at the John F. Kennedy Center as well as at the much smaller Mary Pickford Theater at the Library of Congress.

Commenting on the symposium in the *New York Times*, William Grimes described the panelists' condemnation of the film, then asked, "Throughout the evening, however, the thorny questions were never addressed. Was the Library of Congress right or wrong to leave the film out of its series? Does a reprehensible moral vision fatally impair a work of art?"

QUESTIONS

- How can libraries help the public understand why their collections contain materials that are offensive or controversial?
- How can libraries anticipate controversies over the presence of offensive works in their collections? Can anything be done to mitigate such controversies?
- Does the Library of Congress have different obligations from other libraries in the materials it collects, preserves, and presents to the public?

SOURCES

Brett, Jill. "'The Birth of a Nation' Documents History," [Letter to the Editor responding to letter from William F. Gibson] *Los Angeles Times*, January 4, 1993, F2.

Cutlip, Scott M. "Klan Made Potent Use of 'Birth of a Nation'," [Letter to the Editor] May 12, 1994, *New York Times*, A24.

D'Ooge, Craig, "'The Birth of a Nation': Symposium on Classic Film Discusses Inaccuracies and Virtues." *Library of Congress Information Bulletin* 53 (June 27, 1994): 263–266.

Gibson, William F. "Library of Congress Recognition Undeserved for 'Birth of a Nation'," [Letter to the Editor] Los Angeles Times, December 28, 1992. F3.

Grimes, William, "An Effort to Classify a Racist Classic," *New York Times*, April 27, 1994, C13, C15.

Lennig, Arthur. "Myth and Fact: The Reception of *The Birth of a Nation*," *Film History* 16, no. 2: 117–141.

Library of Congress, Motion Picture, Broadcasting and Recorded Sound Division. "Cinema's First Century, 1893–1993 (Part I), October–December, 1993."

Library of Congress, Motion Picture, Broadcasting and Recorded Sound Division. "Cinema's First Century, 1893–1993 (Part III), April–June 1994 The Birth of a Nation—A Special Symposium & Screening."

Library of Congress Public Affairs Office, "Library of Congress to Screen 'Birth of a Nation,' [Media Advisory] March 25, 1994.

Loughney, Patrick. "A Cinema Century," [Letter to the Editor responding to article by William Grimes] *New York Times*, May 21, 1994, 20.

Ringle, Ken. "Movie Classic Snubbed; Library Excludes 'Nation' Film from Early-Film Series," *Washington Post*, October 25, 1993, C1, C4.

In defining the role of libraries, librarians have to decide whether to collect material in a new format at all. Just as some libraries did not acquire popular fiction because it was incompatible with the library's educational role, some may not collect feature films because of their entertainment qualities or acquire only nonfiction films, documentaries, and public television programs. Others may charge a rental fee for feature films. As libraries continue to report an increasing proportion of their circulation based on DVDs and CDs, the ethics of this balance suggests that libraries are responding to customer demand rather than traditional ideas of quality.

OBSCENITY VERSUS INDECENCY

As we have seen, the Supreme Court has granted films the full protection of the First Amendment. In the area of telecommunications, however, it has applied a decency standard to gauge the appropriateness of content for broadcast over network radio and television. While the direct application to libraries is somewhat limited, librarians need to understand the difference between obscenity and indecency and be aware of the implications of this difference in the early discussions about access to material on the Internet.

Radio/Television

From the early days of radio, many librarians used broadcasts in their libraries as a basis for group discussion and developed their own radio shows to promote books and library service. Radio also played an important role in the extension of library service to new communities of users. In these early days, however, library leaders did not see a relationship between the censorship of radio broadcasts and the censorship of books. In *A History of the American Library Association, 1876–1972*, Dennis Thomison describes discussion within the ALA executive board concerning the censorship by the Federal Communications Commission (FCC) in 1938 of a broadcast of a work by Eugene O'Neill read over station WTCN in

Minneapolis. A majority of the board rejected a resolution protesting this action as a violation of freedom of speech. Ralph Munn, director of the Carnegie Library in Pittsburgh, declared,

I don't think we ought to get mixed up in this radio business. It is one thing to have books which have too many "God damns" per square inch of printed matter on a library shelf, and it is another thing to have it coming into the home by radio.

In contrast, ALA President Milton J. Ferguson saw that the same issue was involved whether the story was told in print or over the airwaves. "It is only a step from saying Eugene O'Neill's book may not be given over the radio to saying you can't put it in your library."[13]

Fearing the greater impact of sound and image in communicating controversial or explicit works, Congress granted the FCC the power to oversee the content of radio and television broadcasts. The FCC in turn has applied a decency standard and determined hours during which indecent material may not be broadcast over the airwaves. Supported by parents' groups, the FCC has sought to protect young people from possible harm, the same spirit that moved those who challenged the presence of explicit books in libraries and explicit scenes on screen.

In this area, the case setting the legal standard is *Federal Communications Commission v. Pacifica Foundation*, decided by the Supreme Court in 1978. It began as a complaint by a father whose son unexpectedly tuned in to a broadcast of George Carlin's "Seven Dirty Words" monologue on a Pacifica Foundation radio station. The FCC took action against the station; the Pacifica Foundation challenged the power of the FCC under the governing statute. In its decision, the court affirmed "indecency" as the appropriate, though stricter, standard. With echoes of nineteenth-century concerns, the court declared,

The concept of "indecent" is intimately connected with the exposure of children to language that describes in terms patently offensive as measured by contemporary community standards for the broadcast medium, sexual or excretory activities or organs, at times of the day when there is a reasonable risk that children may be in the audience.[14]

Thus material that is entitled to full protection of the First Amendment when it appears in print is subject to a different standard when read on the radio or adapted for television. Pacifica Foundation stations were challenged for readings of *Ulysses* on Bloomsday each June, claiming it violated the decency standard. The cost of defending such charges, apart from the outcome, caused a number of stations to forego the custom.

The FCC decides on the hours when "indecent" material may not be broadcast, although the court has struck down a twenty-four-hour "safe harbor." It also can levy fines against offending stations, and under the administration of President George W. Bush, it stepped up enforcement against stations broadcasting "shock jocks" during the morning commute. In the wake of well-publicized incidents involving racial slurs, Congress considered increasing the penalties for indecent radio broadcasts. In response, some disk jockeys moved to satellite radio where, as on cable television, the indecency standard does not apply. In an experiment in Fairfax County, Virginia, that foreshadowed issues with the Internet, librarians installed cable television sets in order to give patrons access to art, culture, and history channels. When patrons used the sets to access pornography, sexually explicit material protected by the First Amendment and permissible on cable but not network television, the sets were allowed to run down and were not replaced.

The Internet

We have already seen how librarians have been quick to adopt new information formats, frequently introducing them to the public and adapting them to library purposes. We have also seen that many of the concerns about information access that arose in a print setting return as information delivered via new technologies seems to pose new hazards for the young and vulnerable. And like judges, librarians have sought to apply existing standards in an environment of increasingly rapid technological change. Writing in 1947, Mary Rothrock, chair of the Audio-Visual Committee of the ALA, described the role of nonprint material in a way that anticipated the role of electronic information more than a half-century into the future. Before the Supreme Court declared in the *Burstyn* case that motion pictures are a medium of ideas entitled to First Amendment protection, Rothrock defended them as a worthy means of communication, not merely a diversion. Just substitute "the Internet" or "electronic information" for "audiovisual materials" in the following paragraph.

Audiovisual materials can never take the place of books, of course. They should not be thought of as devices for building up the circulation of books. They are useful in themselves, but not for stimulating much more reading of library books. Neither should they be used merely to divert with sound and motion. Their function is purposeful communication. Wisely used they can enrich the library's book services by supplementing them. They can take information and ideas to large numbers of people whom books are not reaching. By increasing the volume and intensity of the library's services they can multiply its community contact and increase its effectiveness.[15]

We have seen, as well, how legal standards and professional standards of access have evolved in concert. In the case of the Internet, we will see how librarians participated actively in determining these standards.

Exactly as the Supreme Court struggled to determine whether the First Amendment applied to films, it sought appropriate analogies and definitions to determine what level of protection should govern information accessed on the Internet. Is it a medium of entertainment or education? Should the standard be obscenity or indecency? Is it analogous to the press or to the radio? All the questions we have previously related to the librarian's obligation to provide access reappear as we enter the digital age.

Emerging from a text-based medium designed for defense and research purposes, the Internet has morphed into a multimedia global network making available information in virtually every format—text, sound, and images—and content of every imaginable kind, from the sublime to the obscene. Like earlier visual media, the World Wide Web delivered a more immediate impact as well as access to potentially harmful, controversial, or offensive materials that might appear unbidden and unexpected. Congress responded to these fears when it passed the Communications Decency Act as part of the Telecommunications Act of 1996. Barring obscenity outright, it also incorporated the decency standard and provided criminal penalties for those who knowingly made indecent material available to anyone under the age of eighteen over interactive computer services. Indecency was defined as "any comment, request, suggestion, proposal, or other communication that, in context, depicts or describes, in terms patently offensive as measured by contemporary community standards, sexual, or excretory activities or organs."

The law was struck down by a federal district court in Philadelphia that saw a demonstration of the new technology in the courtroom. Seeking an analogy, the court harkened back to the early printing press and the centrality of information to the democratic process. The Supreme Court agreed and unanimously declared unconstitutional that portion of the law that would give less than full First Amendment protection to material on the Internet. It was, said the court, a "dynamic, multifaceted category of communication" including "not only traditional print and news services, but also audio, video, and still images, as well as interactive, real-time dialogue."

Through the use of chat rooms, any person with a phone line can become a town crier with a voice that resonates farther than it could from any soapbox. Through the use of Web pages, mail exploders, and newsgroups, the same individual can become a pamphleteer. As the District Court found, "the content on the Internet is as diverse as human thought." ... We agree with its conclusion that our cases provide no basis for qualifying the level of First Amendment scrutiny that should be applied to this medium.[16]

Thus, in providing Internet access to patrons, librarians are operating in a global information environment in which only obscene materials may be banned. Material on the Internet is to be judged by the standard of a reasonable adult, not by a lesser standard formulated to protect children.

The power of the Internet has challenged librarians to reconcile their dual commitments to access and service. As co-plaintiffs with the American Civil Liberties Union (ACLU) in a suit against the Communications Decency Act, the ALA demonstrated its willingness to make the whole range of constitutionally permitted information available, regardless of its controversial, offensive, or sexually explicit content. In the electronic age, access is the value that transcends all. At the same time, the infinite and unbridled nature of the Internet evokes the fears of parents and educators of the possible harm lurking in the depths of instantly accessible Web sites. Offering connections to the Internet, librarians must match their commitment to access with their professional expertise to help patrons of all ages find their way in the global network. In one of its first efforts after the favorable decision in *Reno v. ACLU*, the ALA and the Association for Library Service to Children (ALSC) developed a list of the "Great Web Sites for Kids." In the face of legal challenges brought by such groups as Family Friendly Libraries, librarians developed Internet use policies to guide patron behavior in ways appropriate to school, academic, or public library settings without restricting access to material protected by the First Amendment.

CENSORSHIP VERSUS SELECTION

Responding to these same fears, Congress passed the Children's Internet Protection Act (CIPA) that sought to achieve indirectly what it had not been able to accomplish directly in the Communications Decency Act: limit children's access to inappropriate material on the Internet. Using its power of the purse, Congress, in CIPA, required that libraries receiving federal funds install Internet filters. Libraries not complying with this requirement would not be eligible for grants under the Library Services and Technology Act or the discounted E-rate connectivity provided in the Telecommunications Act of 1996. The ALA led the coalition that challenged the constitutionality of this condition. Arguing that filtering software blocked both unprotected and protected speech, the ALA maintained that the government could not condition funding on adherence to a requirement that denied access to material protected by the First Amendment.

The federal district court agreed with plaintiffs. Striking down the law, it heralded the Internet as a "vast democratic forum" facilitating speech "as diverse as human thought."

The architecture of the Internet, as it is right now, is perhaps the most important model of free speech since the founding. Two hundred years after the framers ratified the Constitution, the Net has taught us what the First Amendment means. The model for speech that the framers embraced was the model of Internet-distributed, non-centralized, fully free and diverse.[17]

Because filtering involved content-based restrictions on access, the court subjected them to the strict scrutiny test and found no compelling state interest in requiring the use of filters that blocked access to constitutionally protected material.

The appeal of this decision involved a remarkable consideration by the Supreme Court of the role of libraries in society and the basic values of libraries and librarians. In his decision for the majority, Chief Justice William Rehnquist used the ALA Library Bill of Rights, standards of professional practice, and quotations from library school texts to reverse the ruling of the district court and uphold CIPA. In describing the mission of public libraries, he wrote,

Public libraries pursue the worthy missions of facilitating learning and cultural enrichment. Appellee ALA's Library Bill of Rights states that libraries should provide "[b]ooks and other ... resources ... for the interest, information, and enlightenment of all people of the community the library serves."

Weighing in on the quality side of the long-standing professional debate, Rehnquist quoted the 1980 collection development text by William Katz, that "libraries collect only those materials deemed to have "requisite and appropriate quality," and Frederick Drury's 1930 text that it is "the aim of the selector to give the public, not everything it wants, but the best that it will read or use to advantage."

Rehnquist rejected the role of the public library as a public forum, but harkened to what he considered its traditional mission.

A library's need to exercise judgment in making collection decisions depends on its traditional role in identifying suitable and worthwhile material; it is no less entitled to play that role when it collects material from the Internet than when it collects material from any other source. Most libraries already exclude pornography from their print collections because they deem it inappropriate for inclusion. We do not subject these decisions to heightened scrutiny; it would make little sense to treat libraries' judgments to block online pornography any differently, when these judgments are made for just the same reason.

Because the legislation at issue helped public libraries fulfill their traditional role, and because Congress has the power to require that public funds be spent for the purposes for which they are authorized, the court upheld the act.

Especially because public libraries have traditionally excluded pornographic material from their other collections, Congress could reasonably impose a parallel limitation on its Internet assistance programs. As the use of filtering software helps to carry out these programs, it is a permissible condition ...[18]

It is important to understand that the court did not require filtering. It declared that Congress was within its rights to require the use of filters as a condition of federal aid. It is left to library boards and librarians to decide where the balance lies between providing unfettered Internet access and limiting access in order to receive funds for library services and connectivity.

QUALITY VERSUS DEMAND IN A DIGITAL ENVIRONMENT

Where access is unlimited, the user's need for guidance to inform that access is greater than ever. In a digital environment, librarians have lost much of the prized control that they early sought as emblematic of their professional status. The expertise that they bring to guide patrons' searches for information on the World Wide Web is less exclusive than ever. Blogs give access to specialized resources; amateur reviewers on Amazon.com join those from *Publishers' Weekly* and *Booklist*. Media personalities, like Oprah Winfrey, guide the reading choices of millions of viewers. While calling forth the librarian's strongest affirmation of the principle of access to all information, the Internet has demonstrated the need for the highest level of professional service to identify and evaluate it.

Originally adopted in 1996, in the early years of World Wide Web access, and modified in 2005, after a decade of library experience providing Web access to patrons, the Library Bill of Rights Interpretation on Access to Electronic Information, Services, and Networks synthesizes the legal standards, professional principles, and service obligations required to provide ethical access in an electronic environment.

As in many codes of ethics, it begins with an introduction to the role of libraries and librarians:

Freedom of expression is an inalienable human right and the foundation for self-government.... Libraries and librarians protect and promote these rights by selecting, producing, providing access to, identifying, retrieving, organizing, providing instruction in the use of, and preserving recorded expression regardless of the format or technology.

Users have a right to access that is not restricted or denied for expressing or receiving constitutionally protected speech and also a right to a due process appeal of any denial of access. It is assumed that information is constitutionally protected speech unless a court determines otherwise. Users have a right to training and assistance so that they may find, use, and evaluate information effectively.

To this end, libraries must provide equity of access, bridging information gaps, eschewing fees, and developing policies that ensure that "electronic information, services, and networks provided directly or indirectly by the library [are] equally, readily, and equitably accessible to all library users." Further, it declares that "publicly funded libraries have a legal obligation to provide access to constitutionally protected information," and declares that any technological measure to block access be set at the least restrictive level and disabled in a timely manner on request.

In this new networked world, traditional ethical standards still apply. Librarians must provide access to support user needs regardless of the age of the user or the content of the material. The rights of minors to constitutionally protected speech are recognized as well with a minimum right to request access to erroneously blocked information. Librarians are not to deny access to electronic information because of its controversial content or their own personal beliefs or fears of confrontation. They should provide access to information representing all points of view, recalling that this does not constitute either sponsorship or endorsement.

But it is also clear that in a networked environment, old standards may not apply. Providing connections to global information, services, and networks, the interpretation says, is not the same as selecting and purchasing materials for a library collection. Determining the accuracy or authenticity of electronic information may present special problems. Some information accessed electronically may not meet a library's selection or collection development policy. In an electronic environment, the standard of "best" no longer applies. According to the interpretation, "libraries and librarians should not deny access to electronic information solely on the grounds that it is perceived to lack value." The loss of professional authority and control means that each user must determine what is appropriate, and, as in a print environment, parents remain responsible for guiding their own children in using electronic resources.[19]

Even more than in a print environment, librarians in the age of digital information may provide access to materials with which they profoundly disagree. We turn our attention now to such philosophical conflicts of interest.

END NOTES

1. "'Fanny Hill' Is Banned Again, This Time from an Indiana Computer," *Chronicle of Higher Education*, January 19, 1994, A25.

2. Melvil Dewey, "Next Half-Century," *Library Journal* 51 (October 15, 1926): 888.

3. Wayne Nason, "Community Service of the Library," *Rural America* VI (October 1928): 5–6. Judson T. Jennings, "Sticking to Our Last," *Library Journal* 49 (June 1924): 613–618. "A County Library Film," *Rural America* VI (October 1928): 6.

4. "Louisville's Library," *Newsweek*, March 6, 1950, 80.

5. "Library Bill of Rights," *ALA Bulletin* 42 (July/August 1948): 285. [Adopted by the ALA Council at Atlantic City on June 18, 1948].

6. For a discussion of vice societies, see Paul S. Boyer, *Purity in Print: Book Censorship in America from the Gilded Age to the Computer Age.* Madison, WI: University of Wisconsin Press, 2002.

7. *Mutual Film Corporation v. Industrial Commission of Ohio*, 236 U.S. 230 (1915) at 244–245.

8. Thomas Dixon, "Censorship," *The Publishers' Weekly* 105 (May 24, 1924): 1,698–1,701.

9. *Joseph Burstyn, Inc. v. Wilson*, 343 U.S. 495 (1952).

10. Access for Children and Young Adults to Nonprint Materials: An Interpretation of the Library Bill of Rights, adopted June 28, 1989, amended June 20, 2004, by the ALA Council. *Intellectual Freedom Manual*, 7th ed. Chicago: American Library Association, 2006, 78–80.

11. Labels and Rating Systems: An Interpretation of the Library Bill of Rights, adopted July 13, 1951, amended June 25, 1971, July 1, 1981, June 26, 1990, and January 19, 2005. *Intellectual Freedom Manual*, 7th ed., 171–172, http://www.ala.org/ala/oif/statementspols/statementsif/interpretations/statementlabelingl.htm.

12. Freedom to View Statement. Originally adopted by the Freedom to View Committee of American Film and Video Association (AFVA; formerly Educational Film Library Association) in 1979, and adopted by the AFVA board of directors in February 1979. Updated and approved by the AFVA board of directors in 1989. Endorsed by the ALA Council January 10, 1990.

13. Dennis Thomison, *A History of the American Library Association 1876–1972.* Chicago: American Library Association, 1978, 146.

14. *Federal Communications Commission v. Pacifica Foundation*, 438 U.S. 726 (1978).

15. Mary U. Rothrock, "Wings of Thought," *Library Journal* 74 (March 1949): 458. In 1923, Rothrock defended the inclusion of modern fiction in library collections, applying an adult standard much like that announced in the *Ulysses* decision a decade later.

16. *Reno v. ACLU*, 521 U.S. 150 (1997).

17. *U.S. v. American Library Association*, 201 F. Supp. 2d 401 (E.D. Pa. 2002).

18. *U.S. v. American Library Association*, 539 U.S. 194 (2003) at 6, 11, 15. For the ALA's Web site on the Children's Internet Protection Act, with links to lower court and Supreme Court decisions, see http://www.ala.org/CIPA.

19. Access to Electronic Information, Services, and Networks: An Interpretation of the Library Bill of Rights. Adopted January 24, 1996; amended January 19, 2005, by the ALA Council. *Intellectual Freedom Manual*, 7th ed., 84–88, http://www.ala.org/ala/oif/statementspols/statementsif/interpretations/accesselectronic.htm.

6

———◦—◦◦◦—◦———

CONFLICTS OF INTEREST: PHILOSOPHICAL

Codes of ethics for virtually every professional and vocational group pro-scribe conflicts of interest. The ability to separate personal interests from professional responsibilities is one of the hallmarks of professionalism, with an understanding of potential conflicts deepened by professional training and experience. Using a position of responsibility to enhance oneself at the expense of one's institution is a basic ethical violation.

Personal gain is most often equated with financial gain—using inside in-formation or business contacts for personal enrichment. Like all profession-als, librarians must be wary about using their positions for inappropriate financial benefits. But personal gain can also be achieved in a less tangible form—using a professional position to advance a personal belief or political ideology. Because the central obligation of their work is to collect, organize, and make information available, librarians may face philosophical conflicts of interest in which their personal beliefs conflict with the ideas to which they provide access. In their unique professional role as information providers, librarians must be especially attentive to possible philosophical conflicts of interest. Because this kind of conflict threatens the core values of service and access, we will first examine the ethical obligation to separate personal beliefs and professional duty. In Chapter Seven, we will explore conflicts involving financial gain.

In exploring the ethical dimensions of service, we noted the importance of consistency that frees the provision of information from the identity or influence of the individual librarian who provides it. Attaining a high level of service requires librarians to rely on professional techniques and accepted sources. Similarly, in discussing access, we noted that libraries must provide access to a broad range of points of view. Providing access to information across a spectrum of viewpoints means that some patrons, and by necessity, some staff, may inevitably disagree. An ethical mandate to separate personal beliefs from professional responsibilities is inherent in providing the highest level of service and the freest access to information.

How might such philosophical conflicts arise? In providing service, a public library following the Library Bill of Rights might have no age limits on the materials available to youth. A librarian might personally object to a teenager checking out an adult novel or accessing information about sex on the Internet. Or, in providing access, a public library following the Library Bill of Rights might provide information on both evolution and creationism. Librarians with personal views on either side of the debate might object to making accessible the opposing position. Or the conflict might arise where a library has restricted service to young people or has failed to represent different points of view. In such situations, a librarian may have philosophical differences with the library itself. What is the ethical course of action?

It is not only librarians who face conflicts between their own interests and those of their institutions. Library board members, who govern public libraries, set policy, and choose the library's director, must adhere to their own ethical standards. They, too, must recognize the possible philosophical and financial conflicts of interest inherent in their own duties.

Finally, we must recognize that librarians and libraries play dual roles as information providers and societal players. While ethically required to provide access to diverse points of view, librarians and trustees must also make decisions about their own conduct and policies for their libraries. Unavoidably, this means having to choose sides on issues, such as civil rights or the environment, facing society as a whole. Does the library encourage diversity in its staffing? Does it recycle? Reconciling multiple interests and roles requires librarians and libraries, and professional associations as well, to recognize the duality of their obligations and to separate their particular concerns from their transcendent obligations.

In 1961, arguing why librarianship did not need any code of ethics, Association of College and Research Libraries (ACRL) board member Patricia Paylore expressed her confidence that people will do the right thing and that the power to be ethical is only within each man's heart, governed by individual conscience.[1] Since we cannot be sure, however, that a particular set of strongly held personal beliefs is the best guide to appropriate professional conduct, librarians, like other professionals, require written codes of ethics and explicit cautions against allowing personal beliefs to affect professional practice.

WHAT CODES OF ETHICS TELL US

The obligation to avoid conflicts of interests appears in nearly every version of the codes considered or adopted by the ALA and in the codes of the more specialized library professional organizations. The ALA Code of Ethics approved by the ALA Council in 1995 separates philosophical and financial conflicts.[2] Sections VI declared that

We do not advance private interests at the expense of library users, colleagues, or our employing institutions.

The similar provision in the 1981 Statement on Professional Ethics[3] made this even more explicit, using the imperative "must" to describe the specific duty of librarians.

Librarians must avoid situations in which personal interests might be served or financial benefits gained at the expense of library users, colleagues, or the employing institution.

Section VII in the 1995 code targeted philosophical conflicts.

We distinguish between our personal convictions and professional duties and do not allow our personal beliefs to interfere with fair representation of the aims of our institutions or the provision of access to their information resources.

Again, comparable language in Section V of the 1981 statement provided even more forcefully that

Librarians must distinguish clearly in their actions and statements between their personal philosophies and attitudes and those of an institution or professional body.

Every library school student, librarian, and library trustee has a particular set of political, religious, and personal beliefs, and a worldview shaped by inheritance, experience, demographics, and locality. We have come to welcome and encourage the diversity of our profession and of those we serve. In practice, this means that among practitioners and board members, we should expect the same array of views on such questions as evolution, suicide, war, global warming, and abortion, that we find among library users. We should also expect, however, that librarians and board members share a belief in libraries and the professional values of service and access. The question is how to make certain that decisions about library collections and priorities are determined by shared professional values and not individual, or collective, personal views.

As we have seen, as codes of ethics have been modified over time, they have become more succinct and more focused on values, shedding detail and explanations. When codes call for high levels of service and equitable access to information, we can look to the interpretations of the Library Bill of Rights for a fuller elaboration of these values. The Library Bill of Rights, directed at institutions rather than at professionals, does not cover conflicts of interest.

The obligation to provide access and challenge censorship is unambiguous, but the duty of the librarian to overcome personal beliefs is implicit rather than explicit. Earlier and more detailed versions of library codes of ethics, along with the codes of other professional groups, the Freedom to Read Statement, and *Libraries: An American Value*,[4] suggest how conflicts between beliefs and duty might arise and how they should be resolved.

Personal Beliefs

Acting on personal beliefs can interfere with both service and access. A librarian must not make a decision about what patron to serve on the basis of personal preference or prejudice. Service decisions based the age, race, or other patron characteristics apart from their information need is unethical. A librarian may disagree with a library's policy to make materials available without regard to age but may not act on that belief to impede access to information.

Similarly, personal beliefs may not affect what information is made available or what is not made available, what restrictions are put on access to information, whether labels are attached, or what proportions of different viewpoints are included in a collection. Arthur Bostwick, in his 1908 ALA presidential address, "The Librarian as Censor," noted that in developing public library collections, "it is particularly desirable to avoid here anything in the nature of purely personal opinion and prejudice."[5] Librarians may not be the best judge of their motives in making such decisions. Self-censorship may cloak personal predilections in arguments based on what is in the best interest of the institution or its patrons.

The 1995 code refers to the need to avoid advancing personal interests at the expense of users, colleagues, and institutions. While referring to financial interests, this can also characterize strongly held personal views that might be advanced through the library. As a check, libraries must institute both policies and procedures to ensure that the library is fulfilling its own mission rather than advancing any personal or political agenda. This is done by formulating a mission statement that reflects a consensus of the library's role and a collection development plan that specifies selection criteria, includes a challenge procedure, and invites suggestions for materials to be added. Assigning selection decisions to a committee rather than to an individual also provides some protection against individual bias and increases the likelihood of a more diverse collection.

Intellectual Interests

Intellectual pursuits and academic expertise, as well as personal religious or political beliefs, may cause potential conflicts between personal and institutional interests. Charles Knowles Bolton saw inherent conflicts between personal reading interests and book collecting. In 1909, he wrote that "The librarian should not permit specialized book-collecting or book-reading to narrow his field of interest, nor to bias his judgment in purchasing books."[6] In 1922, Bolton's revised canons declared that "Purchases of books should reflect the needs of the community rather than the personal taste or interest of the librarian. His selection of books should be catholic, and his power to guide be exercised with discretion."[7]

As Bolton envisioned, where librarians, curators, or archivists are subject experts, their personal collecting interests may mirror those of their institution, creating an inappropriate rivalry for the acquisition or use of unique materials. The ACRL Code of Ethics for Special Collections Librarians, based largely on Article VI of the 1995 ALA Code of Ethics, establishes the avoidance of this conflict of interest as its central ethical obligation. Section II declares that

All outside employment and professional activities must be undertaken within the fundamental premise that the special collections librarian's first responsibility is to the library, that the activity will not interfere with the librarian's ability to discharge this responsibility, and that it will not compromise the library's professional integrity or reputation.[8]

Section I provides that "Special collections librarians must not compete with their library in collecting or in any other activity," while Section V asserts that "Special collections librarians may not withhold information about the library's holdings or sequester collection materials in order to further their own research and publications."

Archivists may face similar conflicts between their professional expertise and their personal research and collecting interests. The Code of Ethics for Archivists, adopted by the Council of the Society of American Archivists in 1992, provided this guidance in its section on Conflicts of Interest:

As members of a community of scholars, archivists may engage in research, publication, and review of the writings of other scholars. If archivists use their institution's holdings for personal research and publication, such practices should be approved by their employers and made known to others using the same holdings. Archivists who buy and sell manuscripts personally should not compete for acquisitions with their own repositories, should inform their employers of their collecting activities, and should preserve complete records of personal acquisitions and sales.[9]

In the revision of the Code of Ethics for Archivists adopted in 2005, this matter was handled succinctly in Section III on Judgment:

Archivists should exercise professional judgment in acquiring, appraising, and processing historical materials. They should not allow personal beliefs or perspectives to affect their decisions.

And Section IV on Trust:

Archivists should not profit or otherwise benefit from their privileged access to and control of historical records and documentary materials.[10]

To ensure transparency, some archivists are required not only to refrain from competition with their institution but also to make known and retain records of their personal acquisitions. This is an area in which institutional policy should make explicit such ethical requirements.

Professional Expertise

Professional credentials or expertise in another area may also create potential conflicts of interest that are specifically addressed in the codes of specialized library organizations. The Ethical Principles of the American Association of Law Libraries (AALL), adopted in 1999, using language from the 1995 ALA code, deals with conflicts of interest in sections on "Business Relationships," "Professional Responsibilities," and "Service." Personal and financial conflicts of interest fall under "Business Relationships."

We have a duty to avoid situations in which personal interests might be served or significant benefits gained at the expense of library users, colleagues, or our employing institutions.

The obligation to avoid philosophical conflicts of interest appears under "Professional Responsibilities":

We distinguish between our personal convictions and professional duties and do not allow our personal beliefs to interfere with the service we provide.

Potential conflicts between their roles as librarians and their expertise in legal information appear under "Service."

We acknowledge the limits on service imposed by our institutions and by the duty to avoid the unauthorized practice of law.[11]

All law librarians must draw a line between providing information on legal subjects and offering legal advice. The dilemma is particularly acute for those law librarians who are also trained attorneys. The AALL code makes this ethical obligation explicit. Health sciences librarians might expect to face similar conflicts between providing health information and offering medical advice, especially where the librarian also has nursing or other medical training. Unlike the AALL code, however, the Medical Library Association (MLA) code does not explicitly address this possible conflict. But in each case, the ethical requirement demands functioning as a librarian and not exceeding that professional boundary and role.

Other Professions

We see the same concerns about the potential harm to professional credibility in the codes of other professions, especially where providing information is a central role. For example, in calling on journalists to "Seek the Truth and Report It," the 1996 Code of Ethics of the Society of Professional Journalists declares that journalists should "Examine their own cultural values and avoid imposing those values on others," and "Support the open exchange of views, even views they find repugnant." In the section, "Act Independently," the code specifies that "Journalists should be free of obligation to any interest other than the public's right to know." To remain ideologically independent, journalists should "Avoid conflicts of interest, real or perceived," and "Remain free of associations and activities that may compromise integrity or damage credibility."[12]

PERSONAL BELIEFS VERSUS INSTITUTIONAL AIMS

As the roles of libraries have been further differentiated and their purposes made more explicit in mission statements, library boards may adopt policies at odds with the professional outlook of the library director or staff members. Philosophical conflicts of interest can occur not only in ongoing decisions about providing access to individual patrons or acquiring particular information sources. They may also arise from fundamental disagreements over the nature of service or access. A change in direction to a popular materials focus, a decision to filter Internet access, or a restriction on materials by age may raise basic differences between the board and the staff.

Since board members frequently come from other fields and are not familiar with the philosophical concepts and ethical standards of library service, librarians and library associations should assist board members in understanding the values that undergird library practice. Though public library directors are usually not, and should not be, members of the library board, they can, and do, influence board decisions. Board members need to understand why the collection includes material that may offend members of the community, why access should not be limited by age but left to parents to decide, and why the library needs to reach out to new populations of users. But the board has the final say on library policy.

QUESTIONS

- When the board approves a change in course with which a librarian disagrees, what is the ethical course of action?
- When the board hires a new director to take the library in a different direction, what is the ethical obligation of library staff members who oppose the change?

The 1995 ALA code provides that we "do not allow our personal beliefs to interfere with fair representation of the aims of our institutions." From their earliest codes, librarians have been reminded of their ethical obligations to their institution and to the profession itself. Librarians may not only disagree about the subjects represented in their collections, they may hold fundamentally different views on the role of libraries, the nature of library service, and the extent of information access. In early codes built around relationships, the librarian is called upon to conduct disagreements privately, maintain a loyal stance in publicly defending library policy, and resign in the face of insurmountable differences.

Mary Plummer foresaw such conflicts as early as 1903 when she wrote that a librarian whose natural tendencies conflicted with the best interests of the profession "should be willing to give up the work for the good of the work."[13] In his 1909 canons, Bolton included loyalty among the ethical obligations of the librarian to the library's trustees.

When a librarian cannot in his dealings with the public be entirely loyal to a policy which is clearly upheld by his trustees he should explain his position to the board, and in an extreme case offer to resign.[14]

In the 1922 canons, Bolton warned against a librarian allying himself with one trustee or group of board members, commenting that moderate isolation was preferable to an alliance with one or another faction of board members.[15]

In describing the relationship of the librarian to the library's governing authority, the ALA's first code of ethics in 1938 reiterated that the governing authority held final jurisdiction over the administration of the library. The librarian was to act as a liaison between board and staff, keeping the board informed of library activities, interpreting board policy, and sharing library problems with the staff. The librarian's duty was to carry out board policy. In outlining the relationship of the librarian to the library, the 1938 code limited criticism of library policy only to proper authorities and for the purpose of improvement.[16] More recent codes do not include this level of explicit instruction for situations when conflicts arise between librarian, board, and staff. Based on core professional values, however, they suggest that the librarian must be an advocate for service and access on behalf of the library, its users, and society, while fairly representing the aims of the institution.

TRUSTEE ETHICS

As we have seen, the ALA Code of Ethics sets standards for the members of ALA, not just for librarians. Included in this membership are not only librarians but library staff members, Friends of Libraries, and library trustees. In 1985, the boards of directors of the American Library Trustees Association and the Public Library Association, both constituent parts of the ALA, adopted an Ethics Statement for Public Library Trustees. In addition to requiring that "Trustees must promote a high level of library service while observing ethical standards," the code largely addressed conflicts of interest:

> Trustees must avoid situations in which personal interests might be served or financial benefits gained at the expense of library users, colleagues, or the institution.
>   It is incumbent upon any trustee to disqualify himself/herself immediately whenever the appearance of a conflict of interest exists.
>   Trustees must distinguish clearly in their actions and statements between their personal philosophies and attitudes and those of the institution, acknowledging the formal position of the board even when they personally disagree.[17]

Librarians and library trustees have similar duties to distinguish between their personal interests and professional duty to provide library service and access to information. In the recent controversy over filtering at the Rochester, New York, Public Library, a board member, and former board chair, who was also a member of the clergy, articulated the appropriate response when these values conflict. Although he said that he personally opposed the type of sexually explicit material accessible on the Web, he supported the library's policy of unblocking access to such sites on the request of adult patrons as required by law.[18]

A trustee needs to understand that libraries provide information on a range of viewpoints, that the library does not endorse ideas, and that materials in the collection may provoke controversy. In hiring the library director and determining library policy, trustees must be prepared to defend the librarian who acts in accordance with the ethical values of the profession. The relationship is reciprocal. In honoring the values of the Library Bill of Rights, the Freedom to Read Statement, and the Code of Ethics, trustees support the integrity of libraries and librarianship. In return, librarians must help the board understand these values, advocate on their behalf, but then refrain from public criticism or resign in protest once the board has made a decision with which they disagree.

This reciprocity characterizes the rights to service and access themselves. In getting access to the information we want, we refrain from circumscribing the rights of others to access the information they seek.

PUBLIC CONTROVERSIES

Librarians have increasingly become public figures, and, in fact, early codes of ethics called on librarians to be engaged in their communities in order to determine information needs and build support for the library. As we have seen, the librarian as a representative of the library is required to explain and defend, if necessary, the policies of the library, regardless of any personal disagreement with the policy or reservations about its impact. The same ethical duty applies to trustees.

More difficult is the ethical dilemma posed by the librarian's (or trust-ee's) identification with the library when acting in a personal capacity. As the librarian becomes more widely known, it is more difficult to separate personal from institutional identity and personal beliefs from those of the library. Early codes advised the librarian to maintain a position of public neutrality. In 1909, Charles Knowles Bolton warned that "A librarian should be chary of lending his name to a public controversy."[19] In 1922, he added that the librarian should not "add weight to the contention of a local faction, or to commercial enterprises, even those that have an educa-tional or philanthropic motive." His comment suggested possible dangers involved in siding with one side or another.

[The librarian's] advice will very naturally be sought by his constituents increasingly as his influence grows, but giving for publication a testimonial to a book is likely to lead to serious abuses. Standing on neutral ground, he should be all things to all men.[20]

Quoting librarian poet Sam Walter Foss, Bolton observed, "[The librarian] loves all ideas—even when he despises them and disbelieves in them—for he knows that the ferment and chemic reactions of ideas keep the old world from growing mouldy [sic] and mildewed and effete."[21]

In early ethical codes, the librarian's obligation to take a neutral stand on public controversies was seen as analogous to the library's duty to provide in-formation about all sides of a question. The 1929 draft code, in its section on the librarian and the library's constituency, urged the librarian to take an active part in the life of the community but to "take care not to offend against the standards of decorum that prevail in that community or constituency."

The librarian, representing the governing body, should see that the library serves impartially all individuals, groups, and elements that make up it[s] constituency. In the case of the public library as a non-partisan institution the books purchased should rep-resent all phases of opinion and interest rather than the personal tastes of the librarian or board members. In an official capacity, the librarian and members of the staff should not express personal, religious, or economic issues, especially those of a local nature.[22]

In 1938, reflecting the increasingly public nature of librarianship, the code called on librarians to play an active role in the community as part of the ethi-cal obligation of librarian to society. "Librarians should participate in public and community affairs and so represent the library that it will take its place among educational, social, and cultural agencies."[23]

But again, the 1973 draft Statement on Professional Ethics warned about a possible confusion between personal and professional identity.

The individual should be aware that personal views and activities may be interpreted as representative of the institution in which one is employed. Proper precaution should accordingly be taken to distinguish between private actions and those one is authorized to take in the name of the institution.[24]

And in the "Introduction" to the 1975 American Library Association Statement on Professional Ethics addressed the conflict between the librarian's personal right as a citizen to engage in public activity and the professional obligation of fairly representing the library.

Every citizen has the right as an individual to take part in public debate or to engage in social and political activity.

The only restrictions on these activities are those imposed by specific and well-publicized laws and regulations which are generally applicable. However, since personal views and activities may be representative of the institution in which a librarian is employed, proper precautions should be taken to distinguish between private actions and those one is authorized to take in the name of the institution.[25]

The statement itself provided that "A librarian must avoid any possibility of personal gain at the expense of the employing institution."

Thus, the librarian's ethical obligations regarding philosophical conflicts of interest may be summarized:

- The librarian must not allow personal beliefs or prejudices to affect decisions about services rendered or material acquired or made accessible.

- The librarian must advocate for the adoption of library service and access policies that accord with the Library Bill of Rights, codes of ethics, and other statements of professional values. But, the librarian must refrain from public criticism of library policy or, if in irreconcilable differences with the board, resign.

- The librarian must actively engage in community affairs as a representative of the library. But, the librarian must not allow personal views to be confused with the values and policies of the library.

NEUTRALITY VERSUS SOCIAL RESPONSIBILITY

Thus, librarians are called upon to be players in the public arena and to represent fairly the library, its aims, and its programs to the community, but also to take care lest personal beliefs be attributed to the library itself. Though early codes called on librarians to take neutral positions on public issues, librarians have traditionally been advocates, first, for extending library service to unserved populations, and then for providing access to a wide spectrum of ideas, in an array of media, to a broad audience of library users. Advocacy for service and access has been considered essential to the democratic mission of the public library. The ALA and other professional organizations, especially state library associations, have a long history of lobbying for library service and speaking out against censorship before Congress, state legislatures, and the courts.

Since librarians and library associations have a long history of advocacy on behalf of service and access, how are they to decide which issues they might address? Are there ethical issues in deciding what constitutes a "library issue?"

In the 1960s, the turbulent decade of protests against the war in Vietnam and demonstrations on behalf of civil rights, the library community divided over the question of which issues are "library issues." Is there a duty to neutrality that extends beyond representing diverse points of view in library collections? Proponents of social responsibility within the ALA proposed that the association actively engage with contemporary movements that affected the rights and well-being of underrepresented and marginalized communities and work to expand access to the ideas of ethnic and political minorities.

Those opposing the movement to create a Social Responsibilities Round Table, and later an Office for Social Responsibility within the ALA, feared that active engagement on one side of an issue would undermine the profession's commitment to intellectual freedom. David Berninghausen, dean of the library school at the University of Minnesota, and former chair of the ALA's Committee on Intellectual Freedom, summarized this view in an article "Social Responsibility vs. the Library Bill of Rights." Berninghausen predicted that taking a position on a political issue or social issue would lead to library collections that represented only that point of view, though no one in the social responsibilities movement had suggested this.[26]

The initial debate over social responsibilities was notable in its inattention to the ethical dimensions of the issues at stake. Undertaken when the association was still governed by its long outdated code of 1938, the conversation might have been enriched and the divisions lessened by an ethical analysis of each point of view. Proponents of a more activist posture on social issues were particularly interested in underserved populations, in terms of both library service and information access. The hostile reaction to writings and speeches of political radicals demonstrated the importance of intellectual freedom in giving voice to those whose views were controversial or considered offensive. The list of books involved in the *Pico* case, for example, including works by Eldridge Clever, Richard Wright, and Langston Hughes, reflected the disproportionate censorship attacks on minority writers. In contrast, concerns about the rights of women, African Americans, and other ethnic minorities were consistent with the profession's tradition of extending library service and its long-held ethical commitment to respond to the information needs of all members of the community.

The 1936 decision of the ALA on meeting sites, following its experience with racial segregation at its annual conference in Richmond, is an early example of the kind of issue that requires a more activist response. But, the decision of the ALA to limit its future meetings to sites where all members could participate in conference activities went only part way in addressing the fundamental issues raised by a racially segregated society. As we have seen, the ALA continued to countenance segregated libraries and segregated library associations. The ALA's decision in 1936 had been grounded in the discontinuity between its claim that libraries play a central role in promoting democracy and its practice of condoning racial segregation. Though there was nothing in any of the early ALA drafts or adopted codes on race, and though both the U.S. Constitution and state law upheld racial segregation, the denial of service and access based on race could be viewed as a violation of the profession's fundamental obligation to provide service to the whole community.

The code of ethics drafted in 1968 at the height of the debate over the ALA's social responsibilities, though not adopted, reflected some aspects of this philosophy of more socially engaged librarianship. Unlike early codes, the 1968 draft focused on values, not relationships, and though it proclaimed support for the Freedom to Read and the Library Bill of Rights, its concern was the welfare and dignity of all members of the community. Also, unlike other library codes, its opening declaration was a personal vow:

I pledge according to my best ability and judgment that I will practice my profession with conscience and dignity; the welfare of my patrons will be my first consideration; I will respect the confidences and responsibilities which are bestowed upon me. I will maintain the honor and traditions of the library profession. I will not permit considerations of race, religion, nationality, party politics, personal gain, or social standing to intervene between my duty to my profession and to society. I will maintain the utmost respect for service. Even under threat I will strive for the freedom to read and for the other basic freedoms inherent in a democracy.

Article I, while alluding to the relationships that organized earlier codes, bracketed these responsibilities with an overarching obligation to "render service to society with full respect for the dignity of man" and loyalty "to the cause of democracy and liberty." The explanation elaborated:

A librarian: Recognizes and respects the worth and dignity of each individual in all procedures and actions. He is fair and impartial in the enforcement of library policies and regulations, and does not give preferential consideration to any individual or group because of their special status or position in the community.[27]

As librarians stepped into a more public role, they saw the implications of librarianship in a broader context and interpreted their decisions in light of this expanding consciousness. Decisions impinging on the rights of library users or affecting the ability of libraries to provide service or information access were embraced within the fold of "library issues."

Social issues grounded in the same basic issues reappear in new guises with each generation. Women's rights fell squarely within the ambit of the

ALA. As the professional association of a predominantly female profession, the ALA was an active supporter of the Equal Rights Amendment and arranged its conference schedule to avoid meeting in states that had not adopted the amendment.[28] In 1977, the ALA confronted the complexities posed when commitments to racial justice and to intellectual freedom seemed to be at odds.

ALA AND *THE SPEAKER* (1977)

As the ALA celebrated its centennial in 1976, its Intellectual Freedom Committee proceeded with plans to produce a film on the First Amendment that could be used by civic and educational groups. With approval from the ALA executive board, the committee selected Lee Bobker and Vision Associates to make the film using money from advance orders, a grant from Beta Phi Mu, and $75,000 from the ALA. Robert Wedgeworth, the ALA's executive director, signed the contract; a three-member subcommittee of the Intellectual Freedom Committee, including its chair and Judith Krug, head of the ALA Office for Intellectual Freedom, were to provide oversight. Without widespread consultation within the ALA, Bobker chose a storyline depicting the controversy that erupted when a high school club invited a speaker who espoused a genetic theory of racial inferiority. Suggested by incidents on college campuses involving scientist William Shockley, the script did not involve either a school library or a school librarian.

The subsequent controversy over the completed film involved lapses in oversight, errors in judgment concerning its contents, and difficult questions over what to do with the finished product. Despite requests, members of the Intellectual Freedom Committee and the ALA executive board did not see the script or portions of the film until it was completed in the spring of 1977. When the executive board finally did see the movie, it cautioned against releasing the film until it could be viewed by ALA members at the association's upcoming annual meeting. This decision to withhold the film, challenged at the time as censorship, was reversed on the advice of counsel who was concerned about a possible breach of the contract with Vision Associates.

The contents of the film raised myriad concerns despite its fine acting and production. Among these concerns, opponents noted that though it was commissioned by the ALA, the story omitted libraries and librarians altogether. When controversy arose over the appearance of a speaker espousing views that many found abhorrent, parents, teachers, and the principal all failed to defend First Amendment rights. Nor did the film consider a variety of alternate responses, including the obvious solution of inviting speakers with different points of view. Furthermore, the depiction of characters seemed to follow racial stereotypes in speech and dress, with black students portrayed in an unfavorable light.

Having commissioned and financed the film, the ALA faced the question of what to do with it. At its annual meeting in Detroit in June 1977, the association debated whether to dissociate itself from the film. Lines of division separated proponents of intellectual freedom and defenders of racial justice, with difficult choices confronting those who prized both. Clara Jones, the first African American president of the ALA, argued that the film did not raise a First Amendment issue and objected to treating racial inferiority as an open question. The ALA Black Caucus, supported by *Library Journal*, objected to linking the association with a racist point of view. The membership of the ALA narrowly defeated a resolution to remove the ALA's name from the film. Instead, they passed a resolution introduced by Ella Gaines Yates, an African American librarian who supported the film, to add material from the Black Caucus to the film's discussion guide and a new introduction to the film itself.

Debate about the film continued to reverberate through the profession. Some library educators, like Edward Holley of the University of North Carolina, supported use of the movie because it provoked discussion of the basic issues facing librarians, such as their obligation to make controversial and offensive materials available. Librarian Eli Oboler pointed to the access issue underlying the controversy.

We *all* have feelings about superiority/inferiority—and the *facts* are not easily ascertainable. But denying the rights to *discuss* these facts and feelings and opinions is certainly contrary to any reasonable understanding of the First Amendment or of the Library Bill of Rights.

Reflecting on the *The Speaker*, Clara Jones lamented the lost opportunity, criticized the filmmaker for failing to understand libraries, and wondered whether the failure stemmed from his acceptance of the image of the library profession as "dull and isolated from reality."

Young adult librarian Dorothy Broderick, a strong proponent of the Racism and Sexism Resolution adopted by the ALA a year earlier and chair of the Intellectual Freedom Committee of the Young Adult Services Division (YASD), posed the issue in response to a memo from the Bay Area Social Responsibilities Round Table:

Also, the overriding question seems to be whether the overriding message is a racist's right to speak, or whether the film conveys approval of racism. (That is the question I plan to keep in mind when viewing it. If the former, it meets ALA policy; if the latter, it violates it.)

Prepared to dislike the film, instead Broderick became an advocate of its use despite its flaws. Looking back on the debate over the film at the ALA's 1977 conference, she wrote, "At Detroit, we replayed the film's script," and concluded,

We cannot as an Association devoted to the dissemination of all ideas, be so unsophisticated as to equate defending a racist's right to speak with being a racist. It is the right to be heard that is important, not the quality of the ideas. We cannot allow ourselves to lose sight of the fact that suppression of one unpopular opinion opens to the door to suppression of all unpopular opinions. Nor can we afford to forget that every major improvement in society—including the civil rights movement—began as an unpopular minority opinion. Most of all, out of total self-interest, we should remember that each voice silenced contributes to the possibility of our own voices being silenced.

The resolution to incorporate new material into the film and discussion guide proved impossible to implement. The Black Caucus objected to "patching" the film, and ultimately it was released unchanged. In November 1977, the ALA executive board adopted a "clarifying statement:"

The response to "The Speaker" makes clear that the judgment of a large proportion of the Membership is that this film conveys an inaccurate interpretation of ALA's intent. The reaction of this sector is very strong against what holds to be the film's argument for presenting the subject of the inferiority of Black people's intelligence as an open question.

The American Library Association believes that we must make clear to all who view this film that its sponsorship does not mean that the Association subscribes to the doctrine of racial superiority/inferiority, a concept that has long been discredited, or the implication that the Association is uncertain on the question of the superiority or inferiority of any one race.

In forcefully affirming its official position of insistence on the equality of all people, the Association believes that it is also reaffirming the spirit of the Library Bill of Rights.

By November 1977 more than 200 of 300 prints of the film had been sold. It remained in print for more than two decades and became a touchstone for debates pitting intellectual freedom against social concerns.

QUESTIONS

- In hindsight, how might the production of the film been handled in a way as to avoid some of the conflicts that arose?
- What values divided the proponents and defenders of the film?

- What basis for common ground might have been found?
- How might such a controversy be used to promote ethical values and decision-making?

SOURCES

"ALA ExecBoard Delays Distribution of Film," *Wilson Library Bulletin* 51 (June 1977): 794–795.

Berry, John. "A Whimper for Freedom," *Library Journal* 102 (June 1, 1977): 1,227.

_____. "The 'Lessons' of Detroit," *Library Journal* 102 (August 1977): 1543.

_____. "The Debate Nobody Won," *Library Journal* 102 (August 1977): 1,573–1,580.

"Black Caucus Vetoes 'Patching': *The Speaker* Stands As Is," *American Libraries* 8 (September 1977): 405–406.

Bobker, Lee. "Gratuitous and Bizarre Comments," *Wilson Library Bulletin* 51 (June 1977): 801–802.

Broderick, Dorothy. "Son of *Speaker*," *American Libraries* 8 (October 1977): 502–503.

"Controversy Continues over ALA's *The Speaker*," *School Library Journal* 24 (November 1977): 10.

"'Freedom' Film in Final Editing: Debut Set for Annual Conference," *American Libraries* 8 (April 1977): 205.

"IFC's Film Completed," *Newsletter on Intellectual Freedom* 26 (May 1977): 67, 90.

"Jones Asks for Panel to Review *The Speaker*," *School Library Journal* 24 (December 1977): 9–10.

Jones, Clara S. "Reflections on *The Speaker*," *Wilson Library Bulletin* 52 (September 1977): 51–55.

Oboler, Eli. "Words on *The Speaker*," *Wilson Library Bulletin* 52 (November 1977): 227.

"Other Voices, Other Views," *American Libraries* 8 (October 1977): 504–505.

Plotnik, Arthur. "Freedom of Speech for *The Speaker*," *American Libraries* 8 (June 1977): 337.

_____. "*The Speaker*: Step or Misstep into Filmmaking," *American Libraries* 8 (July 1977): 371–378.

Rosenfeld, H. E. "Overreactions and Reactions," *Wilson Library Bulletin* 51 (March 1977): 591–592.

"*Speaker* to Go Out Unchanged," *Wilson Library Bulletin* 52 (September 1977): 16–17.

And again in 1986 during debates about doing business in South Africa.

DOING BUSINESS IN SOUTH AFRICA (1986)

In 1986, the U.S. Congress passed the Anti-Apartheid Act imposing economic sanctions on South Africa as part of widespread protests against that country's racial segregation and oppression. Books and other information materials were covered by the boycott, along with household products, foodstuffs, and machinery. In support of the anti-apartheid movement, religious organizations, universities, and cultural institutions, including the Smithsonian Institution, divested their shares in companies selling products in South Africa. City councils barred public agencies, including schools and public libraries, from doing business with companies operating in South Africa. Public libraries in cities such as Berkeley, San Francisco, and Houston that enacted anti-apartheid ordinances were required to stop dealing with vendors and publishers that still operated in or traded with South Africa. In turn, publishers withdrew from the South African market. *Village Voice* columnist Nat Hentoff reported that, "Virtually all major American book firms selling textbooks to schools and trade books to public libraries agreed to no longer sell their books to South Africa." The parent company of Baker & Taylor sold two of its plants in South Africa. University Microfilms International stopped providing copies of unpublished research to South African universities.

Judith Krug, head of the American Library Association Office for Intellectual Freedom, argued that a position that endorsed a ban on books was inconsistent with the ALA's commitment to a free flow of information. Krug was hissed at the 1987 meeting of the ALA where a majority of delegates voted down a free flow of information resolution that would have ended the book boycott. In 1989, the Association of American Publishers released a report, *The Starvation of Young Black Minds*, coauthored by Lisa Drew, of the Association of American Publishers (AAP), and Robert Wedgeworth, former ALA executive director and then dean of the Columbia University School of Library Service. After visiting South Africa and conducting extensive interviews, Drew and Wedgeworth urged an end to banning books as part of the sanctions. Though strongly opposed to apartheid, they cited the negative impact of a book boycott on South Africans themselves. The African National Congress was on the record supporting boycotts but did not want to stop the "inflow of progressive cultural products ... and ideas." *American Libraries* reported that ANC leader Nelson Mandela supported a cultural as well as economic ban.

At the ALA midwinter conference in 1990, the International Relations Committee was asked to review a request from AAP to endorse the AAP report. At a hearing on the issue, of seventeen speakers, only Robert Wedgeworth spoke for the report, supporting economic sanctions but not a ban on books. Participants compared the debate to the controversy in 1977 over the film, *The Speaker*. Clara Jones, ALA president at the time, supported complete economic sanctions. The ALA's Intellectual Freedom Committee also reviewed the report but declined to condemn it, finding "inadequate bases in existing policy to respond to the myriad of international situations before us." The ALA Council refused to endorse the AAP report and passed a resolution, introduced by the International Relations Committee, which affirmed existing policies.

QUESTIONS

- What values were at stake in considering what position librarians might take against apartheid?
- Do you see that these values were in conflict?
- What professional expertise or perspective could librarians add to a discussion of apartheid?

SOURCES

"Baker & Taylor's Parent Firm Sells South African Holdings," *American Libraries* 18 (February 1987): 105.

"Guidelines for Librarians Interacting with South Africa," *SSRT [Social Responsibilities Round Table] Newsletter* (September 1989): 7–9.

Hentoff, Nat. "Banning Our Own Books," *Washington Post*, December 5, 1989, A25. Hentoff, Nat. "Fighting Apartheid by Banning Books," *Washington Post*, January 14, 1988, A27.

"In South Africa Boycott, ALA Sides with Mandella [sic]," *American Libraries* 21 (July/August 1990): 640.

"Memorandum on Guidelines for Librarians Interacting with South Africa," *Newsletter on Intellectual Freedom* 39 (March 1990): 72–73 [Intellectual Freedom Committee responds to SRRT guidelines].

The Starvation of Young Black Minds: The Effect of Book Boycotts in South Africa. Report of a Fact-Finding Mission to South Africa, May 18–28, 1989. New York: Fund for Free Expression, Association of American Publishers, 1989. See also, "Dispatch Case," *Chronicle of Higher Education* (November 22, 1989): A29 [describes the report].

Wedgeworth, Robert. "The Book Boycott against South Africa Must End Now," *Chronicle of Higher Education* (February 21, 1990): A52.

An increasing racial awareness and commitment to racial justice within the association led to the cancellation of an ACRL conference in Phoenix. When voters in Arizona turned down a holiday in 1991 in honor of Martin Luther King, Jr., the Association of College and Research Libraries voted to move its conference from Phoenix to register its displeasure. When ACRL then selected Salt Lake City as its alternate conference site, however, feminists within the organization protested against that state's perceived treatment of women. The conference program highlighted women's issues and a diversity theme. Responding to the controversy, the ACRL board adopted three criteria to determine whether a question was one on which the association should take a position.

- When issues of fundamental importance to the profession are in question
- When issues are directly and clearly identified as consistent with the mission and goals of the association's strategic plan
- When issues are ones for which the association is recognized as an authoritative and knowledgeable source by its membership and the national community[29]

Following the adoption of these criteria, the ALA went ahead with its 1993 midwinter meeting in Denver for scheduling reasons although the association objected to the city's adoption of an anti-gay measure. As in Salt Lake City, attendees combined participation in conference sessions with public demonstrations to make their views known. The ALA did cancel Cincinnati as the site of its 1995 midwinter meeting because of the city's anti-gay measure.[30] In 2004, when the ALA expressed its opposition to the war in Iraq, some members who opposed the war nonetheless questioned the wisdom of taking a stand on an issue so far outside its interests and expertise. Whitney Davison-Turley expressed her dismay. "Although I too am appalled by the recent activities of the United States government, I am also certain that the place to express my opinion lies outside of ALA (and I plan to do so in the voting booth in November)."[31]

ACRL MOVES ITS CONFERENCE SITE (1991)

In January 1991, the board of directors of the Association of College and Research Libraries (ACRL) voted unanimously to move its sixth national conference in 1992 from Phoenix after Arizona voters rejected a referendum that would have made the birthday of Martin Luther King, Jr., a state holiday. After considering various locations, in May 1991, the ACRL board agreed to hold the meeting in Salt Lake City, Utah; however, in June, the Women's Studies Section of the association voted to cancel its program to protest Utah's recently enacted, restrictive abortion law. Further, it urged members of the section "to take the issues of reproductive freedom and freedom of information into consideration in reaching individual decisions whether to attend the conference." To protest racial policies in the state, the ACRL's Racial and Ethnic Diversity Committee also decided to boycott the meeting.

Those who went ahead with the 1992 meeting in Salt Lake City emphasized both race and gender issues in conference programming. Julian Bond, the noted civil rights activist and former Georgia legislator, presented the keynote address. Catherine Stimson, feminist and women's study scholar, apologized for her appearance in the face of the boycott and donated part of her honorarium to the National Organization for Women. Attendance fell short of the association's previous meeting in Cincinnati in 1989.

In response to the controversy, the ACRL established a Social Issues Task Force in September 1991 to formulate criteria to determine when the ACRL board should take action on social, political, and economic issues. Based on the task force's report, the ACRL adopted a policy on social issues in January 1993:

The ACRL Board, in deliberating social, political, and economic issues, should take action only when those issues meet the following criteria:
　　Issues are of fundamental importance to the professional of academic librarianship;
　　Issues are directly and clearly identified as consistent with the mission and goals of ACRL and ACRL's Strategic Plan, and
　　Issues are ones for which ACRL is recognized as an authoritative and knowledgeable source by both its membership and the national community (such as issues having to do with intellectual freedom and access to information).

Site-selection questions continued to confront the ALA's conference planners. Because of scheduling difficulties, the association went ahead with its 1993 midwinter meeting in Denver despite the city's approval of an anti-gay ordinance. *Publishers Weekly* quoted the director of the ALA's conference service describing how the association took action. "The ALA made its position quite clear by distributing buttons and flyers at that show protesting the antigay rights bill, and midway through the convention more than 500 of our members marched from the meeting site to the state capitol building, where our president spoke at a rally."

With more lead time, the association did move its 1995 midwinter meeting that was to have taken place in Cincinnati after the city removed "sexual orientation" from its ordinance that prohibited discriminatory practices based on age, race, religion, disability, and other factors. In making the decision, the executive board relied on ALA policies supporting equal employment opportunities for gay librarians and library workers and stating the ALA's commitment to equal-employment opportunity.

QUESTIONS

- In a humorous piece, Will Manley listed all the factors that might make a city or state an inappropriate place for librarians to hold their conference (more Taco Bells than libraries, a senator who belonged to the KKK, etc.). Based on the ALA's ethical values, what kinds of issues might justify a decision to avoid a meeting site?

- During an ALA conference, what actions might attendees take to make known their concerns about local issues? Is this appropriate?

SOURCES

"ACRL Board statement on the ACRL Sixth National Conference in Salt Lake City, Utah, April 12–14, 1992." [dated 6 May 1991] cover letter from Barbara J. Ford, ACRL president, dated May 17, 1991.

"ACRL Board Votes to Withdraw 6th National Conference from Phoenix," [press release] American Library Association, January 13, 1991.

"ACRL Creates Social Issues Task Force," [press release] American Library Association, September, 1991.

DiMattia, Susan S. "Social Issues: Are They Reference and Adult Services Issues?" *RQ* 31 (Winter 1991): 144–145, author president of RASD.

"Executive Board Cancels Cincinnati as Meeting Site [for 1995 Midwinter Meeting]," *American Libraries* 25 (January 1994): 120.

Kniffel, Leonard. "Utah Welcomes ACRL; A Banner Conference Transcends a Sensitive Site Selection Controversy," *American Libraries* 23 (June 1992): 518–519.

Manley, Will. "Where Are We Going?" *Wilson Library Bulletin* 66 (April 1992): 67–69.

Memo from Pat Kreitz, Chair, Women's Studies Section, re: Location of 1992 ACRL National Conference in Utah to ACRL Board of Directors. July 2, 1991.

O'Brien, Maureen. "Pro-gay ALA Says 'No' to Cincinnati for 1995 Meeting," *Publishers Weekly* 240 (December 13, 1993): 9.

"Women's Studies Scholar to Speak at ACRL Sixth National Conference," [press release] American Library Association, October 1991.

The ACRL criteria have been criticized on a variety of grounds. One argues that because libraries have information on all issues, all issues are library issues. Another, advanced by John Buschman and others, is that such criteria shut off debate on certain issues, undermining the democratic process within the ALA, although it is possible to envision a lively debate over the applicability of the criteria to a particular issue.[32] Worse, the criteria have been ignored. At the ALA's annual conference in Orlando in 2004, *Library Journal* editor John

Berry and academic librarian (and future ALA president) James Rettig debated whether the ALA should take a position on social issues such as the war in Iraq. Neither Berry, arguing that all issues are library issues, nor Rettig, arguing in favor of some limits on the issues that the ALA addresses, mentioned the existence of the criteria adopted by the ACRL. Will Manley, librarian and library humorist, while not trivializing the dilemma, demonstrated its complexity by compiling a list of factors that would eliminate a potential conference site. From states that do not have an MLK holiday or did not pass the Equal Rights Amendment to states that do not honor Melvil Dewey's birthday or where there are more Taco Bells than libraries, Manley's column demonstrated how essential it is to identify the core values of the profession on which we are prepared to base decisions and take action.[33]

A professional organization stands in a different position than an individual practitioner. Part of the organization's role is to serve as an advocate for the whole profession, inform policymakers, and work for the advancement of the profession. A library practitioner in providing library service is bound by ethical issues of equity and access. This issue has caused anguish for librarians seeking to differentiate their personal and professional beliefs. In revising its code in 1995, the ALA may have exacerbated this confusion when it focused on the ethical obligations of "we," the members of the association, rather than the ethical responsibilities of professional librarians. Future revisions may attend to these actual and potential differences.

If something like the ACRL criteria are not applied, can the values in the code of ethics be used to gauge the stake of the library community in the issue? Does it affect library users or library service? Does it diminish or impede access? Does war spending take away money from libraries? Does legislation undermine the rights of library workers, library users, or underserved populations? Applying ethical values, so often absent in these discussions, may open the way to consider a broader range of matters as library issues. The ideological pendulum may swing on political issues. Applying the test of professional values to determine library issues may permit an expansive definition of our professional concerns while allowing the kind of consistency required by ethical standards.

QUESTION

- Is booing a speaker, as many librarians booed Al Gore for his vote in support of the first Gulf War, an exercise in free speech or an inappropriate attempt to silence speech?

END NOTES

1. Patricia P. Paylore, "A Note on the Proposed 'A Librarian's Code,'" *College & Research Libraries* 22 (March 1961): 163–164.

2. American Library Association Code of Ethics, adopted by the ALA Council, June 28, 1995.

3. Statement on Professional Ethics, 1981, adopted June 30, 1981, by the ALA Council. *American Libraries* 12 (June 1981): 335; *Intellectual Freedom Manual*, 7th ed. Chicago: American Library Association, 2006, 262.

4. "Libraries: An American Value, adopted by ALA Council, February 3, 1999," *Intellectual Freedom Manual*, 7th ed. Chicago: American Library Association, 2006, 266–267.

5. Arthur E. Bostwick, "The Librarian as Censor," *Library Journal* 33 (July 1908): 263.

6. Charles Knowles Bolton, [1909 canons] reprinted in Jonathan A. Lindsey and Ann E. Prentice, *Professional Ethics and Librarians.* Phoenix, AZ: Oryx Press, 1985, 25.

7. Charles Knowles Bolton, "The Ethics of Librarianship: A Proposal for a Revised Code," *The Annals of the American Academy of Political and Social Science* 101 (May 1922): 146.

8. ACRL Code of Ethics for Special Collections Librarians, approved by the Association of College and Research Libraries, October 2003, http://www.rbms.info/standards/code_of_ethics.shtml.

9. Code of Ethics for Archivists, adopted by the Council of the Society of American Archivists, 1992. Code of Ethics for Archivists, approved the Society of American Archivists Council, February 5, 2005.

10. Code of Ethics for Archivists, approved by the Society of American Archivists Council, February 5, 2005, http://www.archivists.org/governance/handbook/app_ethics.asp.

11. AALL Ethical Principles, approved by the AALL membership, April 5, 1999, http://www.aallnet.org/about/policy_ethics.asp.

12. Code of Ethics of the Society of Professional Journalists, adopted by the SPJ in 1996, http://www.spj.org/ethicscode.asp.

13. Mary W. Plummer, "The Pros and Cons of Training for Librarianship," *Public Libraries* 8 (May 1903): 212.

14. Bolton, [1909 canons] reprinted in Lindsey and Prentice. *Professional Ethics*, 22–23.

15. Bolton, "The Ethics of Librarianship," 141.

16. Code of Ethics for Librarians, adopted by the ALA Council of the American Library Association, December 19, 1938. *ALA Bulletin* 33 (February 1939):129. *Intellectual Freedom Manual*, 7th ed., 257.

17. Ethics Statement for Public Library Trustees [approved by the Public Library Association board of directors and the American Library Trustees Association board of directors, June 8, 1985] in *The Library Trustee: A Practical Guidebook*, 4th ed. Virginia Young, ed. Chicago: American Library Association, 1988, 180. Although the code appeared in an appendix, the implications of the code for trustee conduct were not discussed in the text. The successor volume, Mary Y. Moore, *The Successful Library Trustee Handbook*, Chicago: American Library Association, 2005, included in appendices the ALA resolution on the USA PATRIOT Act, the Freedom to Read Statement, the Library Bill of Rights, and a list of useful Web sites for trustees, but did not include the text of any code of ethics and considered the topic only in passing (page 9).

18. Joseph Spector, "Library Porn Ban Stands for Now," *Rochester Democrat & Chronicle* 1 (March 2007).

19. Bolton, [Canons 1909] reprinted in Lindsey and Prentice, *Professional Ethics* 24.

20. Bolton, "The Ethics of Librarianship," 145.

21. Ibid., 145–146.

22. "Suggested Code of Ethics," *Library Journal* 55 (February 15, 1930): 165.

23. Code of Ethics for Librarians, adopted by the ALA Council, December 19, 1938. *ALA Bulletin* 33 (February 1939): 130. *Intellectual Freedom Manual*, 7th ed., 258.

24. [Draft] Statement on Professional Ethics, 1973, reprinted in Lindsey and Prentice, *Professional Ethics*, 54.

25. "Statement on Professional Ethics, 1975 [draft]," reprinted in Lindsey and Prentice, *Professional Ethics*, 53–54; *Intellectual Freedom Manual*, 7th ed., 259–260.

26. David Berninghausen, "Social Responsibility vs. The Library Bill of Rights," *Library Journal* 97 (November 15, 1972): 3.675–3.681.

27. "1968 Code of Ethics for Librarians: A Draft Proposal," reprinted in Lindsey and Prentice, *Professional Ethics*, 46–48.

28. Kay Ann Cassell, "ALA and the ERA: Looking Back on the Association's Political and Fiscal Involvement," *American Libraries* 13 (December 1982): 690–692, 694, 696.

29. "ACRL Adopts Policy on Social Issues," ALA press release, January 1993.

30. "Executive Board Cancels Cincinnati as Meeting Site [for 1995 Midwinter Meeting]," *American Libraries* 25 (January 1994): 120. Maureen O'Brien, "Pro-gay ALA Says 'No' to Cincinnati for 1995 Meeting," *Publishers Weekly* 240 (December 13, 1993): 9. See also, Grace Anne Andreassi DeCandido, "Send Peggy Four Bucks," *Wilson Library Bulletin* 68 (April 1994): 6.

31. Whitney Davison-Turley, "On My Mind: Differing Opinions Need Not Apply," *American Libraries* 35 (September 2004): 33.

32. John Buschman, Mark Rosenzweig, and Elaine Harger, "The Clear Imperative for Involvement: Librarians Must Address Social Issues," *American Libraries* 25 (June 1994): 575.

33. Will Manley, "Where Are We Going?" *Wilson Library Bulletin* 66 (April 1992): 67–69; see also Herbert S. White, "Selecting Conference Sites for ALA," *Library Journal* 121 (April 15, 1996): 57–58, and Susan S. DiMattia, "Social Issues: Are They Reference and Adult Services Issues?" *RQ* 31 (Winter 1991): 144–145.

7

---·••·---

CONFLICTS OF INTEREST: FINANCIAL

Concern that professional judgment will be improperly influenced by the possibility of financial gain or personal betterment cuts across all fields. Cautions against accepting gifts or other favors appear in codes of ethics of professional organizations of all kinds. The potential dangers involve both the corruption of professional integrity and the resulting harm to patient, client, or institution. Further, such conflicts threaten professional integrity more broadly, undermining the profession's ability to set standards for the conduct of its members that is the very hallmark of professional autonomy. While each profession is subject to different influences and vulnerable to varying harms stemming from conflicts of interest, the general concern is that the quality of service will be compromised. As information professionals, librarians might be swayed by the philosophical influence of a particular interest group, or the commercial allures of an information vendor, or the financial constraints inherent in public funding, or even a combination of these that might lead to diminished service or impeded access.

We saw relationships at the heart of the American Library Association's (ALA) early codes, with the librarian responsible to the library's governing board, colleagues, the public, the profession, and society. We also know that the librarian may be caught between the conflicting demands of these varying constituencies and vulnerable to undue influence, potential sanction, or proffered reward. A philosophical debt to an outside organization or a gift from an outside interest with a stake in the outcome may inappropriately tip the balance.

The more recent casting of ethical codes in terms of values has given librarians a way to make difficult choices by creating a presumption in favor of service and access. But librarians and trustees also need the backing of codes and policies to reinforce their decisions on behalf of library institutions and users. Here again, we cannot depend on individual judgment, instincts, discretion, and good intentions where the highest level of ethical service demands consistency. Just as librarians and trustees have different religious beliefs, political ideas, tastes, and predilections, they also have different ideas about money, perquisites, and what constitutes inappropriate personal gain. Aided by clear guidelines, librarians may more easily refuse gifts or decline opportunities that promise personal benefit but pose institutional risk.

WHAT CODES OF ETHICS TELL US

As with philosophical conflicts of interest, early codes offered greater insight into the type of conflicts that librarians might encounter and provided more specific guidance on right conduct than do more recent codes. While many codes of library ethics conflate philosophical and financial conflicts of interest, early codes tended to focus on financial gain. Coming from an administrative perspective, in an era influenced by the business model of doing things, Charles Knowles Bolton included detailed advice along with general admonitions in his 1922 canons. He warned against librarians accepting library-related employment outside of library hours and called on librarians to make known to the trustees "work which claims much of the librarian's strength and does not add directly or indirectly to his reputation or to that of the institution."[1]

Anticipating the undue influence of vendors, Bolton wrote in the canon on Relation to Agents that "A librarian is bound to expend the funds intrusted to him with the best interest of the library in view," and cautioned that "He should not jeopardize his independence by accepting social favors from business firms." In addition to avoiding overly close contact with members of the board, the librarian was to keep a suitable distance from business agents as well. Again, ethical conduct required transparency. Bolton commented, "If a librarian is in doubt about the propriety of accepting a gift he should at least insist that the gift be public knowledge. Favors often come disguised in a form to flatter the unsuspecting librarian."[2]

The first official Code of Ethics for Librarians adopted by the ALA in 1938 put financial conflicts of interest in Section III, the domain of relations of the librarian within the library.

> 18. A librarian should never enter into a business dealing on behalf of the library which will result in personal profit.
>
> 19. A librarian should never turn the library's resources to personal use, to the detriment of services which the library renders to its patrons.[3]

As we have seen, in the decades following the adoption of the ALA code, librarians focused on their professional commitment to intellectual freedom. The need to avoid conflicts of interest that resulted in personal gain and institutional harm was accepted without elaboration and tucked into codes along with other values. In 1960, the draft of A Librarian's Code combined conflicts of interests with access to information.

In serving the library the librarian will place its needs and those of its readers before personal interests. He will defend the library's freedom to select for its readers the books and other materials needed for a useful and representative collection.[4]

Section 5 of the 1970 draft paired financial conflicts of interest with patron confidentiality as elements of the public trust.

A librarian: Honors the confidence and public trust of his position. He does not permit desire for private gains nor economic interest to affect the discharge of his professional responsibilities.[5]

After cautioning librarians to distinguish between private actions undertaken as an individual and those done on behalf of the library, the 1973 draft Statement on Professional Ethics provided that

The librarian may legitimately engage in various outside activities when and as permitted by the policy of the employing institution. But one must avoid any possibility of personal financial gain at the expense of the institution.[6]

The introduction to the 1975 Statement on Professional Ethics highlighted philosophical conflicts of interest. It declared the right of each citizen to participate in civic affairs but then urged the librarian to take precautions in distinguishing between private and professional actions. The statement itself dealt with financial conflicts. "A Librarian must avoid any possibility of personal gain at the expense of the employing institution."[7]

The proposed revisions in 1977 returned to the problem of outside employment, juxtaposing the librarian's right to pursue such opportunities with a potential loss of professional objectivity, and reiterated the need for transparency.

Librarians have a right to engage in remunerated activities in addition to their regular employment. Whether professional or non-professional in nature, such outside employment should not conflict with or otherwise impair performance of the librarian's ability to serve patrons objectively. The regular employer should be advised by the librarian of any outside employment which contains apparent possibilities of a conflict of interest or other impairment of the librarian's ability to perform assigned responsibilities.[8]

Since 1981, the ALA code has included separate provisions for philosophical and financial conflicts of interest.

V. Librarians must distinguish clearly in their actions and statements between their personal philosophies and attitudes and those of an institution or professional body.

VI. Librarians must avoid situations in which personal interests might be served or financial beliefs gained at the expense of library users, colleagues, or the employing institution.[9]

The possibility remains, however, that a financial conflict can also involve a philosophical one, as we shall see when we discuss some examples.

The only recent draft code that has included specific instances of potential conflicts is the 1968 draft proposal for the Code of Ethics for Librarians. Formulated during the years of intense debate about the social responsibilities of librarians, the draft is the only version to include a personal pledge along with language that seeks to protect the public from the effects of undue outside influence on librarians. Article VII provided that

A librarian does not permit desire for private gain nor personal economic interest to affect the discharge of his professional responsibilities.

The explanation of this provision listed such improprieties as accepting employment in a firm publishing goods or services that the librarian's institution might purchase, allowing free consultative service from a vendor to influence acquisitions, or using for personal profit unpublished materials assembled by others, or inside information for personal profit.[10]

SPECIALIZED CODES

Trustees

As we have seen, ethical standards for library trustees mirror some of those of librarians, but most involve avoidance of conflicts of interest. In addition to promoting a high level of service and distinguishing their personal views from their board responsibilities,

Trustees must avoid situations in which personal interests might be served or financial benefits gained at the expense of library users, colleagues, or the institution. It is incumbent upon any trustee to disqualify himself/herself immediately whenever the appearance of a conflict of interest exists.[11]

Law and Health Sciences Librarians

Conflicts of interest are a special concern for law librarians who wish to avoid overstepping the line between their professional training as librarians and their knowledge of the law. As to financial conflicts, however, the Ethical Principles of the American Association of Law Libraries, approved in 1999, incorporated the language of the ALA code in the section on "Business Relationships":

We have a duty to avoid situations in which personal interests might be served or significant benefits gained at the expense of library users, colleagues, or our employing institutions.[12]

Attention to financial conflicts of interest in the Code of Ethics of the Medical Library Association is implicit rather than explicit in language that calls on health sciences librarians to maintain high standards of professional integrity as part of a duty to the profession.[13]

Archivists and Special Collections Librarians

The more specialized codes of archivists and special collections librarians reflect the particular dilemmas posed by their work with unique and valuable materials and by their personal intellectual interests. In their ethical codes, archivists link financial conflicts of interest with those intellectual and academic interests previously identified as philosophical conflicts of interests. The 1992 Code of Ethics for Archivists specifically provided that archivists may engage in outside scholarly research, some of which might be remunerated, but must receive permission if using the holdings of their own institution for research purposes and must inform others using the same materials. When archivists collect in the same subject area as their institution, possibilities arise for the improper use of inside information or unseemly competition that affects the price the institution must pay or its ability to acquire the material at all. Thus, archivists are cautioned against such personal collecting. To implement this, ethical conduct requires archivists to inform employers about their collecting activities and keep complete records of their personal acquisitions and sales.[14]

Librarians working in special collections face similar intellectual and financial conflicts. In addition to the provisions that govern personal collecting, research, and professional activities, the Association of College and Research Libraries (ACRL) Code of Ethics for Special Collections Librarians, adopted in 2003, addresses specific financial conflicts of interest in Section V:

Special collections librarians must not engage in any dealing or appraisal of special collections materials, and they must not recommend materials for purchase if they have any undisclosed financial interest in them.

Also, Section VI declares:

Special collections librarians must decline all gifts, loans, or other dispensations, or things of values that are available to them in connection with their duties for the library.[15]

Other Professions

Like librarians, journalists may face financial conflicts of interest as well as intellectual ones. Potential financial gain, as well as personal belief, threatens the ability of the journalist to report objectively. The Code of Ethics of the Society of Professional Journalists, organized around values and the overarching obligation of journalists to seek the truth, provides a list of ethical dos and don'ts. In addition to remaining intellectually unfettered, journalists should:

- Avoid conflicts of interest, real or perceived.
  - Refuse gifts, favors, fees, free travel and special treatment, and shun secondary employment, political involvement, public office, and service in community organizations if they compromise journalistic integrity.
  - Disclose unavoidable conflicts.
  - Deny favored treatment to advertisers and special interests and resist their pressure to influence news coverage.
  - Be wary of sources offering information for favors or money; avoid bidding for news.[16]

POLITICAL CONFLICTS

While the need to avoid conflicts of interest, particularly financial ones, seems more clear-cut than ethical duties involving service or access, in practice such conflicts arise in a wide array of situations. In some, the library's ability to provide service may be pitted against its duty to provide access. Ethical librarianship requires that these conflicts, to the extent possible, be anticipated, discussed by board members and staff, and addressed through explicit policies. Conflicts about the level and types of service and access may include financial as well as ideological pressure on libraries, librarians, and board members.

In looking at the kinds of situations in which conflicts of interests might arise, we will revisit some of the topics discussed in earlier chapters on service and access. Underlying basic questions about whom the library serves, what services it provides, what information it makes available, and in what format, lurk possible conflicting choices that could endanger the library's funding or the librarian's job. Like other professionals, librarians may confront situations where the ethical choice in principle endangers another dimension of service or access in practice. We will take a look at some of these situations.

Whom Does the Library Serve?

Even the most basic questions about whom the library serves can pose conflicts of interest. Might the director of a small, independent township library oppose the creation of a county library system for fear of losing her position or her community losing its library even though consolidation would provide efficiencies of scale, shared resources, and enhanced service? As communities have become more resistant to paying taxes for public institutions, public libraries and public schools may face declining voter approval. City and county councils may use circulation statistics as a surrogate measure of popular support. When legislators prefer quantitative measures of success, might a library feel pressure to adopt a popular materials focus and add to its popular DVD collection in order to generate favorable numbers? Or might a library board, sensitive to charges of elitism, prefer a "give 'em what they want" philosophy to one that combines responsiveness to demand with more quality-focused collection policies?

What Service Does It Provide?

If board members do not understand the role of the public library or the library director fails to make the case for the library in the community, citizens and taxpayers may object to policies that are grounded in the ethical principles of librarianship. Controversies arising over the use of public library meeting rooms by groups espousing unpopular points of view, bulletin board exhibits displaying offensive ideas, and public programs on controversial topics may lead to threatened cuts in public support or private donations. In order to quell such restiveness, might a librarian be tempted to adhere to a policy of caution, sticking to a safe midcourse of the accepted, tried, and true?

What Materials Does It Make Available?

Although Dorothy Broderick challenged librarians to include something in their collections to offend everyone, the presence of controversial materials may involve personal and institutional costs that a librarian or library is unwilling to bear. Recall that the controversy over the exhibit of Truth Mission at the meeting of the California Library Association began with a dispute over its inclusion in a collection of banned books at the Torrance Public Library before it escalated into a dispute over the membership of the Los Angeles Public Library in the California Library Association. While challenge or reconsideration procedures allow patrons to question the appropriateness of individual volumes, the community needs to understand that the presence of ideas that one person finds offensive is protected along with the presence of the opposite point of view. Without this understanding, librarians and libraries may be tempted to avoid any dispute that would threaten the surface tranquility of the community and the place of the library in it. Self-censorship to avoid controversy may protect the library's interests in the short run, so as not to offend funders or patrons, but may undercut the library's authority and reputation over time.

What Is the Impact of New Technologies?

Public demand may force library systems to shift the balance of their collections and the allocation of library budgets to new information media. Because the Internet now makes available access to material electronically that would not fall within a library's collection development guidelines for its print collection, libraries face financial dilemmas that pit service against access. As we have seen, the Supreme Court in *Reno v. ACLU* held that material on the Internet was entitled to the full protection of the First Amendment, setting a standard of obscenity rather than indecency for materials disseminated on the World Wide Web. In the case of *U.S. v. ALA*, however, the Supreme Court held that Congress might condition federal aid to libraries and reduced connectivity rates on the installation of filters to block offensive material, even some protected by the First Amendment.

Here is a classic ethical dilemma in which library boards must decide whether to forego federal aid that supports of library services in order to provide maximum access to information. Libraries deciding not to filter experience not only the loss of federal dollars but the additional expense involved in monitoring Internet usage and protecting patrons from exposure to potentially offensive material. In a notable case, the Rochester Public Library was threatened by the county manager with a loss of funding because the library unblocked Web sites on demand, in accordance with federal law.

UNBLOCKING WEB SITES AT THE ROCHESTER PUBLIC LIBRARY (2007)

In February 2007, after seeing a television news report of patrons viewing pornographic Web sites at the Rochester, New York, Public Library, Maggie Brooks, the Monroe County executive, demanded that the library modify its policy or lose its $6.6 million appropriation, 70 percent of the library's budget. Though operating under separate boards, the Rochester Public Library and the Monroe County Library were headed by the same library director, but each library had its own Internet policy. The Rochester Public Library had had an Internet policy in place since 1995. In 2007, its policy provided:

The Rochester Public Library has protective filters on all patron-accessible computers to block sites in the categories of pornography, child pornography, obscene and tasteless, PG-17, and R-rated. Staffers can unblock filtered sites at the request of an adult, age 17 or older. Procedures require that the adult be placed at a computer out of the main traffic flow and given a privacy screen to avoid accidental viewing by the public. Staffers do not unblock computers on the first floor or the children's section, according to the library.

In the previous three years, when more than 1.5 million patrons had used the library, no one had complained about the policy or about exposure to offensive sites.

Lawyers disagreed as to whether librarians were obliged to unblock sites. Brooks, however, emphasized the need to protect children and to use tax money appropriately. "To me, this is not about freedom of speech or hiding behind the Constitution, this is about protecting kids and families. And that's the bottom line: Am I, with public tax money, going to support policies that put kids at risk, or am I going to spend money on policies that protect children? It's an easy choice for me." The local counsel for the ACLU saw the issue in First Amendment terms. "What real significant difference is there between denying an adult patron access to these sites and denying patrons access to *Catcher in the Rye?*"

Although most libraries require that a challenged work remain in circulation while the matter is considered, the Rochester Public Library immediately stopped unblocking sites that might contain graphic material. The president of the county library board defended this moratorium, reiterated the steps the library had taken to protect the public, and noted that much of the blocked material was legally protected. Following a resolution passed by the board, a special task force, made up of trustees from the city and county library boards, was organized to examine the library's policy and report within sixty days.

The dispute prompted a good bit of press coverage and widespread debate. The open meetings of the task force attracted large crowds. Those who made statements tended to support the library, while those who contacted the county executive tended to endorse her point of view. The city's mayor opposed the library policy. The local newspaper printed strong statements of support for the library from a former member of the library foundation board, the president of the Library Friends, and the president of the Rochester Public Library Board. Among those serving on the task force was the Rev. Erol Hunt, a minister and former board president. In explaining his position, Hunt differentiated his personal views and board responsibilities. "Personally, I'm a minister and I do not want my kids exposed to this," he said, "But I can not impose my thinking on what the law is."

The views of many members of the public and the two library boards were tempered by the possible loss of funds. The library's installation of filters enabled it to received federal E-Rate funding. But according to Michael Borgas, the executive director of the New York State Library Association, most libraries in the state had decided against filtering and had foregone federal aid. While each library could determine what was best for its users, Borgas said that "libraries often do not want to be in the position of arbitrating which sites are appropriate or not."

In May, the task force recommended a modification in the library's access policy. An adult patron wishing to see a blocked site would be required to request in writing that it be unblocked. The request would be reviewed by the library director, or a delegate, who would make a determination "without undue delay" and "in accordance with the library's collection development policy." Presumably, since the existing policy did not allow pornography in the library, patrons would not be allowed to view pornographic sites. On May 24, the local paper, under the misleading title "Library Bans Obscene Sites," reported that the county library board had approved the policy. The liaison to the county board rejected the idea that the new policy was a form of censorship. "If adopting the recommendation is censorship, then this library is already in big trouble because the act of choosing books is censorship and because you have a (collection) policy that implies and, in fact, results in rejection of material all the time." The city library board withheld its approval and voted to lift the moratorium that had blocked access to R-rated material, including MySpace.

John Lovenheim, the president of the Rochester Public Library board, took exception to the idea that this was a collection issue:

Some have argued that pornography on the Internet is a collection issue. There is a body of law that has developed that likens the Internet to an encyclopedia. Like an encyclopedia, the library may include or exclude it, but it may not remove portions of the encyclopedia that it does not like based on content.

Others have argued that even though pornography is legally protected speech, the library is not bound to supply it. We do not supply pornography to our patrons, we supply Internet access. There is a big difference.

He concluded, "[The county executive] accused us at the library of hiding behind the First Amendment. We do not hide behind the First Amendment. We stand side by side with it."

Finally, however, faced with the choice of adopting the new policy or losing its local funding, the board of the Rochester Public Library acquiesced. In November 2007, county executive Brooks was overwhelmingly reelected for another term.

QUESTIONS

- What values were at stake in this controversy?
- How do librarians and board members explain why the library provides access electronically to material it would not provide in print?

- How can librarians educate public officials about the meaning and importance of access to information before a controversy arises?
- What are the ethical implications of using the library's collection development policy to determine whether a Web site is to be unblocked?

SOURCES

Carlson, Catherine. "Cutting Off Library Funds Would Curtail Education," [Speaking Out, Guest Essay] *Democrat and Chronicle*, March 5, 2007.

Craig, Gary. "Resounding Wins for Green, Brooks," *Democrat and Chronicle*, November 7, 2007, 1A, 7A.

Lovenheim, John. "Internet Policy, Like Book Policy, Should Be Inclusive," [Speaking Out, Guest Essay] *Democrat and Chronicle*, June 6, 2007, 9A.

Shapiro, Sanford. "Economy Loses if Library Loses Funding," [Speaking Out, Guest Essay] *Democrat and Chronicle*, May 22, 2007, 15A.

Sharp, Brian. "Forum on Web Access at Library Draws 100-Plus," *Democrat and Chronicle*, April 13, 2007, 1B, 4B.

Spector, Joseph. "Brooks' Library Stance Knocked; ACLU May Sue if Adult-Oriented Sites Aren't Unblocked," *Democrat and Chronicle*, February 23, 2007.

____. "Library Access Report Is In," *Democrat and Chronicle*, May 23, 2008, 1A, 8A.

____. "Library Agrees to Internet Limits," *Democrat and Chronicle*, July 4, 2007, 1B, 4B.

____. "Library Bans Obscene Sites," *Democrat and Chronicle*, May 24, 2008, 3B, 4B.

____. "Library Porn Ban Stands for Now; City, County Boards Seek Review of Internet Policy to Satisfy Brooks," *Democrat and Chronicle*, March 1, 2007.

____. "Library Weighs Porn Issue," *Democrat and Chronicle*, March 15, 2007, 1B, 4B.

Wolf, George. "Internet Joint Policy Statement," statement by president of Monroe County Library System board of trustees, joint meeting of the Monroe County Library System and the Rochester Public Library boards of trustees, February 28, 2007.

Librarians may put their positions at risk over any of these questions. In response to this, the LeRoy C. Merritt Humanitarian Fund (http://www.merrittfund.org) was established to provide support to librarians who lose their jobs in defense of intellectual freedom.

DONOR CONFLICTS

Libraries of all kinds have depended on donors to add to their collections. As local and state support for public libraries and for state university systems has declined, public and academic librarians have increasingly become fund-raisers. This new imperative to seek outside support has complicated the ethical dilemmas of financially related conflicts of interest which began with simple gifts of appreciation to librarians from satisfied patrons.

May a Librarian Accept a Gift from a Satisfied Patron?

What is at stake when a librarian accepts a gift from a patron in appreciation of good service? Is such a gift ever acceptable? How much does it depend on the circumstance, the parties involved, or the size of the gift? While expressions of thanks are always welcome, libraries should adopt guidelines on the acceptance of gifts to prevent any appearance of favoritism and to forestall any feeling by patrons that gifts to staff are expected or encouraged. In most situations, a dollar limit on the size of the gift that may be accepted provides an objective standard and a helpful rationale by which a librarian may decline a gift. In a school setting, guidelines for gift giving should be part of an institution or system-wide policy, including teachers and other staff members. A number of alternatives provide objective and easily communicated rules (such as no presents, a dollar limit, only homemade gifts, or gifts to the library rather than to the staff). In keeping with other ethical standards for service, such a policy needs to be communicated and fairly enforced.

Are There Any Unacceptable Donors?

Libraries of all sorts are actively seeking contributions from private donors to augment public funding. Might the acceptance of a contribution from a particular donor threaten the library's reputation in some way? In recent years, academic institutions have experienced embarrassment when major donors have undergone a change of fortune leading to criminal prosecution or disgrace. Are there gifts a library should not accept because of the lifestyle, political views, or conduct of the donor? If the donor's values and those of the library are at odds, is that a sufficient basis for the rejection of a gift?

Must a Library Accept Conditions on a Gift?

A proffered gift that comes with strings attached may present an ethical dilemma to the library director and board members when the donation would enhance the library's collections, services, or capabilities but would require policies or procedures contrary to library practice or values. Schools faced this choice when Channel One offered equipment and programming but required that students view commercial announcements.

CHANNEL ONE (1989)

In 1989, Whittle Communications of Knoxville, Tennessee, piloted a new school program. Each participating school would receive approximately $50,000 worth of equipment including a satellite dish, twenty-five-inch color TV sets, videocassette recorders, wiring, and maintenance. In exchange, the schools agreed to broadcast the Channel One daily news program simultaneously in every classroom. The twelve-minute show included two minutes of ads for products of interest to teens, such as cosmetics, soft drinks, jeans, and fast food. No offensive commercials were shown, and schools could have tapes in advance and delete or skip any offensive or unsuitable content. Whittle would derive its profits from ad revenue, estimated at $85 to $100 million dollars when the program reached its goal of 8,000 participating schools.

Whittle's offer was opposed by a number of parent and education organizations, including Action for Children's Television, the National Parent Teachers Association, and the National School Boards Association. Critics objected to the use of students as a captive audience and the emphasis on material goods in the program's ads. State boards of education in California and New York took action against it. In California, the state superintendent of schools declared that students' minds were not for sale and ruled that state funding would be withheld from schools participating in the program. The New York State Board of Regents banned commercially sponsored television programs in the state's public schools, citing state law against using school property for private gain. To gain support, Whittle removed mandatory viewing requirements and added educational channels. In other states, however, opponents of Channel One were generally defeated in the courts as rulings upheld the power of school boards to reach such agreements.

The American Library Association was slow to take a position on the issue. Jacqueline Morris, president of the American Association of School Librarians (AASL), told the *School Library Journal* that the AASL Executive Committee had discussed Channel One, but "in view of the inadequate funding of most school libraries, chose not to condemn the program outright." In January 1990, the ALA Council adopted a resolution on Channel One that came from the Intellectual

Freedom Committee and focused on the lack of school participation in or control over the content of the news and features shown. Rather than condemn the program outright as a conflict of interest or as a one-sided view of the news, the ALA resolution expressed concern that the programs were not subject to the same selection criteria and review as other school library and curricular materials. It urged librarians to be wary and cautious:

Whereas, The published reports concerning the Whittle Communications "Channel One" project of a television news service with commercials being marketed to schools raises many concerns for various groups within the American Library Association; and

Whereas, The Intellectual Freedom Committee has reviewed these published reports; and

Whereas, The concerns revolve around questions of selection procedures for such commercialized services, enticement to acquire based on equipment offers, mandatory attendance requirements, commercial influence on news reports, and quality of content; and

Whereas, The primary concern of the Intellectual Freedom Committee in this issue is the selection and acquisition of such services in accordance with published materials selection policies; therefore be it

Resolved, That the selection of such services must be made within the established guidelines of written materials selections policies, without regard to gifts or premiums; and be it further

Resolved, That other units of ALA carefully review the implications of such services in light of existing ethical, legal, union and moral policy issues.

Whittle planned to follow up its broadcasting initiative by commissioning a line of books that would be distributed free to 150,000 "opinion leaders" and eventually sold in stores. The books were to be underwritten by paid advertising.

By the time Whittle Communications sold Channel One to Primerica in 1998, more than 100,000 schools were participating, including many private schools in New York and California which had taken the strongest stands against it. The company's new owners planned to increase the presence of Channel One on the Internet and to place a greater emphasis on interactive programming.

QUESTIONS

- If your school had considered participating in Channel One when it was first introduced, what concerns might you have raised?
- In accepting donations from an outside source, how do you decide what conditions are acceptable for your library and which are unacceptable?
- Since advertising is common in magazines and on the Internet, why might advertising in a book be objectionable?

SOURCES

"ALA Urges Caution in Use of Channel One," *School Library Journal* 36 (April 1990): 16.

Bob, Murray L. "Keep Ads Out of Books: Paid Advertisements in a New Line of Commissioned Books Will Undermine Our Freest Vehicle of Expression," *American Libraries* 20 (July/August 1989): 636–637.

"Channel One Forges Ahead Despite Complaints about Ads," *School Library Journal* 35 (July 1989): 9–10.

"Critics of Pilot TV Program Oppose Ads in Schools," *School Library Journal* 35 (March 1989): 91.

"North Carolina Board of Ed Sues to Block Channel One," *School Library Journal* 36 (May 1990): 9; "Future of Channel One Uncertain in Texas," *School Library Journal* 38 (January 1992): 14; "NJ Board of Education Upholds Whittle Decision," *School Library Journal* 39 (February 1993): 11.

"Resolution on Whittle Communications 'Channel One' and Other Such Services," [Adopted by the ALA Council on January 10, 1990] *Newsletter on Intellectual Freedom* 39 (March 1990): 72–73.

The Library of Congress has accepted custody of personal papers on conditions restricting access for a specified period of time. The Smithsonian Institution ultimately rejected a large donation for an exhibit on famous Americans when the donor's continued involvement in the project was deemed to interfere with the institution's professional staff. A donation to a private school conditioned on the removal of *Brokeback Mountain* from the school library media center was similarly rejected.

BROKEBACK MOUNTAIN AT ST. ANDREW'S SCHOOL (2005)

In May 2005, Cary McNair, a parent of students attending St. Andrew's Epicopal School in Austin, Texas, objected to the inclusion of "Brokeback Mountain," a short story by Annie Proulx, as an optional reading in Kimberly Horne's twelfth-grade English class and demanded its removal. The story had originally appeared in the *New Yorker* magazine in 1997 and was reprinted in *Close Range*, a collection of Proulx's stories. McNair, producer of the 2004 film *Killer Diller*, considered the story of a long, romantic relationship between two cowboys to be pornographic and its presence on the reading list to be in conflict with the school's stated mission and values. The story had been discussed in the class for several years without objection. In response to McNair's complaint, the head of the school referred to the school's process for selecting material for class discussion and supported the inclusion of "Brokeback Mountain."

McNair and his wife had earlier pledged $3 million to the school's capital campaign; a new wing of the upper school building was to be named in honor of his family. But in an e-mail to virtue.org, a Web site described as the "voice of global orthodox Anglicanism," McNair declared that if St. Andrew's failed to act in accordance with its values, then the school "by its own action, has removed the McNair funds from the campaign efforts, and accepted the potential risk for other support departures." In September 2005, the school officially released the McNairs from their pledge, citing its policy against accepting conditional gifts of any size.

Following the school's decision, other gifts more than made up the lost donation. Chris Finan, president of the American Booksellers for Free Expression (ABFFE) declared, "Too often the first instinct is to avoid controversy by withdrawing the title. The idea that this school rejected a demand to pull a book and was willing to lose money over it is truly astonishing and very gratifying. I don't know of another case where money has been an issue like this." The principled stand of St. Andrew's in support of its students' freedom to read encouraged others as well. Led by Lisa Yee, young adult authors sent autographed books to the school and formed their own group, Authors Supporting Intellectual Freedom!—AS IF! (http://asifnews.blogspot.com).

In the following academic year, "Brokeback Mountain" no longer appeared on the twelfth-grade reading list. In December 2005, Ang Lee's film version of the story was released to much critical acclaim, and St. Andrew's teacher Kimberly Horne preferred not to explore works in her class that had been made into motion pictures.

QUESTIONS

- What values were at stake in this controversy?
- How does a librarian in a religiously affiliated school reconcile professional obligations to provide access to opposing views with the school's religious and moral values?
- How can a school library resist pressures from parents, donors, or the public who object to material in the library's collection?

SOURCES

Brokeback Mountain, a film by Ang Lee (2005).

Maughan, Shannon. "Donor Pledge Returned to Sender," *Publishers Weekly* 252 (December 5, 2005): 4, 6.

May, Rachel Proctor. "St. Andrew's Defends the Cowboy Way," *The Austin Chronicle*, September 30, 2005, http://www.austinchronicle.com/gyrobase/Issue/story?oid=oid:294035.

Obernauer, Matthew. "St. Andrew's Parents Split over Ending of Short Story," *Austin Statesmen-American*, September 28, 2005: Posted September 29, 2005, at http://www.virtueonline.org/portal/modules/news/article.php?storyid=3046.

Proulx, Annie. "Brokeback Mountain," *New Yorker* 73 (October 13, 1987): 74–80, 82–85.

Proulx, Annie. "Brokeback Mountain," in *Close Range: Wyoming Stories*. New York: Scribner, 1999.

Spong, John. "The Good Book and the Bad Book," *Texas Monthly* 34 (September 2006): 160–165, 238.

"Texas School Keeps Gay-Themed Story," *Advocate* (October 1–October 3, 2005) http://www.advocate.com/news_detail_ektid21231.asp.

Virtue, David W. "Episcopal High School Promotes Gay Sex Book," *VirtueOnline*, August 30, 2005, http://www.virtueonline.org/portal/modules/news/article.php?storyid=2932.

Like policies for the acceptance of gifts by staff members, institutions need to set boundaries for the terms under which they will accept donations, tilting in favor of decisions that free the institution from any suspicion of favored treatment, compromised integrity, or inappropriate influence. In some cases, the intangible harm will outweigh the tangible benefits of the gift.

VENDOR CONFLICTS

Does Corporate Sponsorship Violate Institutional Neutrality?

In discussing philosophical conflicts of interest, we considered whether taking a stand on a social issue violates the role of librarians in providing information reflecting a range of viewpoints. Similar questions may arise when accepting corporate support for library services or programs. Again, we need to differentiate between libraries and librarians, and librarian associations that play different roles but which all fall under the ethical umbrella of the ALA's Code of Ethics.

Several different ethical issues arise. Because information vendors derive a large proportion of their income serving libraries and librarians, it is logical for the library community to turn to them for support of professional activities, meetings, and scholarships. In these cases, there is little danger that corporate interests would conflict with the basic tenets of librarianship. The conflict would arise from a suggestion that too close a relationship with one vendor over another might constitute an endorsement or incline librarians to do business with the corporate sponsor, to the exclusion of other, perhaps better or more competitive companies. When Ameritech sponsored the opening session of an ALA annual conference, the prominence of the corporate name in the hall and on the program drew heavy criticism. The ALA has since broadened the base of its support from vendors and features prominent displays honoring numerous corporate champions.

Library associations and local libraries face a different ethical conflict when choosing whether to solicit or accept donations from a corporation whose product may be objectionable to segments of the library's user population or which is associated with a particular political point of view. The sponsorship of the celebration in 1987 of the bicentennial of the U.S. Constitution by cigarette maker Philip Morris provoked just such a controversy. Though organized by the National Archives, the celebration featured the corporation's logo prominently in bicentennial promotions and educational materials. Corporate sponsorship made possible a much larger and more visible event than would have been possible using only government funds. Assuming that corporate support is essential, how might information organizations avoid the appearance of an endorsement or association with an unpopular or controversial product or cause?

SCHMALTZ BREWING PRESENTS TEEN/TOT STORIES*

Narrator:	The scene is the conference room of the Prospect Public Library where the library board is holding its monthly meeting. Those present include: Robert/Roberta Rules, board chair; Gladys Tidings and Cash Hunter, members of the board's finance committee; Hi N. Dry and Nona Guff, other members of the board; and Stella Page, librarian.
Robert/Roberta Rules:	The first item on the agenda is the report of the finance committee on its effort to secure funding for the library's Teen/Tot Stories Program. Ms. Tidings, I will turn the floor over to you.
Gladys Tidings:	Thank you, Chairman/Chairwoman Rules. As you all know, the library for many years has run a highly successful summer program involving both the town's teenagers and preschoolers. Under

---

*Written by the author for presentation by the ALA Committee on Ethics, "Ethics 'R Us," June 1992.

the direction of our dear Ms. Page (nods appreciatively at the librarian), teenagers learn the art of storytelling and then present story hours at branch libraries, playgrounds, and other recreation department sites.

With the budget cuts ordered by the county, we can no longer afford to pay for this program out of the library's operating budget. We are happy to report, however, that we have found another source of funding! (gleeful) Cash Hunter, another member of the finance committee, will tell you all about it.

Cash Hunter: Well, as you can tell, we've been pretty hard pressed for funds lately, so our distinguished chair, Mr./Ms. Rules, charged our committee to go after some money from local corporations here in Prospect. I must tell you there was a great deal of interest in the Teen/Tot Stories Program, which everyone just loves. Well, the Schmaltz Brewing Company has offered to sponsor the entire program for the coming summer. They will pay a part-time substitute librarian so Ms. Page can hold her training sessions; they will supply materials for puppets, extra copies of the most popular stories, even video equipment to tape story hours. Absolutely everything. I needn't say how thrilled we are. Any questions?

All: (murmurs of enthusiasm) That sounds wonderful. Great work. Congratulations.

Hi N. Dry: (worried) It's almost too good to be true. Aren't there any strings attached?

Gladys Tidings: None at all. It's going to be great publicity for the library. Schmaltz is going to use some of the videotapes of the story hours in its ads. One of the representatives of the brewery gave me this mock-up of a T-shirt that all the teens and tots are going to wear. It says "Schmaltz Brewing Presents Teen/Tot Stories."

Nona Guff:	Wait a minute. Where does it say anything about the library?
Gladys Tidings:	Oh, right down here at the bottom.
Hi N. Dry:	Do you really think it's appropriate for the brewery to be sponsoring a children's program? We may be sending the wrong message to our young people. We in the schools have been trying awfully hard to keep children from drinking. Might this just encourage them?
Cash Hunter:	What do you mean? A lot of people in this town work at the brewery. Why, the Schmaltz family is one of the oldest families in Prospect. We're hoping this will get them real interested in the library. We could use their help in our capital campaign.
Nona Guff:	I know the Schmaltzes are a fine family, but I certainly do not appreciate the way women are pictured in the brewery ads. I think they need to show more respect for women. They ought to put more women in management positions over at the brewery.
Robert Rules:	What do you think, Ms. Page?
Stella Page:	Well, we really do need the money. Teen/Tot Stories is one of our most popular programs.
Narrator:	What should the board do? How should it go about deciding on a course of action?

May Libraries and Librarians Appear in Ads? Endorse Products?

Since librarians are now called on to be more visible and to promote both their libraries and librarianship, are ethical issues involved when a librarian appears in an advertisement for a library-related product? One of the longest-running ad campaigns by a library vendor was the Interlaken Bindery series "Great American Libraries" that ran in *Library Journal* from 1942 to 1961.[17] Each full-page advertisement featured black-and-white photos of a library, usually a public library, but also academic and special libraries, and of its librarian. The text included information about the library's history and the librarian's professional background but not a specific product endorsement.

In more recent ads for library systems and products, librarians have testified to their library's satisfaction with a vendor's database, integrated library system, or customer service representatives. Assuming this to be the case, are there any ethical concerns raised by such an explicit affiliation between librarian and vendor? Are there any mitigating factors that would counter what seems on its face to be a conflict of interest?

A more subtle conflict arises where a library appears in an advertisement as the backdrop for a product. The company takes advantage of the beauty of the library setting; the library receives payment for allowing its facility to serve as an advertising locale. The relationship gives a specific library visibility, serves as a general reminder of the beauty of libraries, and generates additional revenue for the library. Even if there is no linkage between the library and the advertised product, does this constitute an implicit endorsement? Does it matter whether the library is identified by name?

Librarians need to be aware of all of the possible ramifications of relationships with commercial enterprises, with both library vendors and local corporations. As the need for funding grows and the ingenuity of corporate sponsors devises new linkages, librarians must weigh each offer for real and apparent conflicts of interest. A too-close affiliation with a company, product, or cause may undermine the library's claim to represent all points of view and the librarian's obligation to steer clear of compromising relationships.

ANALOGIES TO COLLECTIONS

What is striking about our discussion of financial conflicts of interests is the way in which ethical principles formulated in the context of library service and access seem newly relevant. While the avoidance of financial conflicts is one of most basic ethical obligations, it takes on particular meaning in a library setting. By exploring analogies with library services and collections, we can gain new insight into how librarians might view the unique aspects of this ethical obligation for their profession.

Like policies on categories of which patrons are to be served, what services are to be provided, what materials are to be collected, what issues are to be considered library issues, conflicts of interest arise across library practices. We see them in policies on service, use of meeting rooms, and provisions for access.

Defining Categories

Equitable service policies require that all library users falling within the same category receive comparable treatment. Rules may differentiate between groups of users, but the service provided may not be extended or withheld because of personal favoritism or prejudice. Might the same be true in defining policies about conflicts of interest? Decisions about relationships with donors or vendors should be based on the type of organization, not approval or disapproval of their point of view. Strictures against accepting gifts from vendors, for example, would apply to all vendors, without exceptions for those with whom a library has contracts.

Eschewing Endorsements

Are there unacceptable donors? In making decisions about collections, ethical conduct requires that librarians not consider the personal lives or affiliations of authors. Is the same true about the personal lives and affiliations of donors? If so, then how is the library to make distinctions? The Freedom to Read Statement reminds us that the library does not endorse the works in its collection. Is it also true that libraries do not endorse the lifestyles or conduct of those from whom it accepts donations and whose names appear on donor walls and in annual reports?

Adhering to Neutrality

In policies about personal attire, exhibits, and meeting spaces, libraries must devise policies that are content-neutral. If religious or political groups are allowed to use space or facilities, then all religious or political groups are entitled to the same privileges regardless of point of view. If dress rules allow religious or patriotic symbols, the privilege extends to all points of view. If the library has accepted a gift from the Methodist Church, must it also accept a gift from the Church of Scientology? Just as public television struggled with accepting sponsorship from the Ku Klux Klan, libraries may wish to avoid associations that may lead to controversy, but to do so requires content-neutral policies that govern other areas of library conduct.

Anticipating Problems/Setting Limits

Libraries need policies on conflicts of interests, donations, and gifts for the same reason they need collection development policies. By drafting clear-cut guidelines, a library works through possible scenarios in advance, averts problems, and avoids surprises.

Valuing Consistency

Such policies mitigate differences caused by varying personal standards and preferences on the part of staff. With a policy in place, it is easier for staff to resist a demand, decline a gift, or avoid outside pressure in a consistent way.

Making Principled Exceptions

While it is not true that rules are made to be broken, professional judgment requires knowing when to make exceptions. If the policies of the library are well understood, then a librarian making an exception should be able to articulate which alternative library value is enhanced. It should be possible to articulate an exception so that it may be applied should a similar, analogous situation arise.

Maintaining Transparency

Underlying each of these principles is the paramount need for library dealings to remain transparent. In avoiding conflicts of interest, as in developing collections, policies need to be known and publicized to staff, the community, policymakers, and potential funders. From the earliest provisions dealing with conflicts of interests, codes have required that librarians divulge their personal interests and financial ties. Again, information is the key to more ethical conduct.

END NOTES

1. Charles Knowles Bolton, "The Ethics of Librarianship: A Proposal for a Revised Code," *The Annals of the American Academy of Political and Social Science* 101 (May 1922): 146.

2. Bolton, "The Ethics of Librarianship," 146.

3. "Code of Ethics for Librarians [adopted by the ALA Council December 29, 1938]." *ALA Bulletin* 33 (February 1939): 130. *Intellectual Freedom Manual*, 7th ed. Chicago: American Library Association, 257.

4. "A Librarian's Code [1960 draft]," reprinted in Jonathan A. Lindsey and Ann E. Prentice, *Professional Ethics and Librarians*. Phoenix, AZ: Oryx Press, 1985, 46.

5. "Code of Ethics (Proposed Revision) [1970]," reprinted in Lindsey and Prentice, *Professional Ethics*, 52.

6. "Statement on Professional Ethics, 1973 [draft]," reprinted in Lindsey and Prentice, *Professional Ethics*, 54.

7. "Statement on Professional Ethics, 1975," reprinted in Lindsey and Prentice, *Professional Ethics*, 54; *Intellectual Freedom Manual*, 7th ed., 260.

8. 1975 Statement on Professional Ethics [with newly suggested revisions to 1975 statement], 1977, reprinted in Lindsey and Prentice, *Professional Ethics*, 60.

9. Statement on Professional Ethics, 1981, adopted June 30, 1981 by the ALA Council. *American Libraries* 12 (June 1981): 335; *Intellectual Freedom Manual*, 7th ed. Chicago: American Library Association, 2006, 262.

10. "1968 Code of Ethics for Librarians: A Draft Proposal" reprinted in Jonathan A. Lindsey and Ann E. Prentice, *Professional Ethics and Librarians*. Phoenix, AZ: Oryx Press, 1985, 51.

11. Ethics Statement for Public Library Trustees [approved by the Public Library Association board of directors and the American Library Trustees Association board of directors, June 8, 1985] in *The Library Trustee: A Practical Guidebook*, 4th ed., Virginia Young, ed. Chicago: American Library Association, 1988, 180.

12. AALL Ethical Principles, approved by the AALL membership, April 5, 1999, http://www.aallnet.org/about/policy_ethics.asp.

13. Code of Ethics for Health Sciences Librarianship, adopted by the Medical Library Association, 1994, http://www.mlanet.org/about/ethics.html.

14. Code of Ethics for Archivists, adopted by the Council of the Society of American Archivists, 1992.

15. Code of Ethics for Special Collections Librarians, approved by the Association of College and Research Libraries, October 2003, http://www.rbms.info/standards/code_of_ethics.shtml.

16. Code of Ethics of the Society of Professional Journalists, adopted by the SPJ in 1996, http://www.spj.org/ethicscode.asp.

17. Interlaken Bindery, "Great American Libraries," *Library Journal* 67 (April 15, 1942) to *Library Journal* 86 (December 15, 1961). In total, the series numbered 428.

8

CONFIDENTIALITY

The protection of confidential information is one of the oldest ethical values and one most commonly shared among the professions. Essential to the relationship between doctor and patient, clergy and confessor, and lawyer and client, the duty to keep in confidence what is learned from or about a person in the course of providing service is a hallmark of professionalism. In becoming professionals, librarians somewhat belatedly incorporated the ethical obligation to protect confidences without fully realizing the extent of its reach or its implications for practice.

At the same time, the protection of patron confidentiality is the most currently relevant and debated ethical requirement of library practice. As changing technologies facilitate storing and sharing patron information, librarians must rethink what part of that information is essential to providing service. As heightened concerns about terrorism prompt intensified government interest in patron information, librarians must deal with new legal obligations that impinge upon traditionally protected confidentiality. Like ensuring access to information, protecting patron confidentiality is an ethical obligation increasingly defined by legal requirements.

WHY PROTECT PRIVACY?

The need to protect patron privacy is part of a paradox of access. Protecting confidences also encourages the revelation of information that might not otherwise be made known. Society, as well as the individual, benefits when patients get treatment, sinners repent, and defendants provide information to aid their defense.[1] Similarly, society benefits when its citizens obtain information and ideas to better their lives and communities. To create a climate where library users feel safe to access information, librarians withhold information about who those users are and what materials they seek and borrow. In earlier chapters, we have seen many ways in which ethical values are interconnected. In honoring patron privacy and protecting confidential information, librarians further their obligations to provide the highest level of service and the greatest degree of access.

Awareness of the importance of protecting patron privacy has grown along with the profession's expanding commitment to intellectual freedom. Where other professionals protect information about a patient's condition, a penitent's lapses, or a client's misconduct, a librarian protects the patron's thoughts and interests from outside scrutiny. Knowing that the librarian will not divulge information about books borrowed, databases searched, materials examined, Web sites visited, or questions asked, a library user may freely explore the realm of ideas, ranging into the unfamiliar, unpopular, or controversial. The intellectual quest for information is protected by assurances that the patron's explorations will not be revealed.

Many of the ethical dilemmas we have considered in the context of service, access, and conflicts of interest reappear as we examine issues of patron privacy. Here is another case where a librarian may have information sought by a patron or a public official but must decline to provide it. The greater good of providing access to all information is served by the short-term denial of access to protected information. And again we see how the Code of Ethics and the Library Bill of Rights illuminate and reinforce each other. For example, the protection of confidentiality is an ethical obligation. The librarian's duty to provide service without regard to age appears in the Library Bill of Rights. Taken together, they extend the protection of privacy to all library patrons, including children and young adults.

Although now one of librarianship's basic ethical requirements, the librarian's duty to protect patron privacy may not be known or understood by either library users, trustees, or policymakers. Like the presence of offensive works in a collection, the refusal to reveal who a patron is or what that patron has been reading may embroil the library in unwanted controversy. Librarians must educate themselves, trustees, and staff members about the right to privacy and the library's duty to protect it.

As with access to information and philosophical conflicts of interest, assuring patron privacy may require librarians to differentiate personal beliefs from professional responsibilities. Why shouldn't the library provide law enforcement officers with information about suspicious-looking patrons? Here again, because we cannot assume a shared understanding of the obligation or its implications, guidelines and procedures are essential to assure fair and equitable protection of the right in practice. Thus, ethical issues become management ones. Librarians must make sure that the library has in place proper policies, approved by the library board, to protect patron privacy, and that all library employees and volunteers understand the right to privacy and are prepared to defend it.

In the interest of patron privacy, librarians have been educators, advocates, lobbyists, and activists. They have campaigned for state laws protecting the confidentiality of library records and protested legislation eroding this right. Forty-eight states now have such laws; in the remaining two, opinions by the state attorneys general secure the right.[2] When faced with a police request for information about a patron, the librarian may have to educate law enforcement officers and prosecutors about the existence of such laws and their requirements. Librarians have been among the most outspoken opponents of the USA PATRIOT Act, passed in 2001 in the wake of the September 11 terrorist attacks. Because the act reduced the standard for protecting confidentiality in investigations involving terrorism threats and barred librarians from revealing that they had received requests for patron information, librarians challenged the act in court and lobbied against reenacting provisions affecting libraries.

In this chapter, we will first examine how confidentiality figures in library codes of ethics and then trace how a right long overlooked has been thrust center stage into debates about twenty-first-century professional practice and public policy.

QUESTIONS

- In a small town, where everybody knows each other, why not share information about what the neighbors have been reading?
- In a public library, why not tell parents what books their children have checked out?
- In the wake of a crime, why not tell a police officer what books a suspect borrowed from the library?
- In an academic community, why not tell one scholar which manuscripts in the university library another researcher has been using?

WHAT CODES OF ETHICS TELL US

The ALA's 1995 Code of Ethics distinguished between privacy and confidentiality:

III. We protect each library user's right to privacy and confidentiality with respect to information sought or received and resources consulted, borrowed, acquired, or transmitted.[3]

While part of the same process of information gathering and use, one centers on the patron, the other on the library. In protecting privacy, the library assures that the library user may freely roam in the physical or virtual world of information without fear of scrutiny. In protecting confidentiality, the library pledges not to reveal information about library patrons or their information interests or use. Though the code of ethics itself is rarely amplified or interpreted, we will see that the unstated exception is when the library is confronted with a valid request for information from a law enforcement agency in a pending criminal or other legal proceeding.

Strangely, the earliest proposed codes of library ethics did not include specific strictures against divulging information received from or about library patrons. Given the preoccupation of early librarians with asserting their professional status, their failure to include confidentiality as an ethical obligation may be explained by a general lack of acceptance of privacy as a societal value at the time. It was only in 1890 that future Supreme Court Justice Louis Brandeis published his influential *Harvard Law Review* article asserting such a right.[4] Or librarians may not have felt that information about patron borrowing or information requests involved anything worth protecting. Sharing information about what others were reading may have been seen as an element of service or a natural part of exchanging community news with little apparent risk or harm.

Mary Plummer's suggestions for a code in 1903 did not mention patron privacy or confidentiality. Charles Knowles Bolton's canons in 1909 and 1922, and the 1929 ALA draft code based on them, likewise did not address the matter. These early codes did, however, consider the possibility that a librarian's treatment of a patron might have adverse consequences. Under Canon XIV in 1922, Bolton made this connection under "Personal Obligation":

Each assistant should realize his own personal obligation as a public servant to each library patron. He should strive always to be courteous and pleasant, remembering that the staff stands as the interpreter of the library to the public and that it may be materially helped or harmed by his individual conduct.

In his comment, Bolton noted that patrons might be scared away from library use by an inappropriate staff attitude, including making derisive remarks about library users to other staff members:

An assistant sometimes fails to realize that some of the more desirable constituents who use the library are shy. To the mind of such a user of books the friendly assistant personifies the library. Habitual ridicule in private of mistakes or ignorance on the part of the public will affect, eventually, the conduct of the assistant.[5]

In the 1929 draft, this obligation appears in the staff's relations to the public.

The members of the staff are interpreters of the library to the public, and its service may be materially helped or harmed by their individual contacts.[6]

That draft, as we have seen, calls on staff to provide a cordial welcome and impartial, courteous service to all those using the library, without favoritism or distinctions based on race, color, creed, or condition. But in a section where protection of confidentiality might logically appear, it is conspicuously absent.

The ALA Code of Ethics formally adopted in December 1938 was the first to include the protection of confidentiality as an ethical obligation. As part of the relationship between the librarian and the library's constituency, it declared in Section 11 that

It is the librarian's obligation to treat as confidential any private information obtained through contact with library patrons.[7]

While this almost sounds like ethical boilerplate, the Cold War witch hunts of the 1950s and the political turmoil of the 1960s demonstrated the dangers of being associated with subversive, unpopular, or radical causes. To ensure the freedom to read, librarians needed to protect their patrons from guilt by association with controversial works. According to the Library Bill of Rights and the Freedom to Read Statement, a library does not endorse all the ideas in the books it makes available. Protection of patron reading from scrutiny is necessary to protect library users from accusations that they subscribe to all of the ideas in the books they read.

Drafts and codes considered or adopted after 1938 all provided for confidentiality with varying degrees of explication and priority, asserting the obligation but also providing exceptions. The 1968 draft Code of Ethics for Librarians included the obligation in its opening pledge:

I pledge according to my best ability and judgment that I will practice my profession with conscience and dignity; the welfare of my patrons will be my first consideration; I will respect the confidences and responsibilities which are bestowed upon me.

It reiterated this duty in Article III, "A librarian honors the confidence and the public trust of his position," and then explained:

A librarian respects the trust under which confidential or privileged information is exchanged in the course of executing the affairs of the library. **These confidences shall be revealed only as the law or courts may require.**

It is proper for a librarian to discuss confidential information with his superiors or the governing board in executive session.[8]

Thus, the protection of patron confidentiality is not absolute. Under certain circumstances, information received as part of a protected relationship may be shared with colleagues similarly bound to maintain confidentiality and as required by law enforcement officials. The 1973 draft Statement on Professional Ethics for the first time linked the reader and the works consulted:

The Librarian should seek to safeguard the essential privacy of the relationship between user and material, being careful not to divulge anything one may have learned about individual clients in the course of one's professional activities unless required to do so by competent legal authority.[9]

The Statement on Professional Ethics adopted in 1975 linked the library user and the library, removing any explicit exceptions. "A Librarian must protect the essential confidential relationship which exists between a library user and the library." But a proposed revision in 1977, while retaining the same language, based the librarians' ethical obligation on the patron's *right* to privacy and equated the position of the librarian with that of other professionals.

As an institution for democratic living, the integrity of the library in regard to matters of privacy must be unquestionable. Right to privacy is one of the basic human rights, and abrogation of the right can only result in irreparable damage to the service ability of the library. Information which is confidential in nature consists of circulation records and professional services. Any information gained by a librarian in serving an individual is deemed confidential as in the cases of lawyers and doctors.[10]

The commentary provided two circumstances when such information might be released: first, when presented "a properly issued process, order, or subpoena issued for good cause according to federal, state, or local law, as part of a discovery or investigatory procedure in a civil, criminal, or administrative matter." Second, the library might also reveal such information when given the written consent of the person to whom the records pertained.

For the first time, in 1981, the ALA incorporated a *right* of privacy in its official code. Section 3 of its Statement on Professional Ethics required that "Librarians must protect each user's right to privacy with respect to information sought or received, materials consulted, borrowed, or acquired."[11] In its comparable section, the 1995 ALA Code of Ethics provided for confidentiality in the era of electronic information, protecting a patron's right to both privacy and confidentiality "with respect to information sought or received and resources consulted, borrowed, acquired, or transmitted."[12]

HOW POLICIES AMPLIFY THE CODE

Although the ALA Code of Ethics specifically protects patron privacy and confidentiality, we must look to other ALA policies to understand fully the dimensions of this obligation. Because of the possible interest of law enforcement officials in information obtained from or about library patrons, the ALA, since 1971, has issued a series of policy statements on confidentiality. The introduction to its "Policy on Confidentiality of Library Records" adopted when U.S. Treasury agents sought to examine circulation records in a number of cities, declared:

... the efforts of the federal government to convert library circulation records into "suspect lists" constitute an unconscionable and unconstitutional invasion of the right of privacy of library patrons and, if permitted to continue, will do irreparable damage to the educational and social value of the libraries of this country.

Since 1970, forty-eight states have enacted "Confidentiality of Library Records" statutes. In the remaining two, Hawaii and Kentucky, state attorneys general have issued opinions that library records are entitled to more protection than business records.[13] The ALA's 1991 Policy Concerning Confidentiality of Personally Identifiable Information about Library Users describes such personally identifiable information appearing in various library records but generally of two kinds:

- Information about the patron that would be required to obtain library service and to be eligible to borrow materials. This might include such things as proof of residency.
- Information about the patron's reading and information interests. According to the policy, these might include requests for specific materials or on specific subjects, information provided in a reference interview to help a staff member answer a question or facilitate a search on a particular topic.[14]

Of particular concern are records that include information about a patron's reading habits, research interests, and tastes. When data do not link a certain individual with particular materials or services, such records may be used by the library to study user trends or evaluate its services.

HOW OTHER CODES TREAT CONFIDENTIALITY

Protection of patron privacy and confidential information now appears in virtually all library codes of ethics. The 1985 Ethics Statement for Public Library Trustees declares that

A trustee must respect the confidential nature of library business while being aware of and in compliance with applicable laws governing freedom of information.[15]

The Code of Ethics for Health Sciences Librarianship, adopted in 1994, includes the protection of confidentiality in its obligations to clients. "The health sciences librarian respects the privacy of clients and protects the confidentiality of the client relationship."[16] Like medical librarians who work with health professionals bound by strict tenets of patient privacy, law librarians work with lawyers bound by attorney-client privilege. The Ethical Principles of the American Association of Law Libraries, approved in 1999, considers protection of confidentiality to be an aspect of service. Following immediately upon the obligation to provide open and effective access to legal and related information, it states that "We uphold a duty to our clientele to develop service policies that respect confidentiality and privacy."[17]

As we have seen, special collections librarians and archivists interpret ethical values in the context of their particular institutions and professional roles. The ACRL Code of Ethics for Special Collections Librarians, approved in 2003, states that

Special collections librarians are responsible for protecting the confidentiality of researchers and materials as required by legal statutes, donor agreements, or policies of the library.

Commentary declares that this article is based on Article III of the 1995 Code of the American Library Association: "We protect each user's right to privacy and confidentiality with respect to information sought or received and resources consulted, borrowed, acquired, or transmitted." Its language, however, points to specific sources that may impose additional restrictions on confidential information, particularly donor agreements that might protect identifying information in manuscripts or other unique materials.[18]

Similarly, the Code of Ethics for Archivists, adopted in 1992, called for protecting the privacy of individuals who created or are the subjects of documentary material. Archivists, for whom facilitating the research process is a high priority, also included in that code the possibility that archivists may, with permission, share with each other the names of researchers using the same archival records. Unique among codes, the 1992 Code of Ethics for Archivists provided for waiving the right to privacy in the interest of furthering the use of records and promoting research.[19] The revised Code of Ethics for Archivists approved by the Society of American Archivists in 2005 provided for privacy in Section VII.

Archivists protect the privacy rights of donors and individuals or groups who are the subject of records. They respect all users' rights to privacy by maintaining the confidentiality of their research and protecting any personal information collected about them in accordance with the institution's security procedures.[20]

Although the Special Libraries Association does not have its own ethical code, its Competencies for Information Professionals of the 21st Century, revised in 2003, provides for confidentiality in its competencies related to Applying Information Tools & Techniques, Section D.3, "Protects the information privacy of clients and maintains awareness of, and responses to, new challenges to privacy."[21]

INTERPRETATIONS OF THE LIBRARY BILL OF RIGHTS

Although privacy is not mentioned in the Library Bill of Rights, recent interpretations demonstrate its importance in protecting the patron's ability to access information. The Intellectual Freedom Principles for Academic Libraries, an interpretation of the Library Bill of Rights adopted by the ACRL in 1999, and approved by the ALA Council in 2000, calls for the protection of privacy to foster free thought in a university setting.

A2. The privacy of library users is and must be inviolable. Policies should be in place that maintain the confidentiality of library borrowing records and of other information relating to personal use of library information and services.[22]

In 2002, the ALA adopted an interpretation to the Library Bill of Rights on privacy itself, noting that "privacy is essential to the exercise of free speech, free thought, and free association." A patron's access to information may be compromised or impeded by fears that the subject of their research or data about themselves might be examined or scrutinized by others.

In all areas of librarianship, best practice leaves the user in control of as many choices as possible. These include decisions about the selection of, access to, and use of information. Lack of privacy and confidentiality has a chilling effect on users' choices. All users have a right to be free from any unreasonable intrusion into or surveillance of their lawful library use.[23]

To make this right a reality, librarians must inform patrons about the policies and procedures governing the retention of personally identifiable information, ensure that library policies are consistent with applicable law, inform all staff members about their responsibility to protect patron privacy, and maintain only information that is essential to fulfill the mission of the library.

From this look at library codes of ethics over time and across the profession, and at ALA policies and interpretations of the Library Bill of Rights, we can draw these conclusions:

- Protecting confidentiality, although basic to most codes of ethics, did not appear until fairly late in the evolution of the ethical principles of librarians.
- Protecting patron confidentiality came to be seen as an important means to protect the right of access to information.
- Codes now provide for the protection of both patron privacy and confidential information.
- Protection of patron privacy allows library users to freely explore the universe of information without unwanted scrutiny, intrusion, or documentation.
- Protection of confidential information ensures that libraries do not retain information received from or about a patron unnecessarily or divulge it without proper legal justification.
- More recent codes of ethics regard patron privacy as a right.
- Awareness of confidentiality has increased as the legal implications of protecting patron information have become more apparent.

- The confidentiality of patron information is protected by statute or the opinion of attorneys general in every state.
- The importance of protecting privacy and confidentiality grows as new fears and new technologies provide motives and means for invading patron privacy.
- Special collections librarians and archivists are concerned with protecting confidential information that appears in documents in their care.
- Under certain conditions, the right of privacy may be waived.

PROTECTING PRIVACY IN PRACTICE

Libraries and Reading Are Both Communal and Individual

Perhaps because libraries are communal institutions, protecting confidentiality may seem at odds with the library's role as a center for community conversation and debate. In the free marketplace of ideas, citizens can exchange views and delve into topics out of favor or fashion. Adult education in libraries involves both group activities and individual consultations with a readers' advisor. Reading, while perceived to be a solitary activity, has public dimensions as well. Libraries sponsor book discussion groups; summer reading programs reward those who read the most; librarians and patrons blog about the books they recommend. Members of social networks such as Facebook and MySpace reveal the details of their personal lives. But all these involve a voluntary sharing of information that implicitly waives any protection of confidentiality. Why then, should librarians be concerned about it?

As we have seen, librarians were slow to add confidentiality to their ethical canon. Few librarians establish a one-to-one relationship with patrons, conducting most reference transactions at a public service desk within earshot of other library users. Historically, only reader's advisors have met with patrons privately and by appointment, sometimes over an extended period, establishing the kind of professional-client relationship that might suggest a need for confidentiality. For their part, patrons generally do not bring an expectation of privacy to the library.

Practice Must Reflect Privacy Values

Protection of confidentiality requires both an awareness that a privacy right is at risk and a willingness to incur the additional costs or make the requisite changes in policies or procedures. Indeed, the right to confidentiality is often more honored in the breach than in the observance. In early libraries, openness about patron records was reinforced by book circulation systems in which a patron's name remained on the charge card for other users to see. Such personally identifiable information, now specifically covered by ALA policy, has been a boon to historical researchers studying the reading habits of various segments of the community. Librarians sent post-cards to remind patrons about overdue books even though the borrowed titles could be seen by the postman, family members, or neighbors picking up the mail. Easy alternatives were at hand to protect confidential information: assign patrons an ID number to put on a charge card rather than a name, mail overdue notices in envelopes. But if no one is complaining, why take the trouble and incur the expense?

Technology has both enhanced and further complicated issues of confidentiality. Integrated library systems, combining cataloging and circulation data, make it possible to store and retrieve extensive information about a patron's borrowing record. The maintenance of records of database or Web searches similarly makes it possible to access a detailed account of what information has been sought and accessed electronically. On the other hand, the introduction of self-charging systems, often installed as a cost-cutting measure, allows patrons to check out materials without revealing them to either circulation staff or other patrons waiting in line.

The ability of patrons to access sexually explicit material on the Web may cause conflicts between the values of access and confidentiality. When a library chooses not to install Internet filters, library users and staff members may object to the exposure to pornographic material on another patron's computer screen. Some libraries have sought to discourage accessing such material by installing terminals in plain view even though this clearly violates patron privacy. Alternatives such as privacy screens and more secluded terminal locations, away from children's areas, provide some privacy protection, though some patrons may resent special accommodations for those viewing this material. In such cases, the library has two values to protect, access and confidentiality, and may incur both expense and controversy in the process of defending them.

Policies Must Presume Protection of Privacy

To those unfamiliar with the right of privacy in libraries and the rationale behind it, efforts to protect confidentiality may seem to defy common sense. Editorial writers and columnists have had a field day writing about a library's refusal to tell parents what books their children have borrowed or spouses about each other's overdue books. The general public may share this disbelief. But young people may wish to read about sex, health, family problems, religion, or even works written for children that have created controversy, without parental oversight or disapproval. Similarly, an adult may wish to explore a topic or a writer's works, for whatever reason, that might cause suspicion or ill-feeling if discovered by another family member.

As with other core values of librarianship, protecting patron confidentiality must begin with a presumption in its favor. The standard to overcome such a presumption must be high, and exceptions must be applicable in similar circumstances. In this case, the presumption is that the privacy protection extends to all library users regardless of age or relationship. Parents may feel that such a policy interferes with their ability to guide their children's reading by refusing them access to their children's borrowing records.

What is needed in such a situation then is a policy that honors the primary value of privacy while providing an alternate means to provide the requested information. To accomplish this, some libraries offer family borrowing cards or, at the request of parents, limit borrowing to certain parts of the collection. In essence, the parents have waived their children's right to privacy. The presumptive protection of privacy stays in place, while parents achieve the desired result for their own family. Thus, a policy that requires family borrowing cards or parental permission for children to access the entire collection is an inappropriate approach which dishonors the obligation to protect confidentiality. Requiring families to opt out of privacy protection, rather than asking them to opt in, is the ethical approach to confidentiality, service, and access.

Protecting Student Privacy in School Libraries

The protection of patron privacy extends to schools as well. Since students are entitled to access information in school library media centers, they also have a right to privacy that protects their information seeking and use from scrutiny by school officials, teachers, or parents.[24] School librarians, for example, should be careful not to indicate the name of the resource borrowed when sending an overdue notice to parents or teachers. Because school library media specialists become better acquainted with students than public librarians do with a larger and changing population, they may have a closer relationship and greater responsibility to individual student needs. Library media specialist and privacy expert Helen R. Adams suggests that there may be times when an exception to privacy protection is justified. After citing Section III of the 1995 ALA Code of Ethics, she notes

… there may be times when a library media specialist must apply common sense rather than the ALA policy and ethics statements because of concern for the student's welfare. Just as educators are required to report cases of child abuse, there are times when concern for a student may move the library media specialist to seek the advice of another school professional bound by confidentiality such as a guidance counselor. Intervening to potentially save the life of a student transcends student privacy.[25]

This is an excellent example of establishing a presumption in favor of privacy as an ethical value while acknowledging that there may be circumstances of sufficient gravity to overcome the presumption. Consultation with another professional bound by strictures on confidentiality further honors student privacy.

Professional judgment is required to make this determination. Neverthe-less, because individuals may disagree about situations that may require divulging confidential information, school media specialists, in consultation with principals and teachers, should consider guidelines for making such exceptions, as for example, evidence of a physical condition or unusual behavior. Also, library media specialists, like all librarians, may ask the patron for permission to share confidential information with another pro-fessional, reiterating that the student's privacy is protected while asking for a waiver of that protection. Just as public librarians must educate board members and the community about privacy privileges, school librarians must be sure that principals, teachers, and parents understand the nature of their ethical as well as statutory obligations.[26]

Hauptman's Hypothetical Revisited

This might be a good time to revisit Robert Hauptman's ethical experi-ment in 1976 which included not only elements of service and access but also issues of confidentiality. Hauptman was concerned about the response of librarians to his request for information about a bomb that could blow up a suburban house.[27] His disappointment at the willingness of librarians to provide the information stemmed from what he considered their willing-ness to put duty to their profession ahead of duty to society. In making his request, Hauptman apparently did not say what he intended to do with the information, nor did the librarians ask. Reexamining these exchanges, we see that Hauptman did not consider either the specific code of ethics in place at the time or how standards protecting patron privacy and confiden-tial information might apply.

Here are some thoughts. Hauptman's article appeared in the *Wilson Library Bulletin* in April 1976, shortly after the ALA adopted its 1975 Statement on Professional Ethics. Although he refers to language in the ALA code of ethics about a "higher duty to society in general," the code did not include such a phrase. It did, however, provide for "the essential confidential relationship which exists between a library user and the library."[28] Protection of patron privacy ensured that Hauptman, in his experimental guise, could have searched on his own for information about explosives without scrutiny or staff intervention. By the mid-1970s, however, librarians were already interested in setting standards for situations in which they might be asked by law enforce-ment agents to relinquish patron information. Even though Hauptman's experiment was inspired by FBI statistics on recent bombings, he did not con-sider under what circumstances the librarians he approached might have reported him to law enforcement officers. In the absence of additional infor-mation or clearly antisocial conduct, what were librarians to do besides refuse to provide assistance? Leaving librarians to determine their duty to society, beyond the realm of professional obligation, surrenders all claims to professionalism, consistency, or principled decision-making.

Librarians have determined that the presentation of a subpoena or court order in a pending criminal case overcomes the presumption in favor of protecting confidential patron information. State laws and attorneys' general opinions now embody this ethical standard. This sets a high bar and draws a clear line between situations when information is to be protected and when it is to be released. It is not dependent on individual discretion or subject to varying interpretations. It applies to all library staff and frees them from having to decide what to do when law enforcement officers appear without the requisite court order.

Janis Lee, librarian of the Swarthmore Public Library, recounts how she lobbied for Pennsylvania's law protecting the confidentiality of library records and then relied on it when local police demanded the borrowing records of a patron who was accused of a mall shooting. The law declared:

Records related to the circulation of library materials which contain the names or personally identifying details regarding the users of the State Library or any local library which is established or maintained under any law of the Commonwealth or the library of any university, college, or educational institution chartered by the Commonwealth or the library of any public school or branch reading rooms, deposit station or agency operated in connection therewith, shall be confidential and shall not be made available to anyone except by a court order in a criminal proceeding.[29]

Despite the heinous nature of the crime, the library refused to release the records until the police, after three months spent questioning and pressuring the librarian, finally obtained the court order required by law. As in many instances, an alternative source of the sought-after information was at hand. In his account, borough attorney Guy Smith, who represented the library, pointed out that the books themselves were found in the trunk of the suspect's car, which the police had impounded, making the request to the library unnecessary.[30]

Suspicious Patrons

Efforts by Internal Revenue Service agents in the 1970s to secure information about suspicious library patrons interested in explosive devices not only inspired Hauptman's experiment but spurred lobbying efforts for laws to protect library records.[31] But even as the protection of patron privacy appeared in codes of ethics and state statutes, law enforcement officials continued to test the resolve of librarians and trustees. The FBI Library Awareness Program in 1980s demonstrated that the protection of patron confidentiality had not been regularized by libraries, internalized by librarians, or understood and accepted by law enforcement officials. Though the

Cold War was winding down, the FBI targeted academic libraries to inquire about subversives seeking to access unclassified technical information. Dispatched to libraries without advance notice or appointment, agents approached lower-level staff members to ask about "suspicious patrons." Without any court order identifying a particular individual, agents described a generic suspect, usually a swarthy man with a dark complexion and an Eastern European accent.

Proceeding for several years, the FBI effort was revealed only after the visit of an agent to the engineering library of Columbia University was reported by its librarian, Paula Kaufman. Although the FBI claimed that its investigation was limited to the metropolitan New York area, other universities as far away as the engineering library at the University of Maryland reported similar visits.[32] An outcry in the library community led to Congressional hearings but no legislation establishing federal protection of library records. The library community was particularly concerned when Jerald R. Newman, chairman of the National Commission on Library and Information Science (NCLIS), voiced his support of the FBI effort. In a transcript of a meeting with the FBI, Newman was quoted as saying, "I'm supposed to be impartial, but I'm inclined on behalf of what the Bureau is doing.... We have the responsibility as Commissioners, of being sure there's freedom of access of information, but I think we have another responsibility in upholding the Constitution of the United States ... which is a higher responsibility, and that includes citizens protecting our democracy and our republic." ALA president Margaret Chisholm responded, "At worst such statements exhibit a cavalier disregard for privacy rights of all library patrons as a fundamental ethical principle of the library profession. These privacy rights are vital to effective access to information and, moreover, are protected by statute in thirty-eight states and in the District of Columbia."[33]

These episodes revealed that academic as well as public libraries have issues with patron privacy, that training frontline, public service staff is essential to the protection of confidentiality, and that law enforcement officers need to be better informed about the legal and ethical responsibilities of libraries and librarians. Responding to the FBI Library Awareness Program, the Association of Research Libraries adopted a Statement on Library Users' Right to Confidentiality, affirming its commitment to unrestricted information access and dissemination. It concluded,

The ARL condemns the efforts of any government agency to violate the privacy of library users, to subvert library patron records, and to intimidate or recruit library staff to monitor so-called "suspicious" library patrons or report on what or how any individual uses library resources. Such actions are an affront to First Amendment freedoms, individual privacy, and all citizens' right to know. These actions violate the basic tenets of a democratic society.[34]

Allies in Protecting Privacy

Episodes during the George H. W. Bush and Bill Clinton presidential administrations in the late 1980s and 1990s demonstrated the common interest of libraries, bookstores, and video stores in protecting patron and customer privacy. As we have seen in the statements on the Freedom to Read and the Freedom to View, these groups already share a commitment to First Amendment rights and free access to information. The Library Bill of Rights calls on libraries to cooperate with other organizations in the fight against censorship. This joint effort implicitly extends to protecting the records of those who borrow, buy, or rent materials in any format.

Revelations in 1987 by the Washington, D.C., *City Paper* of videos rented by Supreme Court nominee Robert Bork showed the interest of retailers in protecting customer confidentiality. Had Bork borrowed the same videos from the D.C. Public Library, the records would have been protected by local ordinance. Calls for a federal law resulted in the introduction of a bill to protect the confidentiality of video rental outlets. Efforts by the library community to include libraries in the legislation were met with a series of draconian amendments that would have imposed a gag order on libraries approached by federal agents. The provisions affecting libraries did not pass but give a chilling foreshadowing of provisions of the USA PATRIOT Act.[35]

ROBERT BORK AND VIDEO PRIVACY (1987)

In September 1987, amid a contentious Senate confirmation hearing, the Washington, D.C., *City Paper* published an article by Michael Dolan revealing videos rented by Supreme Court nominee Robert Bork. Dolan had inquired about Bork's video-rental transactions at Erol's, where a clerk willingly provided the information and made a copy for Dolan's use. Had Bork borrowed the same videos from the D.C. Public Library, the records would have been protected by local ordinance. In fact, the proprietor of Erol's had a policy in place to prevent the release of rental information. A spokesman described such press inquiries as rare and attributed the lapse to a young, part-time employee who "ignored the owner's directive." In fact, the account was in the name of Bork's wife. Had Bork himself inquired about her account at the public library, his request would have been denied.

The widely publicized incident prompted calls for a federal law to protect the confidentiality of the records of video rental outlets. In May 1988, Senator Patrick Leahy of Vermont introduced a bill that would protect the privacy of patrons of both video stores and libraries "to ensure that the choice of the books we read and the movies we view will be protected against unlawful disclosure." Private information contained in library records was protected by law in most states, but there was no comparable federal law.

The proposed legislation contained parallel provisions protecting patron confidentiality in libraries and video rental stores and delineated specific circumstances in which personally identifiable information could be revealed. These included release to a law enforcement agency pursuant to a court order. The provision set a high standard, including notice to the patron and an opportunity to contest the order:

(C) to a law enforcement agency pursuant to a court order authorizing such disclosure if (i) the patron is given reasonable notice, by the law enforcement agency, of the court proceeding relevant to the issuance of the court order and is afforded the opportunity to appear and contest the claim of the law enforcement agency; and (ii) such law enforcement agency offers clear and convincing evidence that the subject of the information is reasonably suspected of engaging in criminal activity and that the information sought is highly probative and material to the case.

Provision for court orders in civil proceedings included similar notice and challenge safeguards. The legislation also provided for the destruction of old records, no later than a year from the date the information was no longer needed for the purposes for which it was collected.

Efforts of the library community to include libraries in the legislation were countered with proposed amendments that would have imposed a gag order on libraries approached by federal agents. The ALA's Washington office reported in its October 24, 1988, newsletter that the FBI had informally approached the House Judiciary Subcommittee on Courts, Civil Liberties, and the Administration of Justice seeking an amendment that would give the FBI director or his designee the ability to issue a "national security letter" without having to get a court order. Thus, years before the attacks of September 11, 2001, or the earlier bombing of the World Trade Center in 1993, federal agents sought powers to access library records with only an assertion of a national security need, without the need to show cause, or without the protections of notification and challenge. In response to these amendments, the library provisions were stripped from the bill, which was then passed into law. The Video Privacy Protection Act 18 USC 2710 (1988) forbids video rental and sales outlets from disclosing borrowing or purchase information or personal data without the customer's written consent. Library patrons would have to continue to rely on state laws protecting the confidentiality of library records.

Michael Dolan continued to view his article as a humorous attempt to show Bork's human side and as an analysis of Bork's taste in movies (Bork seemed to like films with "man" in the title) rather than a

violation of his privacy. Surprisingly for a journalist whose own professional ethics includes a willingness to go to jail to protect a confidential
source, Dolan, writing in May 1988, was still not concerned about the
privacy implications of his tongue-in-cheek "parody." If video rentals
were to be protected, he asked, why not protect the records of other
retail establishments? Why draw the line at video stores and libraries?
What about bookstores? Will we soon have a law making it a crime for a
bookseller to let slip what books I have bought? What about movie theaters? Should we have a law forbidding a ticket-taker from mentioning
who went to what at Cinema 42 last night? How about lingerie sellers?

Dolan could not have anticipated that within a decade, a special
prosecutor would seek records of the purchases of White House intern Monica Lewinsky at two Washington, D.C., bookstores. The
protest of this invasion of privacy was led by a law librarian.

QUESTIONS

- How are the roles of libraries, video rental places, and bookstores similar
  or different?
- What ethical values do bookstores, libraries, and video rental places have
  in common? When might their values diverge?
- Is it unethical to give information that a particular patron was in a store or
  library at a particular time?
- What circumstances might overcome a presumption in favor of the confidentiality of patron information?
- How can institutions prevent the inappropriate or illegal disclosure of confidential information about their patrons?

SOURCES

Bork, Robert H., Jr. "The Secrecy of Video Rentals: 'Another Example of
    How His Privacy Was Being Trampled'," *Washington Post* [Letter to the
    Editor], February 21, 1988, B8.

Dolan, Michael. "America Was Ready for a Chuckle," *Washington Post*
    [Letter to the Editor], February 21, 1988, B8.

Dolan, Michael. "The Bork Tapes: Never Mind His Writings on *Roe v. Wade*. The
    Inner Workings of Robert Bork's Mind Are Revealed by the Videos He
    Rents." *City Paper* 7, no. 9 (September 25–October 1, 1987): 1, 12, 14, 16, 18.

Patrick Leahy. Remarks on S. 2361 Video and Library Privacy Protection Act
    of 1988. Congressional Record, 100th Congress, 2nd session, Senate,
    May 10, 1988.

"Video and Library Privacy Protection Act," *ALA Washington Newsletter* 40,
    no. 10 (October 24, 1988): 2–3

During the inquiry into the conduct of President Bill Clinton leading to impeachment proceedings, independent counsel Ken Starr sought to force bookstores to reveal purchases made by White House intern Monica Lewinsky. When an independent bookstore in Washington, D.C., initially acquiesced, a law librarian led a picket line protesting this invasion of privacy.[36] Unlike libraries, bookstores and video rentals do not have a natural constituency, nor do their employees have codes of ethics protecting patron confidentiality. But in a democratic society, they play a key role in providing information and are vulnerable to the same chilling effects if they are known to reveal patron reading and borrowing choices to even informal law enforcement or journalist inquiries.

Responding to New Threats to Privacy

Before September 11, 2001, librarians had reconciled their ethical obligation to protect patron confidentiality with the need of law enforcement officials for information in criminal and other legal matters. Librarians did not claim an absolute privilege of confidentiality. Instead, they based their obligation on an implicit presumption of privacy protection that could be overcome only in particular circumstances, generally defined in state law. The federal government's response to the terrorist attacks of September 11 upset this balance, putting new pressures on libraries and challenging the commitment of librarians to patron privacy.

The USA PATRIOT Act ("Uniting and Strengthening America by Providing Appropriate Tools Required to Intercept and Obstruct Terrorism"), which passed without significant debate on October 26, 2001, gave law enforcement authorities broader investigatory powers in cases involving suspected terrorism. Of particular significance for libraries, Section 215 authorized access to business records, including library circulation records, on the basis of National Security Letters. Unlike court-issued search warrants or subpoenas, these could be issued on the basis of mere suspicion, did not need to identify particular subjects or acts, and did not require prior court approval. In the past, librarians had divulged library records when subpoenaed or presented with a court order naming a specific patron suspected of or charged with a specific act. Under the USA PATRIOT Act, agents might seek information about books borrowed or searches conducted by all of the library's patrons on a certain day or at a certain time without identifying a particular suspect. Thus, the records of any library user might be scrutinized by federal agents.

In addition, the USA PATRIOT Act included a gag order that prevented those who received National Security Letters from sharing that information with anyone save the organization's own legal counsel. Under state laws that do not include gag orders, librarians could notify the subject of the inquiry as a courtesy or could contact the ALA Office for Intellectual

Freedom to report the incident or request advice. The USA PATRIOT Act provided criminal sanctions for such activities. Further, the U.S. Department of Justice was not required to report how many National Security Letters it had sent to libraries.

The passage and implementation of the USA PATRIOT Act presented classic ethical dilemmas in dramatic new circumstances. Two ethical values were at stake: patron privacy was jeopardized by the lowered standard for law enforcement demands for information and the broadened scope of queries. Access to information was impinged by gag orders preventing librarians from exercising their First Amendment rights to discuss their situation and seek outside assistance. In the 1980s, it had been the willingness of librarians to go public about the FBI Library Awareness Program and their freedom to do so that had led to professional and public outrage, press coverage, and a Congressional hearing. As with all political and societal issues, the war on terror evoked myriad responses, especially as the United States undertook the war in Iraq in its campaign against al Qaeda. Like the war itself, the USA PATRIOT Act divided the country, posing another situation where a librarian's personal view might be at odds with ethical values or legal responsibilities. For many librarians, efforts to combat terrorism threatened some of the nation's basic civil liberties.

As it had responded to the FBI Library Awareness Program, the library community presented a remarkably united front in its opposition to the USA PATRIOT Act. In individual libraries and through their professional organizations, librarians registered their opposition to the strictures the law imposed on them and the risks to their patrons. In the past, state laws had protected patron confidentiality, facilitating ethical practice; here, the law threatened patron confidentiality, conflicting with a core ethical value.

Barred by gag orders from the court of public opinion, librarians devised alternatives that honored their legal obligation while protecting patron rights and registering their objections to the law. Information itself was at the heart of their response.

- Signs posted prominently in public libraries informed patrons about the law and what it required of libraries.[37]

- Library record-keeping policies were streamlined, eliminating the collection of unnecessary patron information and deleting other data from library systems as quickly as possible.

- Some libraries, barred from reporting that they had received a request for information under the USA PATRIOT Act, posted a sign that they had NOT received such a request.

- The ALA and state library organizations issued guidelines and hosted programs to inform librarians of their obligations under the law and the need to train all library staff members and volunteers of their responsibilities as well.

- The ALA led the effort to modify the provisions of the act when it came up for reauthorization.
- Individual librarians, with the support of the ALA, booksellers, publishers, and the American Civil Liberties Union (ACLU) brought suit challenging the constitutionality of the act itself.

JOHN DOES CHALLENGE THE USA PATRIOT ACT (2005)

In July 2005, agents of the Federal Bureau of Investigation delivered a National Security Letter to the executive director of the Library Connection, a consortium providing integrated library services to twenty-six public and academic libraries in the Hartford, Connecticut, area. The letter was issued under the terms of the USA PATRIOT Act, enacted on October 26, 2001, in the wake of the September 11 terrorist attacks. (The act's acronym stands for Uniting and Strengthening America by Providing Appropriate Tools Required to Intercept and Obstruct Terrorism.) The letter requested "any and all subscriber information, billing information, and access logs of any person or entity" using a specific IP (Internet protocol) address during a specific forty-five-minute period on February 15 of that year. Although it was later revealed that the request was prompted by a threat against a government official alleged to have been sent via e-mail over a library computer, the letter did not name a specific suspect. Compliance would have revealed information about all patrons using the computer at that time. Under the terms of the act, the information requested was deemed "relevant to an authorized investigation to protect against international terrorism or clandestine intelligence activities," and "not conducted solely on the basis of activities protected by the First Amendment of the Constitution of the United States." The letter requested delivery of the records in person and cautioned against disclosing the substance of the request.

After consultation, four members of the executive committee of the Library Connection's executive board sought legal assistance from the American Civil Liberties Union to challenge the act itself and the gag order it imposed on recipients of National Security Letters. With the USA PATRIOT Act up for reauthorization by Congress, the four librarians, known collectively as "John Doe," argued that the gag order impeded their ability to participate in the debate over the act. When librarians had objected to provisions of the law, then-Attorney General John Ashcroft had dismissed their concerns as "hysteria." The experience of the Library Connection vindicated their misgivings. In making their case, the plaintiffs cited their ethical obligation to keep library records confidential unless served with a court-ordered subpoena, as provided by state law.

A federal district court judge agreed with plaintiffs that the gag order violated their First Amendment right to free speech and enjoined the government from barring disclosure of their identities. Her order was stayed pending appeal and upheld by the 2nd Circuit Court of Appeals. Supreme Court Justice Ruth Bader Ginsburg turned down an emergency appeal by the plaintiffs, in order to let the 2nd Circuit Court make its decision, but also indicated her own concerns with the government's position. The American Library Association, along with the Freedom to Read Foundation, the American Booksellers Foundation for Free Expression, and the Association of American Publishers, filed an amicus brief urging the Supreme Court to overturn the stay and allow the plaintiffs to reveal their identities.

In the meantime, however, the identity of John Doe had already been made public in the *New York Times* on September 2, 2005, using information in court documents that the government had failed to redact. Nonetheless, the government continued to defend the gag order through the passage of a somewhat modified version of the USA PATRIOT Act that was signed into law on March 9, 2006. When the testimony of the plaintiffs about their experience could no longer affect the reauthorization debate, federal prosecutors in April 2006 agreed to allow the Library Connection to identify itself as the recipient and challenger of the National Security Letter. The government claimed that the new law gave them the discretion to make this information public and revealed that an independent investigation had determined that the e-mail threat had been without basis. Plaintiffs reiterated their concern that the timing had been politically motivated.

In June 2006, the four Connecticut librarians identified as John Doe, namely George Christian, executive director of the Library Connection; Barbara Bailey, director of the Welles-Turner Memorial Library in Glastonbury; Peter Chase, director of the Plainville Public Library; and Janet Nocek, director of the Portland Library, were the honored recipients of the Robert B. Downs Intellectual Freedom Award presented by the Graduate School of Library and Information Science at the University of Illinois at Urbana-Champaign. Because of the gag order, they had been unable to accept the award at the 2006 midwinter meeting of the American Library Association. In June 2006, their identities revealed, the four also received the Roger Baldwin Medal of Liberty, the highest award of the American Civil Liberties Union.

On August 2, 2006, Justice Ginsburg ordered that all documents related to the case be made public.

QUESTIONS

- Librarians in Connecticut had abided by subpoenas requesting information about patron use of libraries in criminal cases. What was different about this case?
- How does opposition to the USA PATRIOT Act fit criteria for determining what is a library issue?

SOURCES

"Bush Signs Reauthorization of USA PATRIOT Act," *Freedom to Read Foundation News* 31, no. 1, March 2006. Issue also includes USA PATRIOT Act Litigation Summary.

"John Does Allowed to Speak, Receive Belated Robert Downs Award" [press release posted by the American Library Association, June 27, 2006].

For complete court documents related to the case, go to http://www.aclu.org/safefree/nationalsecurityletters/index.html.

For documents related to the case on the ALA Web site, go to http://www.ala.org/ala/oif/ifissues/usactlibrarians.htm.

For national news coverage, see Cowan, Alison Leigh, "Hartford Librarians Watch as U.S. Makes Demands," *New York Times*, September 2, 2005; "Connecticut Librarians See Lack of Oversight as Biggest Danger in Antiterror Law," *New York Times*, September 3, 2005; "Judges Question Patriot Act in Library and Internet Case," *New York Times*, November 3, 2005; "A Court Fight to Keep a Secret that's No Real Secret at All," *New York Times*, November 18 2005; "Librarian Is Still John Doe, Despite Patriot Act Revision," *New York Times*, March 21, 2006; "Four Librarians Finally Break Silence in Records Case," *New York Times*, May 31, 2006; "U.S. Ends a Yearlong Effort to Obtain Library Records Amid Secrecy in Connecticut," *New York Times*, June 27, 2006.

O'Connor, Anahad, "Librarians Win as U.S. Relents on Secrecy Law," *New York Times*, April 13, 2006.

Despite herculean efforts by the library community urging modification of the most objectionable sections of the USA PATRIOT Act, the law was reauthorized in March 9, 2006, with major provisions intact. The law still authorizes generalized, rather than specific, inquiries and continues to impose a gag order on those contacted for information. Just as the library community responded to the act by making information about it available, the modifications of the law it did secure made implementation of the act slightly more transparent.[38]

PROFESSIONAL ROLES REVISITED

Exploring the ethical dimensions of access, we have seen how individual librarians resisted censorship efforts and proclaimed the centrality of information access in a democratic society. Government threats to patron confidentiality under the USA PATRIOT Act called forth the same public commitment of librarians to a core professional value. Gag orders authorized by the law muted such a public defense, and the climate of fear surrounding the war on terror might have chilled the profession's willingness to risk public disapproval. How far have we come in our defense of privacy? Is there an element comparable to the self-censorship we observed in information access?

In May 2006, shortly after reauthorization of the USA PATRIOT Act, the identity of four Connecticut librarians who had challenged the act and its gag-order provision were made public. George Christian, Barbara Bailey, Peter Chase, and Janet Nocek, members of the executive board of Library Connection, a consortium of academic and public libraries in Connecticut, had been the "John Doe" plaintiffs in a suit brought by the ACLU against U.S. Attorney General Alberto Gonzales. At issue was a National Security Letter ordering the Library Connection to provide "all subscriber information, billing information, and access logs of any person or entity related to" a specific Internet protocol address for a forty-five-minute period on February 15, 2005. Acting on an apparent terrorist threat made by e-mail to a government agency from a library computer terminal, the FBI wanted to know about *every* person using a library computer at the time.

In protecting ethical values, librarians have become expert litigators as well as advocates and educators. While Congress debated the reauthorization of the USA PATRIOT Act, a federal district court judge lifted the gag order on the grounds that it prevented the plaintiffs who had experienced its reach from participating in the debate on the act's renewal. When the appellate court issued a stay of this order, the ALA, joined by the Freedom to Read Foundation, the American Booksellers for Freedom of Expression, and the Association of American Publishers, filed a friend-of-the-court brief seeking to overturn it, a request denied by Justice Ruth Bader Ginsburg. In June 2006, the Justice Department announced that it had concluded independently that the threat had no merit, allowing the plaintiff "John Does" to speak about their experience and to accept the University of Illinois Graduate School of Library and Information Science's Robert B. Downs Award for their defense of intellectual freedom.[39]

The response of librarians to the USA PATRIOT Act in defense of confidentiality demonstrates the importance of interpreting traditional ethical values in the context of new, and sometimes unimaginable, threats. Although many professions have a duty to protect client or patient confidentiality, librarians were on the frontlines defending against the incursions of National Security Letters and general requests for information about which patrons had accessed what data. Many professed surprise at the library community's response while a few expressed disappointment that it was not even stronger. One such complaint, from anthropologist David H. Price, felt librarians had been too willing to comply with FBI demands and called for a complete refusal to respond. In an article in *CounterPunch* in March 2003, Price interpreted the ALA Code of Ethics as requiring an absolute refusal to obey.

While the legal issues involved in the FBI's latest invasion of patrons' privacy may seem complex, the ethical issues are quite simple. My interpretation of the ethical dilemma faced by librarians when given the obvious contradictions between the American Library Association's ethical commitment to protecting the privacy of patrons and the FBI's reckless quest for information on the reading preferences and thought processes of American citizens is that the ALA code of ethics demands that librarians refuse to comply with FBI requests for patron records. Ethical librarians have no choice but to engage in civil disobedience and thus must refuse to comply with the FBI's (temporarily) legal, but unethical request. Librarians have an ethical duty to protect their patrons that trumps the legal issues confronting them. Period. If they are not prepared to uphold their own basic ethical principles of patron advocacy then they should be prepared to reap the scorn and suspicions of other patrons.[40]

Deriding librarians as minions of the FBI, Price gave examples of the chilling effect of the act on scholars who rephrased reference questions, feared their previous use of potentially suspicious documents, and removed materials without checking them out to avoid leaving a record in the system. According to Price, the protection of privacy does not involve a presumption that can be overcome; it is absolute.

In contrast, Illinois Senator Richard Durbin hailed the efforts of ALA to protect patron privacy. During the debate on the reauthorization of the USA PATRIOT Act, Durbin lauded the association's grassroots effort. Speaking on the floor of the Senate, Durbin said,

Let me say a word as I close. One of the most unlikely groups became so important in this debate—the American Library Association. I cannot recall a time in recent memory when this organization showed such leadership. Time and again, they came forward to tell us that they wanted to protect the privacy of their patrons at libraries across America who might come in and take out a magazine or book, and they certainly didn't want to do that with the knowledge that the Government could sweep up all of the library records and sift through them to see if anybody had checked out a suspicious book. They sent us petitions gathered from libraries across the Nation, and I think they really did good work on behalf of our Constitution and our rights and liberties guaranteed under the Bill of Rights.[41]

Should Senator Durbin have been surprised at the role of librarians in this debate? We have seen that over more than a century, librarians have expanded their understanding of ethical requirements for professional library service. The highest quality of service now depends on maximum access to data of all sorts using every information medium. Librarians have come to see that free access to information depends on the protection of patron confidentiality. The USA PATRIOT Act has given librarians the opportunity to make this case to the public, Congress, and the courts.

As ethical standards are embodied in law and also threatened by it, librarians must continuously reexamine, reinterpret, and defend these core values. Similarly, as we enter the world of Library 2.0, the new possibilities of information sharing made possible by social networking Web sites, blogs, instant messaging, and wikis both challenge our understanding of these values and demonstrate their continued relevance, as we shall see in the next chapter.

END NOTES

1. A similar paradox underlies copyright law: the use of copyrighted information is limited for a certain period in order to protect the interests of the copyright holder but also to inspire others to create works, thus benefiting society as a whole.

2. American Library Association, State Privacy Laws Regarding Library Records, http://www.ala.org/ala/oif/ifgroups/stateifcchairs/stateifcinaction/Default1819.htm.

3. American Library Association Code of Ethics adopted by the ALA Council June 28, 1995.

4. Samuel D. Warren and Louis D. Brandeis, "The Right to Privacy," *Harvard Law Review* 4: 193 (1890).

5. Charles Knowles Bolton, "The Ethics of Librarianship: A Proposal for a Revised Code," *The Annals of the American Academy of Political and Social Science* 101 (May 1922): 143.

6. "Suggested Code of Ethics," *Library Journal* 55 (15 February 1930): 165.

7. "Code of Ethics for Librarians [adopted by ALA Council December 29, 1938]." *ALA Bulletin* 33 (February 1939): 129. *Intellectual Freedom Manual*, 7th ed., Chicago: American Library Association, 2006, 257.

8. "1968 Code of Ethics for Librarians: A Draft Proposal" reprinted in Jonathan A. Lindsey and Ann E. Prentice. *Professional Ethics and Librarians.* Phoenix, AZ: Oryx Press, 1985, 47.

9. Statement on Professional Ethics, 1973 [draft] reprinted in Lindsey and Prentice, *Professional Ethics and Librarians*, 55.

10. Proposed revisions to the 1975 Statement on Professional Ethics, 1977, Lindsey and Prentice, *Professional Ethics*, 59.

11. Statement on Professional Ethics, 1981, adopted June 30, 1981, by the ALA Council. *American Libraries* 12 (June 1981): 335; *Intellectual Freedom Manual*, 7th ed. Chicago: American Library Association, 2006, 262.

12. American Library Association Code of Ethics, adopted by the ALA Council, June 28, 1995.

13. American Library Association, State Privacy Laws Regarding Library Records, http://www.ala.org/ala/oif/ifgroups/stateifcchairs/stateifcinaction/Default1819.htm.

14. Policy Concerning Confidentiality of Personally Identifiable Information about Library Users, http://www.ala.org/alaorg/oif/pol_user.html.

15. Ethics Statement for Public Library Trustees, approved by the Public Library Association board of directors and the American Library Trustees Association board of directors, July 8, 1985.

16. Medical Library Association, Code of Ethics for Health Sciences Librarianship, adopted by the Medical Library Association, 1994, http://www.mlanet.org/about/ethics.html.

17. AALL Ethical Principles, approved by the AALL membership, April 5, 1999, http://www.aallnet.org/about/policy_ethics.asp.

18. Code of Ethics for Special Collections Librarians, approved by the Association of College and Research Libraries, October 2003, http://www.rbms.info/standards/code_of_ethics.shtml.

19. Code of Ethics for Archivists, adopted by the Council of the Society of American Archivists, 1992.

20. Code of Ethics for Archivists, approved the Society of American Archivists Council, February 5, 2005, http://www.archivists.org/governance/handbook/app_ethics.asp.

21. Special Libraries Association, Competencies for Information Professionals of the 21st Century, rev. 2003, http://www.sla.org/content/learn/comp2003/index.cfm.

22. Association for College and Research Libraries. Intellectual Freedom Principles for Academic Libraries: An Interpretation of the Library Bill of Rights, 1999. *Intellectual Freedom Manual*, 7th ed. Chicago: American Library Association, 2006, 166–168, http://www.ala.org/ala/oif/statementspols/statementsif/interpretations/intellectual.htm.

23. Privacy: An Interpretation of the Library Bill of Rights, adopted June 19, 2002 by the ALA Council. *Intellectual Freedom Manual*, 7th ed., 190–194, http://www.ala.org/ala/oif/statementspols/statementsif/interpretations/privacy.htm.

24. American Association of School Librarians, Position Statement on the Confidentiality of Library Records, revised July, 1999. The AASL policy incorporates ALA Policy 52.4 Confidentiality of Library Records.

25. Helen R. Adams, "The Age of the Patron: Privacy for Middle and High School Students," *School Library Media Activities Monthly* 23 (April 2007): 38.

26. Helen R. Adams, "Principals and Confidentiality of Library Records," *School Library Media Activities Monthly* 23 (September 2006): 32. See also Helen R. Adams, et al. *Privacy in the 21st Century: Issues for Public, School, and Academic Libraries.* Westport, CT: Libraries Unlimited, 2005.

27. Robert Hauptman, "Professionalism or Culpability? An Experiment in Ethics." *Wilson Library Bulletin* 50 (April 1976): 626–27.

28. "Statement on Professional Ethics, 1975," reprinted in Lindsey and Prentice, *Professional Ethics*, 54; *Intellectual Freedom Manual*, 7th ed., 260.

29. Pennsylvania State Act 1984–90, protecting the confidentiality of library records, quoted in Janis Lee, "Confidentiality: From the Stacks to the Witness

Stand: A State Law Shields a Librarian from Prosecutors Trying to Convict a Murder Suspect," *American Libraries* 19 (June 1988): 444–448, 450.

30. G. Guy Smith, "A Lawyer's Perspective on Confidentiality," *American Libraries* 19 (June 1988): 453.

31. Policy on Confidentiality of Library Records, *Intellectual Freedom Manual*, 7th ed., 295–299.

32. Herbert N. Foerstel, *Surveillance in the Stacks: The FBI's Library Awareness Program*. New York: Greenwood Press, 1991.

33. "ALA Board Expresses 'Grave' Concern on NCLIS Response to FBI Program," [press release] American Library Association, May 1988.

34. "ARL Adopts Statement on Library Users' Right to Confidentiality," [press release] Association of Research Libraries, May 5, 1988.

35. The Video Privacy Protection Act 18 USC 2710 (1988) forbids video rental and sales outlets from disclosing information about rentals or sales except in specific circumstances.

36. Ann Gerhart and Annie Groer, "Ken Starr's Reading List," *Washington Post*, March 26, 1998, B3; Bill Miller, "Starr Office Defends Book Inquiry: Bombing Probes Cited as Precedent for Subpoenas," *Washington Post*, April 4, 1998, C1, C3.

37. The Santa Cruz, California, Public Library posted a warning that under the law, the FBI could confiscate library records and prohibit the library from informing patrons that federal agents had obtained borrowing information. Kathy Ishizuka, "Warning: Uncle Sam Watching?" *School Library Journal* 49 (April 2003): 23.

38. For specific provisions of the USA PATRIOT Act and their applicability to libraries, go to http://www.ala.org/ala/oif/ifissues/usapatriotactlibrary.cfm

39. "John Does Allowed to Speak, Receive Belated Downs Award," ALA, posted June 27, 2006; "PATRIOT Act Litigation Summary." *Freedom to Read Foundation News* 31, no. 1 (March 2006): 1–2.

40. David H. Price, "Prostrate to the Patriot Act [sic]: Librarians as FBI Extension Agents," *CounterPunch* 6 March 2003. http://www.counterpunch.org/price03062003.html. Price is the author of *Threatening Anthropologists: McCarthyism and the FBI's Surveillance of Activist Anthropologists*. Durham, NC: Duke University Press, 2004.

41. "Senator Durbin Dedicates PATRIOT Success to ALA" ALA Washington Office *Newsline* 14, no. 74 (August 2, 2005).

9

———◆•◦•◆———

FUTURE

As we saw with the successive introduction of film, radio, and the Internet, the expanding array of social-networking capabilities enables libraries to expand both service and access. A promotional device as well as an information source, each new medium extends the reach of the library while posing a potential threat to it. Entering the world of Library 2.0, we can revisit the core values we explored in earlier chapters to see how they apply in an interactive, participatory information environment, one in which communication is central and users become content providers.

SERVICE

In Library 2.0, service is once again central. As wikis, blogs, chat, e-mail, YouTube, and social-networking sites have transformed the World Wide Web from the static model of Web sites and online databases to the dynamic possibilities of Web 2.0, librarians have been quick to see the possibilities for libraries. Writing in *Library Journal* in September 2006, Michael Casey and Laura Savastinuk introduced the concept of Library 2.0 as a means to revitalize a library's service and its interaction with customers. In this new formulation, it is service and not technology that is key, although new technologies enable such new services as virtual reference, personalized OPAC interfaces, and downloadable media. As Casey and Savastinuk define it,

The heart of library 2.0 is user-centered change. It is a model for library service that encourages constant and purposeful change, inviting user participation in the creation of both the physical and the virtual services they want, supported by constantly evaluating services. It also attempts to reach new users and better serve current ones through improved customer-driven offerings. Each component by itself is a step toward better serving our users; however, it is through the combined implementation of all of these that they can reach Library 2.0.[1]

All innovation, however, does not constitute Library 2.0. Casey and Savastinuk continue,

Any service, physical or virtual, that successfully reaches users, is evaluated frequently, and makes use of customer input is a Library 2.0 service. Even older, traditional services can be Library 2.0 if these criteria are met. Similarly, being new is not enough to make a service Library 2.0.[2]

In short order, librarians across the profession have employed the tools of Library 2.0 to involve library users in the enhancement of customer service: in reference through user contributions to wikis, in readers' advisories through reader reviews, and in technical services through user suggestions to improve subject access.[3]

As librarians have been quick to embrace the possibilities of this interactive environment, we have seen little consideration of its potential ethical implications. In each of these areas, where traditionally librarians have held control by their positions or expertise, the tools of Library 2.0 might be seen as undermining their professional role or undercutting their professional values. In defining the highest level of service, we asked first, "Service by whom?" In a Library 2.0 environment, the answer is librarians working in conjunction with library users. In asking, "Service for whom?" we saw that librarians have continuously sought to expand the audience for library service. In Library 2.0, everyone is not just a potential recipient of information but an active participant in its creation.

ACCESS

The ready accessibility of wikis, chat, blogs, and Web sites means that users do not need to go to the library or consult a librarian in their quest for information. In response to the question, "What information?" we again encounter questions about the quality of information. In a highly democratized environment, information that is easily available may not be the most accurate or authoritative. Librarians stamp their imprimatur of quality on the links they select and the blogs and wikis they support, but they also allow the free marketplace of ideas to function as readers contribute ideas, suggestions, and corrections. As librarians open the process of information gathering and sharing to user participation, they will need to reemphasize their role in pointing users to reliable information and educating users to become critical information consumers.

In this digital marketplace, conversation ranges far beyond ideas into the full panoply of interactive communication. As did the World Wide Web before it, Library 2.0 invites access to information that in the past was not part of a library's domain. This includes the details of personal lives available on social networking sites such as Facebook and MySpace and interchanges on blogs expressed in the vituperative language of personal insult. Protected by the First Amendment, participants in Library 2.0 are also subject to its exceptions, including obscenity laws, libel, and slander. But where participant identity is cloaked in anonymity, there is no legal recourse for those injured by false accusations or smeared by inaccurate reports. Student requests that social networking sites such as juicycampus.com be blocked have so far been turned down by university administrators reluctant to serve as institutional filters.[4]

In addition to concerns about child safety, some public libraries, such as the Manatee County Public Library in Florida, have prohibited chat rooms, e-mail, and social-networking sites as incompatible with their educational mission.[5] In other cases, the very popularity of such sites has led libraries to question the wisdom of providing access, as in Wake County, North Carolina, where the library blocked access to MySpace, pending review, because the site was attracting patrons who used the site "to recruit gang members, to sell or purchase drugs, or to view or post pornography."[6]

CONFLICTS OF INTEREST

The dilemmas posed by social-networking sites illustrate a new kind of philosophical conflict of interest, a long-standing concern of librarians that is now being experienced by school and academic officers as well. Tensions arise that are related to both service and access. On the one hand, libraries and schools wish to provide a high-demand service that greatly expands access to information in print, audio, and visual formats. On the other, they worry that much of this information is antithetical to the standards for quality and civility they have traditionally maintained.[7] Library 2.0 has thus added a whole new dimension to the question of filtering.

These philosophical conflicts of interest may confound individual practitioners as well as library institutions. Libraries may see providing access to Internet e-mail sites, chat, and social networks as enhancing service to an expanded audience of users. A practitioner may see these services as akin to providing access to pornographic Web sites, material that is protected by the First Amendment but inconsistent with the traditional role of libraries, as was the view of the Supreme Court in the Children's Internet Protection Act (CIPA) case. As more and more libraries make use of Library 2.0 tools, how is a librarian to reconcile personal reservations about such services with a library's decision to provide them?

PRIVACY

We may be seeing the most serious challenges to core library values in the interpretation of privacy protections in the Library 2.0 environment, with heightened protection in some areas and a diminished respect for confidentiality in others. By protecting the anonymity of bloggers, we see a classic expansion of access to information as participants feel free to express views that they might not otherwise have shared. We have also seen how this has led to higher levels of online incivility. Some newspapers, alarmed by the invective in reader feedback, are requiring commenters to register before sharing their views online. So while privacy has traditionally been regarded as a positive library value that protects the reader and promotes the free use of library and online resources, it has a negative side as well. While committed to protecting patrons in the use of information, libraries face challenges when protecting the identity of patrons as content providers threatens to diminish rather than enhance the information exchange.

A related concern tilts in the opposite direction. Social-networking sites by their very nature encourage the sharing of personal information. Access is provided only upon divulging certain identifying elements. Successful participation stems from sharing ideas and creations that attract the attention and approval of other site participants. But because identities are cloaked, participants may not be who they claim to be,[8] with underage youngsters or overage predators assuming a false identify in order to make online "friends."

The enormous amount of personal information available on these sites presents tempting commercial possibilities. And while it has been assumed that young people participating in social networks were not concerned about protecting their privacy, a decision by Facebook to share information about user purchases prompted a storm of criticism expressed through an online group organized to protest it. In response, Facebook now allows users to refuse to authorize the release of such information.[9]

An environment in which participants have to opt out in order to protect their privacy turns the presumption in favor of confidentiality on its head. The privacy of a library patron using a library and the confidentiality of that user's library records are protected as a matter of course and revealed only on the presentation of a court-issued subpoena, or, under the USA PATRIOT Act, on receipt of a National Security Letter. While Facebook, for example, has a similar privacy policy requiring law enforcement officials to obtain subpoenas,[10] in a social-networking environment, the presumption generally seems to be that information may be shared unless the subject of the information blocks its release.

LIBRARY ETHICS 2.0

The question of ethics in this new information environment has generated little discussion in the many articles about libraries in the digital age, virtual libraries, and Library 2.0. What is striking, however, is how applicable the core ethical values of the profession that have developed over the last century seem newly relevant and applicable. Presumptions in favor of service, access, the protection of confidentiality, and the avoidance of conflicts of interest should continue to provide librarians with an ethical approach to practice.

This continuity of values is apparent in "A Librarian's 2.0 Manifesto" posted by Web librarian Laura Cohen in November 2006.[11] Much like Mary Wright Plummer's suggestions for a library code of ethics in 1903, Cohen's manifesto is a strong statement of professional identify drafted by a single, committed librarian. Further, while it encompasses the user-centered, participatory nature of Library 2.0, it also reflects the ethical obligations manifested in past and present codes of library ethics. In Cohen's declaration, the 2.0 librarian is aware of the fast-changing universe of information culture, continues to learn about that culture and those who use it, is active in moving the library forward, is courageous in designing new services, and is experimental, risk-taking, collaborative, and fun-loving. The 2.0 librarian is an advocate and an honest observer of library practices. Plummer would approve of the manifesto's conclusion, "I will validate through my actions, librarians' vital, relevant, professional role in any type of information culture that evolves." Charles Knowles Bolton, on the other hand, might be bemused by its intention to "encourage my library's administration to blog."

In providing service, the 2.0 librarian in Cohen's manifesto responds to the changing environment by offering resources and services that users want and need, even if they are not perfect, and modifies them based on user feedback. The 2.0 librarian is willing to go wherever users are, online or in physical space, and sees the library through the eyes of its users rather than in library terms. Both Helen Haines and Charles Robinson could agree with Cohen's declaration that, "I will educate myself about the information culture of my users and look for ways to incorporate what I learn into library service."

Though the manifesto mentions service many times, it makes no specific mention of access. It does provide, however, that the 2.0 librarian takes advantage of new technologies in order to benefit users. Melvil Dewey would concur in its statement that, "I will not fear Google or related services, but rather will take advantage of these services to benefit users while providing excellent library services that users need." In the view of the 2.0 librarian, service is enhanced when users contribute to content. Sanford Berman would applaud its call for "an open catalog that provides personalized interactive features that users expect in online information environments." And though it does not mention intellectual freedom, the manifesto's emphasis on openness accords with the Library Bill of Rights in stating that, "I will create open Web sites that allow users to join with librarians to contribute content in order to enhance their learning experience and provide assistance to their peers."

BEST READING FOR THE LARGEST NUMBER AT THE LEAST COST

Unlike the ALA's interest in library ethics that started slowly at the beginning of the twentieth century and accelerated as the profession evolved and faced new challenges, the association's motto, "The best reading for the largest number at the least cost," languished on letterheads and in professional consciousness. In January 1988, however, on a motion at the ALA's midwinter meeting by Norman Horrocks, honorary life member and ALA parliamentarian, and Marvin Scilken, long time ALA council member, the association voted to reinstate it.[12] Nonetheless, at midwinter 2004, a new member of the ALA Executive Board proposed that the motto be abandoned because "it no longer adequately reflects the aims, mission, and activities of the association." In the year that the phrase Web 2.0 was coined, the ALA Council rejected the move to mothball its motto. In approving this decision, John Berry, editor of *Library Journal*, noted the continuing validity of the motto in the digital age.

Old Dewey got it right. "Best reading" is either a value judgment, or it simply means collections carefully selected by librarians to meet that most basic criterion, that they best serve the library users. It may seem like a stretch, but "reading" can mean electronic databases, DVDs, or printed books, as long as we accept the kinds of "literacy" libraries promote these days.

"The largest number" clearly means librarians believe in doing what libraries have always done: provide something for everyone, from youngest child to the oldest patron.

Finally, ... "least cost" pertains to carefully managed purchasing and skillfully negotiated licenses and contracts.... [Dewey] would have cheered our modern consortia and the tough negotiators who get their users the most bang for the buck for library resources.[13]

Although Berry did not comment on the ethical implications of the ALA's motto, its focus on service to library users and access to information in all formats embodies two of the profession's core ethical values. Along with protecting patron confidentiality and avoiding conflicts of interest, these ethical obligations have survived a century of debates, drafts, resolutions, interpretations, practice, and revisions in an ongoing cycle. Across time and professional specialties, they reflect how the understanding of our core values has been able to adapt to changes in society, technology, and practice. Their applicability to practice in the world of Library 2.0 attests to their continued relevance and importance.

END NOTES

1. Michael E. Casey and Laura C. Savastinuk, "Library 2.0," *Library Journal* *(1976)* 131 (September 1, 2006): 40–42.

2. Casey and Savastinuk, "Library 2.0," 242.

3. See, for example, Neal Wyatt, "2.0 for Readers," *Library Journal* (1976) 132 (November 1, 2007): 30–33. Kimberly Bolan, Meg Canada, and Rob Cullin, "Web, Library, and Teen Services 2.0," *Young Adult Library Services* 5 (Winter 2007): 40–43. Diane Murley. "What Is All the Fuss about Library 2.0?" *Law Library Journal* 100 (Winter 2008): 197–204.

4. Jeffrey R. Young, "How to Combat a Campus-Gossip Web Site (and Why You Shouldn't)," *The Chronicle of Higher Education* (March 28, 2008): A16.

5. "Manatee County Pulls the Plug on MySpace," *American Libraries* 38 (January 2007): 26–27.

6. Oder, Norman. "NC System Blocks MySpace," *Library Journal (1876)* 132 (April 1, 2007): 18.

7. For a work exploring the negative impact of the Internet, see Andrew Keen, *The Cult of the Amateur: How the Internet is Killing Our Culture.* New York: Doubleday/Currency, 2007.

8. For a humorous example, see Peter Steiner's cartoon, "On the Internet, Nobody Knows You're a Dog," *The New Yorker* 69 (July 5, 1993): 61.

9. Siva Vaidhyanathan, "Naked in the 'Nonopticon," *The Chronicle of Higher Education* (February 15, 2008): *Chronicle Review* 54 at 7.

10. Facebook Privacy Principles, effective as of December 6, 2007, http://www.facebook.com/policy.php (accessed March 30, 2008).

11. "A Librarian's 2.0 Manifesto," http://www.tinyurl.com/ybwq6s. John N. Berry III, "Library 2.0 Comes into View," *Library Journal* (1976) 132 (April 15, 2007): 10. The text of the manifesto can also be found in a mashup at http://www.youtube.com/watch?v=ZblrRs3fkSU. Many bloggers responded enthusiastically to "A Librarian's 2.0 Manifesto," although one accused its author of being a library school student. Cohen was at the time was nearing retirement as a Web support librarian at the State University of New York at Albany.

12. Lillian N. Gerhardt, "That Motto of ALA: On What Occasion Will It Ever Again Be Appropriate?" *School Library Journal* 34 (April 1988): 4.

13. John N. Berry III, "Dewey's ALA Motto Still Works Fine," *Library Journal (1876)* 129 (February 15, 2004): 8.

LIBRARY ETHICS TIMELINE

This timeline brings together the codes of ethics, interpretations of the ALA Library Bill of Rights, legislation, and court decisions that establish the ethical framework for library practice. Codes of ethics appear in shaded circles, interpretations of the Library Bill of Rights in white oblongs, and court decisions and legislation in black rectangles. Sources generally can be found in the text. Documents related to ALA codes of ethics and Interpretations of the Library Bill of Rights can be found at http://www.ala.org/oif.

Ethics Timeline 1791-1972

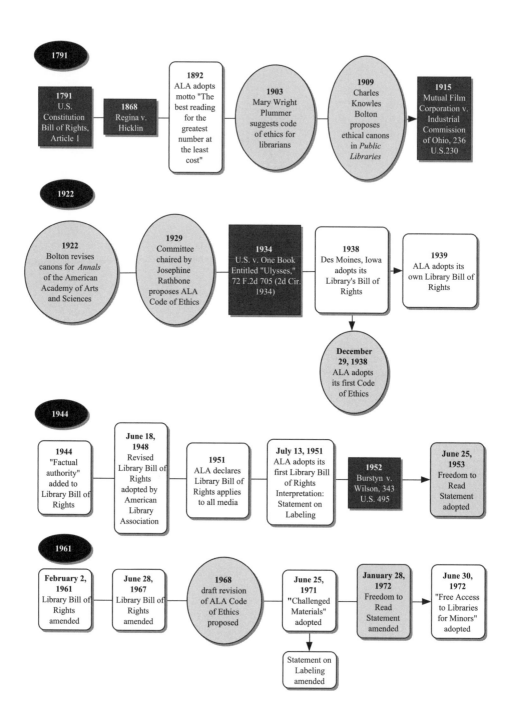

1791

1791
U.S. Constitution Bill of Rights, Article 1

1868
Regina v. Hicklin

1892
ALA adopts motto "The best reading for the greatest number at the least cost"

1903
Mary Wright Plummer suggests code of ethics for librarians

1909
Charles Knowles Bolton proposes ethical canons in *Public Libraries*

1915
Mutual Film Corporation v. Industrial Commission of Ohio, 236 U.S.230

1922

1922
Bolton revises canons for *Annals* of the American Academy of Arts and Sciences

1929
Committee chaired by Josephine Rathbone proposes ALA Code of Ethics

1934
U.S. v. One Book Entitled "Ulysses," 72 F.2d 705 (2d Cir. 1934)

1938
Des Moines, Iowa adopts its Library's Bill of Rights

1939
ALA adopts its own Library Bill of Rights

December 29, 1938
ALA adopts its first Code of Ethics

1944

1944
"Factual authority" added to Library Bill of Rights

June 18, 1948
Revised Library Bill of Rights adopted by American Library Association

1951
ALA declares Library Bill of Rights applies to all media

July 13, 1951
ALA adopts its first Library Bill of Rights Interpretation: Statement on Labeling

1952
Burstyn v. Wilson, 343 U.S. 495

June 25, 1953
Freedom to Read Statement adopted

1961

February 2, 1961
Library Bill of Rights amended

June 28, 1967
Library Bill of Rights amended

1968
draft revision of ALA Code of Ethics proposed

June 25, 1971
"Challenged Materials" adopted

January 28, 1972
Freedom to Read Statement amended

June 30, 1972
"Free Access to Libraries for Minors" adopted

Statement on Labeling amended

Ethics Timeline 1973-1987

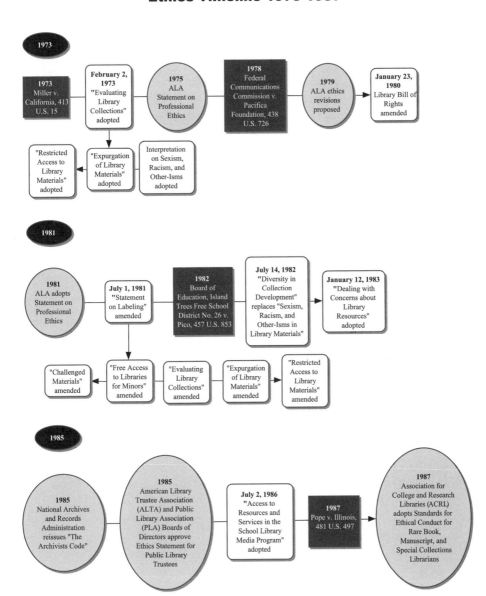

1973

1973
Miller v. California, 413 U.S. 15

February 2, 1973
"Evaluating Library Collections" adopted

1975
ALA Statement on Professional Ethics

1978
Federal Communications Commission v. Pacifica Foundation, 438 U.S. 726

1979
ALA ethics revisions proposed

January 23, 1980
Library Bill of Rights amended

"Restricted Access to Library Materials" adopted

"Expurgation of Library Materials" adopted

Interpretation on Sexism, Racism, and Other-Isms adopted

1981

1981
ALA adopts Statement on Professional Ethics

July 1, 1981
"Statement on Labeling" amended

1982
Board of Education, Island Trees Free School District No. 26 v. Pico, 457 U.S. 853

July 14, 1982
"Diversity in Collection Development" replaces "Sexism, Racism, and Other-Isms in Library Materials"

January 12, 1983
"Dealing with Concerns about Library Resources" adopted

"Challenged Materials" amended

"Free Access to Libraries for Minors" amended

"Evaluating Library Collections" amended

"Expurgation of Library Materials" amended

"Restricted Access to Library Materials" amended

1985

1985
National Archives and Records Administration reissues "The Archivists Code"

1985
American Library Trustee Association (ALTA) and Public Library Association (PLA) Boards of Directors approve Ethics Statement for Public Library Trustees

July 2, 1986
"Access to Resources and Services in the School Library Media Program" adopted

1987
Pope v. Illinois, 481 U.S. 497

1987
Association for College and Research Libraries (ACRL) adopts Standards for Ethical Conduct for Rare Book, Manuscript, and Special Collections Librarians

Ethics Timeline 1988-1996

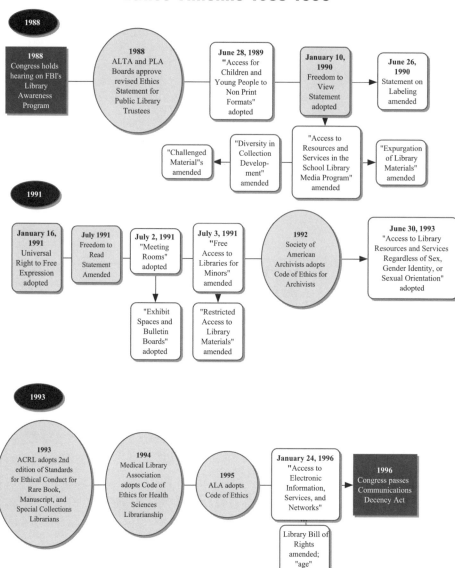

Ethics Timeline 1996-2008

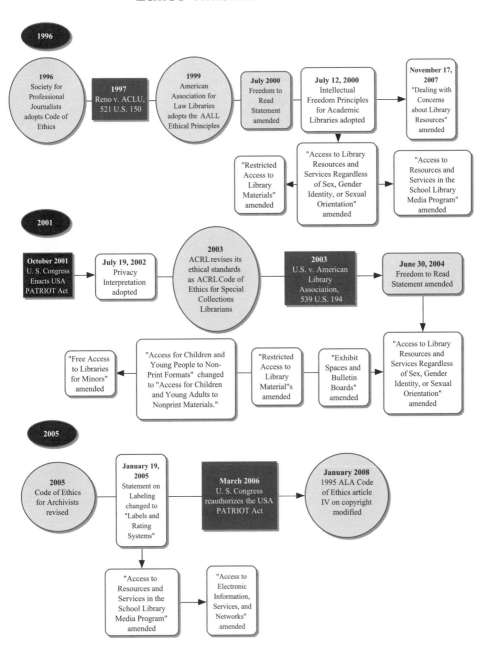

APPENDIX: CODES OF ETHICS

AMERICAN LIBRARY ASSOCIATION

ALA Code of Ethics for Librarians (1938) http://www.ala.org/ala/oif/statementspols/codeofethics/coehistory/1939code.pdf

ALA Statement on Professional Ethics (1981), *Intellectual Freedom Manual*, 7th ed. Chicago: American Library Association, 262–63.

Code of Ethics of the American Library Association (1995, modified 2008) http://www.ala.org/ala/oif/statementspols/codeofethics/codeethics.htm

Library Bill of Rights (1948, amended 1961, 1980, reaffirmed, 1996) http://www.ala.org/ala/oif/statementspols/statementsif/librarybillrights.htm

American Association of Law Libraries Ethical Principles (1999) http://www.aallnet.org/about/policy_ethics.asp

Association of College and Research Libraries (ACRL) Code of Ethics for Special Collections Librarians (2003) http://www.rbms.info/standards/code_of_ethics.shtml

Medical Library Association (MLA) Code of Ethics for Health Sciences Librarianship (1994) http://www.mlanet.org/about/ethics.html

Society of American Archivists Code of Ethics for Archivists (2005) http://www.archivists.org/governance/handbook/app_ethics.asp

A Librarian's 2.0 Manifesto (2006) http://liblogs.albany.edu/library20/2006/11/a_librarians_20_manifesto.html

ALA CODE OF ETHICS FOR LIBRARIANS (1938)

Preamble

1. The library as an institution exists for the benefit of a given constituency, whether it be the citizens of a community, members of an educational institution, or some larger or more specialized group. Those who enter the library profession assume an obligation to maintain ethical standards of behavior in relation to the governing authority under which they work, to the library constituency, to the library as an institution and to fellow workers on the staff, to other members of the library profession, and to society in general.

2. The term librarian in this code applies to any person who is employed by a library to do work that is recognized to be professional in character according to standards established by the American Library Association.

3. This code sets forth principles of ethical behavior for the professional librarian. It is not a declaration of prerogatives nor a statement of recommended practices in specific situations.

I. Relation of the Librarian to the Governing Authority

4. The librarian should perform his duties with realization of the fact that final jurisdiction over the administration of the library rests in the officially constituted governing authority. This authority may be vested in a designated individual, or in a group such as a committee or board.

5. The chief librarian should keep the governing authority informed on professional standards and progressive action. Each librarian should be responsible for carrying out the policies of the governing authority and its appointed executives with a spirit of loyalty to the library.

6. The chief librarian should interpret decisions of the governing authority to the staff, and should act as liaison officer in maintaining friendly relations between staff members and those in authority.

7. Recommendations to the governing authority for the appointment of a staff member should be made by the chief librarian solely upon the basis of the candidate's professional and personal qualifications for the position. Continuance in service and promotion should depend upon the quality of performance, following a definite and known policy. Whenever the good of the service requires a change in personnel, timely warning should be given. If desirable adjustment cannot be made, unsatisfactory service should be terminated in accordance with the policy of the library and the rules of tenure.

8. Resolutions, petitions, and requests of a staff organization or group should be submitted through a duly appointed representative to the chief librarian. If a mutually satisfactory solution cannot be reached, the chief librarian, on request of the staff, should transmit the matter to the governing authority. The staff may further request that they be allowed to send a representative to the governing authority, in order to present their opinions in person.

II. Relation of the Librarian to His Constituency

9. The chief librarian, aided by staff members in touch with the constituency, should study the present and future needs of the library, and should acquire materials on the basis of those needs. Provision should be made for as wide a range of publications and as varied a representation of viewpoints as is consistent with the policies of the library and with the funds available.

10. It is the librarian's responsibility to make the resources and services of the library known to its potential users. Impartial service should be rendered to all who are entitled to use the library.

11. It is the librarian's obligation to treat as confidential any private information obtained through contact with library patrons.

12. The librarian should try to protect library property and to inculcate in users a sense of their responsibility for its preservation.

III. Relation of the Librarian Within His Library

13. The chief librarian should delegate authority, encourage a sense of responsibility and initiative on the part of staff members, provide for their professional development, and appreciate good work. Staff members should be informed of the duties of their positions and the policies and problems of the library.

14. Loyalty to fellow workers and a spirit of courteous cooperation, whether between individuals or between departments, are essential to effective library service.

15. Criticism of library policies, service, and personnel should be offered only to the proper authority for the sole purpose of improvement of the library.

16. Acceptance of a position in a library incurs an obligation to remain long enough to repay the library for the expense incident to adjustment. A contract signed or agreement made should be adhered to faithfully until it expires or is dissolved by mutual consent.

17. Resignations should be made long enough before they are to take effect to allow adequate time for the work to be put in shape and a successor appointed.

18. A librarian should never enter into a business dealing on behalf of the library which will result in personal profit.

19. A librarian should never turn the library's resources to personal use, to the detriment of services which the library renders to its patrons.

IV. Relation of the Librarian to His Profession

20. Librarians should recognize librarianship as an educational profession and realize that the growing effectiveness of their service is dependent upon their own development.

21. In view of the importance of ability and personality traits in library work, a librarian should encourage only those persons with suitable aptitudes to enter the library profession and should discourage the continuance in service of the unfit.

22. Recommendations should be confidential and should be fair to the candidate and the prospective employer by presenting an unbiased statement of strong and weak points.

23. Librarians should have a sincere belief and a critical interest in the library profession. They should endeavor to achieve and maintain adequate salaries and proper working conditions.

24. Formal appraisal of the policies or practices of another library should be given only upon the invitation of that library's governing authority or chief librarian.

25. Librarians, in recognizing the essential unity of their profession, should have membership in library organizations and should be ready to attend and participate in library meetings and conferences.

V. Relation of the Librarian to Society

26. Librarians should encourage a general realization of the value of library service and be informed concerning movements, organizations, and institutions whose aims are compatible with those of the library.

27. Librarians should participate in public and community affairs and so represent the library that it will take its place among educational, social, and cultural agencies.

28. A librarian's conduct should be such as to maintain public esteem for the library and for library work.

Approved by the ALA Council, December 29, 1938

ALA STATEMENT ON PROFESSIONAL ETHICS (1981)

Introduction

Since 1939, the American Library Association has recognized the importance of codifying and making known to the public and the profession the principles which guide librarians in action. This latest revision of the CODE OF ETHICS reflects changes in the nature of the profession and in its social and institutional environment. It should be revised and augmented as necessary.

Librarians significantly influence or control the selection, organization, preservation, and dissemination of information. In a political system grounded in an informed citizenry, librarians are members of a profession explicitly committed to intellectual freedom and the freedom of access to information. We have a special obligation to ensure the free flow of information and ideas to the present and future generations.

Librarians are dependent upon one another for the bibliographical resources that enable us to provide information services, and have obligations for maintaining the highest level of personal integrity and competence.

Code of Ethics

   I. Librarians must provide the highest level of service through appropriate and usefully organized collections, fair and equitable circulation and service policies, and skillful, accurate, unbiased, and courteous responses to all requests for assistance.

  II. Librarians must resist all efforts by groups or individuals to censor library materials.

 III. Librarians must protect each user's right to privacy with respect to information sought or received, materials consulted, borrowed, or acquired.

 IV. Librarians must adhere to the principles of due process and equality of opportunity in peer relationships and personnel actions.

  V. Librarians must distinguish clearly in their actions and statements between their personal philosophies and attitudes and those of an institution or professional body.

 VI. Librarians must avoid situations in which personal interests might be served or financial benefits gained at the expense of library users, colleagues, or the employing institution.

Adopted by the ALA Council, June 30, 1981.

ALA CODE OF ETHICS (1995, MODIFIED 2008)

As members of the American Library Association, we recognize the importance of codifying and making known to the profession and to the general public the ethical principles that guide the work of librarians, other professionals providing information services, library trustees and library staffs.

Ethical dilemmas occur when values are in conflict. The American Library Association Code of Ethics states the values to which we are committed, and embodies the ethical responsibilities of the profession in this changing information environment.

We significantly influence or control the selection, organization, preservation, and dissemination of information. In a political system grounded in an informed citizenry, we are members of a profession explicitly committed to intellectual freedom and the freedom of access to information. We have a special obligation to ensure the free flow of information and ideas to present and future generations.

The principles of this Code are expressed in broad statements to guide ethical decision making. These statements provide a framework; they cannot and do not dictate conduct to cover particular situations.

I. We provide the highest level of service to all library users through appropriate and usefully organized resources; equitable service policies; equitable access; and accurate, unbiased, and courteous responses to all requests.

II. We uphold the principles of intellectual freedom and resist all efforts to censor library resources.

III. We protect each library user's right to privacy and confidentiality with respect to information sought or received and resources consulted, borrowed, acquired or transmitted.

IV. We respect intellectual property rights and advocate balance between the interests of information users and rights holders.

V. We treat co-workers and other colleagues with respect, fairness, and good faith, and advocate conditions of employment that safeguard the rights and welfare of all employees of our institutions.

VI. We do not advance private interests at the expense of library users, colleagues, or our employing institutions.

VII. We distinguish between our personal convictions and professional duties and do not allow our personal beliefs to interfere with fair representation of the aims of our institutions or the provision of access to their information resources.

VIII. We strive for excellence in the profession by maintaining and enhancing our own knowledge and skills, by encouraging the professional development of co-workers, and by fostering the aspirations of potential members of the profession.

Adopted by the ALA Council June 1995, modified January 22, 2008.
Reprinted by permission of the American Library Association

ALA LIBRARY BILL OF RIGHTS (1948, 1961, 1980, 1996)

The American Library Association affirms that all libraries are forums for information and ideas, and that the following basic policies should guide their services.

I. Books and other library resources should be provided for the interest, information, and enlightenment of all people of the community the library serves. Materials should not be excluded because of the origin, background, or views of those contributing to their creation.

II. Libraries should provide materials and information presenting all points of view on current and historical issues. Materials should not be proscribed or removed because of partisan or doctrinal disapproval.

III. Libraries should challenge censorship in the fulfillment of their responsibility to provide information and enlightenment.

IV. Libraries should cooperate with all persons and groups concerned with resisting abridgment of free expression and free access to ideas.

V. A person's right to use a library should not be denied or abridged because of origin, age, background, or views.

VI. Libraries which make exhibit spaces and meeting rooms available to the public they serve should make such facilities available on an equitable basis, regardless of the beliefs or affiliations of individuals or groups requesting their use.

Adopted June 18, 1948.
Amended February 2, 1961, and January 23, 1980,
Reaffirmed January 23, 1996,
by the ALA Council

AMERICAN ASSOCIATION OF LAW LIBRARIES
ETHICAL PRINCIPLES (1999)

Preamble

When individuals have ready access to legal information, they can participate fully in the affairs of their government. By collecting, organizing, preserving, and retrieving legal information, the members of the American Association of Law Libraries enable people to make this ideal of democracy a reality.

Legal information professionals have an obligation to satisfy the needs, to promote the interests and to respect the values of their clientele. Law firms, corporations, academic and governmental institutions and the general public have legal information needs that are best addressed by professionals committed to the belief that serving these information needs is a noble calling and that fostering the equal participation of diverse people in library services underscores one of our basic tenets, open access to information for all individuals.

Service

We promote open and effective access to legal and related information. Further we recognize the need to establish methods of preserving, maintaining and retrieving legal information in many different forms.

We uphold a duty to our clientele to develop service policies that respect confidentiality and privacy.

We provide zealous service using the most appropriate resources and implementing programs consistent with our institution's mission and goals.

We acknowledge the limits on service imposed by our institutions and by the duty to avoid the unauthorized practice of law.

Business Relationships

We promote fair and ethical trade practices.

We have a duty to avoid situations in which personal interests might be served or significant benefits gained at the expense of library users, colleagues, or our employing institutions.

We strive to obtain the maximum value for our institution's fiscal resources, while at the same time making judicious, analytical and rational use of our institution's information resources.

Professional Responsibilities

We relate to our colleagues with respect and in a spirit of cooperation.

We distinguish between our personal convictions and professional duties and do not allow our personal beliefs to interfere with the service we provide.

We recognize and respect the rights of the owner and the user of intellectual property.

We strive for excellence in the profession by maintaining and enhancing our own knowledge and skills, by encouraging the professional development of co-workers, and by fostering the aspirations of potential members of the profession.

Approved by the AALL membership, April 5, 1999.
Reprinted by permission of the American Association of Law Libraries

ASSOCIATION OF COLLEGE AND RESEARCH LIBRARIES CODE OF ETHICS FOR SPECIAL COLLECTIONS LIBRARIANS (2003)

NOTE: "Standards for Ethical Conduct for Rare Book, Manuscript, and Special Collections Librarians" first appeared in 1987 and was designed to amplify and supplement the ALA Code of Ethics. A second edition of the Standards was approved by ACRL in 1993. This version, recast as a simplified "Code of Ethics for Special Collections Librarians" with commentary, was approved by ACRL in October 2003.

Preamble

Special collections librarians share fundamental values with the entire library profession. They should be thoroughly familiar with the ALA Code of Ethics and must adhere to the principles of fairness, freedom, professional excellence, and respect for individual rights expressed therein. Furthermore, special collections librarians have extraordinary responsibilities and opportunities associated with the care of cultural property, the preservation of original artifacts, and the support of scholarship based on primary research materials. At times their commitment to free access to information may conflict with their mission to protect and preserve the objects in their care. When values come into conflict, librarians must bring their experience and judgment to bear on each case in order to arrive at the best solution, always bearing in mind that the constituency for special collections includes future generations.

Other stresses arise naturally from the fact that special collections often have great monetary as well as documentary and aesthetic value. Special collections librarians must exercise extreme caution in situations that have the potential to allow them to profit personally from library-related activities. The highest standard of behavior must be maintained, as propriety is essential to the maintenance of public trust in the institution and in its staff.

Definitions

Special collections librarian: An employee of a special collections library or any library staff member whose duties involve work with special collections materials. The principles in this Code relate primarily to professional staff (typically librarians, curators, archivists, and conservators), but all library staff members must be aware of the need to avoid potential and even apparent conflicts of interest.

Special collections library: A library, or an administrative unit (such as department) of a larger library, devoted to collecting, organizing, preserving, and describing special collections materials and making them accessible. Also referred to as "the institution."

Special collections materials: The entire range of textual, graphic and artifact primary source materials in analog and digital formats, including printed books, manuscripts, photographs, maps, artworks, audio-visual materials, and realia.

Code of Ethics

I. Special collections librarians must not compete with their library in collecting or in any other activity.

II. All outside employment and professional activities must be undertaken within the fundamental premise that the special collections librarian's first responsibility is to the library, that the activity will not interfere with the librarian's ability to discharge this responsibility, and that it will not compromise the library's professional integrity or reputation.

III. Special collections librarians must not engage in any dealing or appraisal of special collections materials, and they must not recommend materials for purchase if they have any undisclosed financial interest in them.

IV. Special collections librarians must decline all gifts, loans, or other dispensations, or things of value that are available to them in connection with their duties for the library.

V. Special collections librarians may not withhold information about the library's holdings or sequester collection materials in order to further their own research and publication.

VI. Special collections librarians are responsible for protecting the confidentiality of researchers and materials as required by legal statutes, donor agreements, or policies of the library.

Approved by ACRL, October 2003.
Reprinted by permission of the American Library Association

MEDICAL LIBRARY ASSOCIATION CODE OF ETHICS
FOR HEALTH SCIENCES LIBRARIANSHIP (1994)

Goals and Principles for Ethical Conduct

The health sciences librarian believes that knowledge is the sine qua non of informed decisions in health care, education, and research and the health sciences librarian serves society, clients, and the institution, by working to ensure that informed decisions can be made.

Society

- The health sciences librarian promotes access to health information for all and creates and maintains conditions of freedom of inquiry, thought, and expression that facilitate informed health care decisions.

Clients

- The health sciences librarian works without prejudice to meet the client's information needs.
- The health sciences librarian respects the privacy of clients and protects the confidentiality of the client relationship.
- The health sciences librarian ensures that the best available information is provided to the client.

Institution

- The health sciences librarian provides leadership and expertise in the design, development, and ethical management of knowledge-based information systems that meet the information needs and obligations of the institution.

Profession

- The health sciences librarian advances and upholds the philosophy and ideals of the profession.
- The health sciences librarian advocates and advances the knowledge and standards of the profession.
- The health sciences librarian conducts all professional relationships with courtesy and respect.
- The health sciences librarian maintains high standards of professional integrity.

Self

- The health sciences librarian assumes personal responsibility for developing and maintaining professional excellence.

Reprinted by permission of the Medical Library Association

SOCIETY OF AMERICAN ARCHIVISTS CODE OF ETHICS FOR ARCHIVISTS (2005)

Preamble

The Code of Ethics for Archivists establishes standards for the archival profession. It introduces new members of the profession to those standards, reminds experienced archivists of their professional responsibilities, and serves as a model for institutional policies. It also is intended to inspire public confidence in the profession.

This code provides an ethical framework to guide members of the profession. It does not provide the solution to specific problems.

The term "archivist" as used in this code encompasses all those concerned with the selection, control, care, preservation, and administration of historical and documentary records of enduring value.

I. Purpose

The Society of American Archivists recognizes the importance of educating the profession and general public about archival ethics by codifying ethical principles to guide the work of archivists. This code provides a set of principles to which archivists aspire.

II. Professional Relationships

Archivists select, preserve, and make available historical and documentary records of enduring value. Archivists cooperate, collaborate, and respect each institution and its mission and collecting policy. Respect and cooperation form the basis of all professional relationships with colleagues and users.

III. Judgment

Archivists should exercise professional judgment in acquiring, appraising, and processing historical materials. They should not allow personal beliefs or perspectives to affect their decisions.

IV. Trust

Archivists should not profit or otherwise benefit from their privileged access to and control of historical records and documentary materials.

V. Authenticity and Integrity

Archivists strive to preserve and protect the authenticity of records in their holdings by documenting their creation and use in hard copy and electronic formats. They have a fundamental obligation to preserve the intellectual and physical integrity of those records.

Archivists may not alter, manipulate, or destroy data or records to conceal facts or distort evidence.

VI. Access

Archivists strive to promote open and equitable access to their services and the records in their care without discrimination or preferential treatment, and in accordance with legal requirements, cultural sensitivities, and institutional policies. Archivists recognize their responsibility to promote the use of records as a fundamental purpose of the keeping of archives. Archivists may place restrictions on access for the protection of privacy or confidentiality of information in the records.

VII. Privacy

Archivists protect the privacy rights of donors and individuals or groups who are the subject of records. They respect all users' right to privacy by maintaining the confidentiality of their research and protecting any personal information collected about them in accordance with the institution's security procedures.

VIII. Security / Protection

Archivists protect all documentary materials for which they are responsible and guard them against defacement, physical damage, deterioration, and theft. Archivists should cooperate with colleagues and law enforcement agencies to apprehend and prosecute thieves and vandals.

IX. Law

Archivists must uphold all federal, state, and local laws.

Approved by the SAA Council, February 5, 2005.
Reprinted by permission of the Society of American Archivists

A LIBRARIAN'S 2.0 MANIFESTO (2006)

I will recognize that the universe of information culture is changing fast and that libraries need to respond positively to these changes to provide resources and services that users need and want.

I will educate myself about the information culture of my users and look for ways to incorporate what I learn into library services.

I will not be defensive about my library, but will look clearly at its situation and make an honest assessment about what can be accomplished.

I will become an active participant in moving my library forward.

I will recognize that libraries change slowly, and will work with my colleagues to expedite our responsiveness to change.

I will be courageous about proposing new services and new ways of providing services, even though some of my colleagues will be resistant.

I will enjoy the excitement and fun of positive change and will convey this to colleagues and users.

I will let go of previous practices if there is a better way to do things now, even if these practices once seemed so great.

I will take an experimental approach to change and be willing to make mistakes.

I will not wait until something is perfect before I release it, and I'll modify it based on user feedback.

I will not fear Google or related services, but rather will take advantage of these services to benefit users while also providing excellent library services that users need.

I will avoid requiring users to see things in librarians' terms but rather will shape services to reflect users' preferences and expectations.

I will be willing to go where users are, both online and in physical spaces, to practice my profession.

I will create open Web sites that allow users to join with librarians to contribute content in order to enhance their learning experience and provide assistance to their peers.

I will lobby for an open catalog that provides personalized, interactive features that users expect in online information environments.

I will encourage my library's administration to blog.

I will validate, through my actions, librarians' vital and relevant professional role in any type of information culture that evolves.

Posted November, 2006 by Laura Cohen, web support librarian, University of Albany, NY, Laura's blog Library 2.0 An Academic Perspective. http://www. tinyurl.com/ybwq6s

Reprinted by permission of Laura Cohen

FURTHER READING

TOOLS

ALA Office for Intellectual Freedom. *Intellectual Freedom Manual*. 7th ed. Chicago: American Library Association, 2006. See also materials at http://www.ala.org/ala/oif.

———. American Library Association. History of the Code of Ethics, http://www.ala.org/ala/oif/statementspols/codeofethics/coehistory.

Lindsey, Jonathan A., and Ann E. Prentice. *Professional Ethics and Librarians*. Phoenix, AZ: Oryx Press, 1985.

Minow, Mary, and Tomas A. Lipinski. *The Library's Legal Answer Book*. Chicago: American Library Association, 2003.

Moore, Mary Y. *The Successful Library Trustee*. Chicago: American Library Association, 2005.

PHILOSOPHICAL AND LEGAL

Aiken, Julian. "Outdated and Irrelevant? Rethinking the Library Bill of Rights—Does It Work in the Real World?" *American Libraries* 38 (September 2007): 54–56.

Budd, John M. "Toward a Practical and Normative Ethics for Librarianship." *Library Quarterly* 76 (July 2006): 251–269.

Hauptman, Robert. "Professionalism or Culpability? An Experiment in Ethics." *Wilson Library Bulletin* 50 (April 1976): 626–27.

———. "Professional Responsibility Reconsidered. *RQ* 35 (Spring 1996): 327–29.

Hauptman, Robert, ed. "Ethics and the Dissemination of Information," *Library Trends* 40 (Fall 1991): 199–375.

Koehler, Wallace C., and J. Michael Pemberton. "A Search for Core Values: Towards a Model Code of Ethics for Information Professionals." *Journal of Information Ethics* 9 (Spring 2000): 26–54.

Swan, John, and Noel Peattie. *The Freedom to Lie: A Debate about Democracy.* Jefferson, NC: McFarland, 1989.

Wengert, Robert, ed. "Ethical Issues of Information Technology." *Library Trends* 49 (Winter 2001): 391–537.

Wiegand, Wayne A., ed. "The Library Bill of Rights." *Library Trends* 45 (Summer 1996): 1–127.

CASE STUDIES

White, Herbert S. *Ethical Dilemmas in Libraries: A Collection of Case Studies.* New York: G. K. Hall, 1992.

Zipkowitz, Fay. *Professional Ethics in Librarianship: A Real Life Casebook.* Jefferson, NC: McFarland, 1996.

IDENTITY

Gorman, Michael. *Our Enduring Values: Librarianship in the 21st Century.* Chicago: American Library Association, 2000.

———. *The Enduring Library: Technology, Tradition, and the Quest for Balance.* Chicago: American Library Association, 2003.

Kranich, Nancy, ed. *Libraries and Democracy: The Cornerstone of Liberty.* Chicago: American Library Association, 2001.

Lancaster, F. W., ed. *Ethics and the Librarian.* Urbana-Champaign, IL: University of Illinois Graduate School of Library and Information Science, 1991.

SERVICE

Alire, Camila A., and Jacqueline Ayala. *Serving Latino Communities*, 2nd ed. New York: Neal-Schuman, 2007.

American Library Association. *Unattended Children in the Public Library: A Resource Guide.* Chicago: 1999.

Dewey, Barbara I., and Loretta Parham, eds. *Achieving Diversity.* New York: Neal-Schuman, 2006.

Dowd, Frances Smardo. *Latchkey Children in the Library and the Community: Issues, Strategies, and Programs.* Phoenix, AZ: Oryx Press, 1991.

Geiszler, Robert W. "Patron Behavior in the Public Library: *Kreimer v. Morristown* Revisited," *Journal of Information Ethics* 7 (Spring 1998): 54–67.

Honnold, Rosemary, and Saralyn A. Mesaros. *Serving Seniors.* New York: Neal-Schuman, 2004.

McNeil, Beth, and Denise J. Johnson. *Patron Behavior in Libraries: A Handbook of Positive Approaches to Negative Situations.* Chicago: American Library Association, 1996.

Sarkodie-Mensah, Kwasi, ed. *Helping the Difficult Library Patron: New Approaches to Examining and Resolving a Long-Standing and Ongoing Problem.* New York: Haworth Information Press, 2002. (*The Reference Librarian*, no. 75–76)

ACCESS

American Booksellers Foundation for Free Expression. Banned Books Week, http://www.abffe.org/.

Doyle, Robert P. *Banned Books: 2007 Resource Guide*. Chicago: American Library Association, 2007.

Random House. "First Amendment First Aid Kit: What to Do if Someone Challenges a Book," 2004, http://www.randomhouse.com/teens/firstamendment/strategies.html.

Historical Perspective

Boyer, Paul. *Purity in Print: Book Censorship in America from the Gilded Age to the Computer Age*. 2nd ed. Madison, WI: University of Wisconsin Press, 2002.

Garrison, Dee. *The Apostles of Culture: The Public Librarian and American Society, 1876–1920*. New York: Free Press, 1979.

Geller, Evelyn. *Forbidden Books in American Public Libraries, 1876–1939: A Study in Cultural Change*. Westport, CT: Greenwood Press, 1984.

Lingo, Marci. "Forbidden Fruit: The Banning of *The Grapes of Wrath* in the Kern County Free Library," *Libraries & Culture* 38 (Fall 2003): 351–377.

Robbins, Louise B. *Censorship and the American Library: The American Library Association's Response to Threats to Intellectual Freedom, 1939–1969*. Westport, CT: Greenwood Press, 1996.

Selection Versus Censorship

Asheim, Lester. "The Librarian's Responsibility: Not Censorship, But Selection." *Wilson Library Bulletin* 28 (September 1953): 63–67.

———. "Not Censorship, But Selection: A Reappraisal." *Wilson Library Bulletin* 58 (November 1983): 180–184.

Fialkoff, Francine. "Selection, Not Censorship." *Library Journal (1976)* 129 (May 15, 2002): 69.

Intner, Sheila S. "Censorship Versus Selection, One More Time." *Technicalities* 24 (May/June 2004): 1, 7–10.

Self-Censorship

Berman, Sanford. "'Inside' Censorship," *Progressive Librarian* 18 (Summer 2001): 48–63. See also http://www.sanfordberman.org.

Broderick, Dorothy M. "About the Self-Righteous among Us," *Voice of Youth Advocates* 20 (October 1997): 233–234 [librarians as censors and self-appointed citizen groups].

Coley, Ken P. "Moving toward a Method to Test for Self-Censorship by School Library Media Specialists," *School Library Media Research* 5 (2002).

Hole, Carol. "Who Me, Censor?" *Top of the News* 40 (Winter 1984): 147–153.

———. "Yeah, Me Censor: A Response to Various Critics," *Top of the News* 41 (Spring 1985): 236–247.

Hunter, Dorothea, and Madsen, Winifred. "The Enemy Within," *School Library Journal* 39 (March 1993): 140.

Moody, Kim. "Censorship by Queensland Public Librarians: Philosophy and Practice," *APLIS* 17 (December 2004): 168–185.

———. "Covert Censorship in Libraries: A Discussion Paper," *Australian Library Journal* 54 (May 2005): 138–147.

Schrader, Alvin. "Why You Cannot 'Censorproof' Your Public Library," *APLIS* 10 (September): 143–159.

SCHOOLS

Gerhardt, Lillian. "Chewing on ALA's Code" *School Library Journal* 36 (January 1990): 4; "Ethical Back Talk," *School Library Journal* 36 (1990) [discussing each element of the ALA's 1981 Statement on Professional Ethics in the context of school librarianship]: "I [Service]" (February 1990): 4; "II [Resist Censorship]" (April 1990): 4; "III [Respect Privacy]" (June 1990): 4; "IV [Peer Relationships]" (August 1990): 4; "V [Distinguish Personal Philosophies]" (October 1990): 4; "VI [Avoid Conflicts of Interest]" (December 1990): 4.

Lukenbill, W. Bernard, and James F. Lukenbill. "Censorship: What Do School Library Media Specialists Really Know? A Consideration of Students' Rights, the Law, and Implications for a New Education Paradigm," *School Library Media Research* 10 (November 2007): 1–31.

Reichman, Henry. *Censorship and Selection: Issues and Answers for Schools*. 3rd ed. Chicago: American Library Association, 2001.

Scales, Pat R. *Teaching Banned Books: 12 Guides for Young Readers*. Chicago: American Library Association, 2001. See also Random House Teaching Guides, http://www.randomhouse.com/educator (accessed March 31, 2008).

Simpson, Carol. "School Library Ethics—A Battle of Hats," *Library Media Connection* 22 (January 2004): 22–23.

Simpson, Carol, ed. *Ethics in School Librarianship: A Reader*. Worthington, OH: Linworth Publishing, 2003.

FORMATS

Pinnell-Stephens, June. "Lester Asheim in Cyberspace: A Tribute to Sound Reasoning," *American Libraries* 33 (October 2002): 70, 72.

Film

Butters, Gerald R., Jr. *Banned in Kansas: Motion Picture Censorship, 1915–1966*. Columbia, MO: University of Missouri Press, 2007.

Cripps, Thomas. *Slow Fade to Black: The Negro in American Film, 1900–1942*. New York: Oxford University Press, 1993.

De Grazia, Edward, and Roger K. Newman. *Banned Films: Movies, Censors, and the First Amendment*. New York: R. R. Bowker, 1982.

Fleener-Marzec, Nickieann. *D. W. Griffith's* The Birth of a Nation: *Controversy, Suppression, and the First Amendment as It Applies to Filmic Expression, 1915–1973.* New York: Arno Press, 1980.

Gardner, Gerald C. *The Censorship Papers: Movie Censorship Letters from the Hays Office, 1934–1968.* New York: Dodd, Mead, 1987.

Moley, Raymond. *The Hays Office.* Indianapolis: Bobbs-Merrill, 1945.

FILTERS

Auld, Hampton. "Filters Work: Get Over It," *American Libraries* 34 (February 2003): 38–42.

———. "Filtering Materials on the Internet Does Not Contradict the Value of Open Access to Material," *Public Libraries* 44 (July/August 2005): 196–198.

Brennan Center for Justice. "Internet Filters: A Public Policy Report," 2nd ed. New York: 2006, http://www.fepproject.org/policyreports/filters2.pdf. See also "Internet Filters Screen Out Political, Scientific Material Well Beyond Stated Intent, Report Finds," *Newsletter on Intellectual Freedom* 55 (July 2006): 178–179.

"Court Overturns CIPA; Government Will Appeal," *American Libraries* 33 (August 2002): 18; "*American Library Association v. United States,*" *Newsletter on Intellectual Freedom* 51 (July 2002): 147, 158–160 [excerpts from lower court opinion overturning CIPA]; "Supreme Court Upholds CIPA," *Newsletter on Intellectual Freedom* 52 (September 2003): 173, 187–191.

Cronin, Blaise. "Whatever Happened to Common Sense?" *Library Journal* (1976): 125 (September 1, 2000): 177; Burek Pierce, Jennifer, "Blaise Cronin: Defender of CIPA," *American Libraries* 34 (February 2003): 41.

Dilevko, Juris, and Lisa Gottlieb. "Selection and Cataloguing of Adult Pornography Web Sites for Academic Libraries." *The Journal of Academic Librarianship* 30 (January 2004): 36–50.

Jaeger, Paul T., John Carlo Bertot, and Charles R. McClure. "The Effects of the Children's Internet Protection Act (CIPA) in Public Libraries and Its Implications for Research," *Journal of the American Society for Information Science and Technology* 55 (November 2004): 1,131–1,139.

Kranich, Nancy. "Filtering Materials on the Internet Contradicts the Value of Open Access to Material," *Public Libraries* 44 (July/August 2005): 198–200.

———. "Why Filters Won't Protect Children or Adults." *Library Administration & Management* 18 (Winter 2004): 14–18.

Minow, Mary. "Lawfully Surfing the Net: Disabling Public Library Internet Filters to Avoid More Lawsuits in the United States," *First Monday* (online at http://www.firstmonday.org/issues/issue9-4/minow/index.html) 9 (April 5, 2004): 1–13.

Radom, Rachel. "Internet Filtering Companies with Religious Affiliations in the Context of Indiana Public Libraries," *LIBRES* 17 (September 2007): 1–19; Comer, Alberta Davis. "Studying Indiana Public Libraries' Usage of Internet Filters," *Computers in Libraries* 25 (June 2005): 10–15.

Schneider, Karen G. "Let's Begin the Discussion Right Now," *American Libraries* 34 (August 2003): 14–16.

SOCIAL RESPONSIBILITY

Berninghausen, David K. *The Flight from Reason: Essays on Intellectual Freedom in the Academy, the Press, and the Library.* Chicago: American Library Association, 1975.

Horn, Zoia. *Zoia! Memoirs of Zoia Horn, Battler for the People's Right to Know.* Jefferson, NC: McFarland, 1995.

"Intellectual Freedom and Social Responsibility," [Special Issue] *School Libraries in Canada* 26, no. 2 (February 2007): 43–51. [Follow-up to "Intellectual Freedom and Social Responsibility," *School Libraries in Canada* 24, no. 4 (2004)], http://www.clatoolbox.ca/casl/slic/slicindex.html.

Samek, Toni. *Intellectual Freedom and Social Responsibility in American Librarianship, 1967–1974.* Jefferson, NC: McFarland, 2001.

———. "Library Ethics, Rights, and Values: Provocative Commentary on the Utility of Library Rhetoric," *PNLA Quarterly* 65 (Spring 2001): 15–17.

Samek, Toni, Edgardo Civallero, and Kenneth D. Gariepy. *Librarianship and Human Rights: A Twenty-First Century Guide.* Oxford: Chandos, 2007.

CONFLICTS

Herrada, Julie. "Letters to the Unabomber: A Case Study and Some Reflections," *Archival Issues* 28, no. 1 (2003/2004): 35–46.

Matacio, Lauren R. "Intellectual Freedom: Challenges and Responsibilities of Seventh-Day Adventist Academic Libraries," *Journal of Research on Christian Education* 12 (Fall 2003): 171–192.

Oder, Norman. "Monroe Cty Adopts Tough Net Policy," *Library Journal (1976)* 132 (June 15, 2007): 16–17.

O'Sullivan, Michael K., and Connie J. O'Sullivan. "Selection or Censorship: Libraries and the Intelligent Design Debate," *Library Review* 56, no. 3: 200–207.

Preer, Jean. "Special Ethics for Special Librarians?" *Special Libraries* 82 (Winter 1991): 12–18.

Raphael, Molly. "A Challenging Decision in a Changing Environment: Options for Internet Access at the Multnomah County Library," *OLA Quarterly* 11 (Fall 2005): 8–9, 20.

Yakel, Elizabeth. "Museums, Management, Media, and Memory: Lessons from the *Enola Gay* Exhibition," *Libraries & Culture* 35 (Spring 2000): 278–310.

CONFIDENTALITY

Adams, Helen R., et al. *Privacy in the 21st Century: Issues for Public, School, and Academic Libraries.* Westport, CT: Libraries Unlimited, 2005.

American Library Association Office for Intellectual Freedom. "Model Policy: Responding to Demands for Library Records," *American Libraries* 38 (September 2007): 48–49.

Foerstel, Herbert N. *Refuge of a Scoundrel: The Patriot Act in Libraries.* Westport, CT: Libraries Unlimited, 2004.

———. *Surveillance in the Stacks: The FBI's Library Awareness Program.* New York: Greenwood Press, 1991.

———. *The Patriot Act: A Documentary and Reference Guide*. New York: Greenwood Press, 2007.

Riehl, Donna. "Students' Privacy Rights in School Libraries: Balancing Principles, Ethics, and Practice," *School Libraries in Canada (Online)* 26 (February 2007): 32–42.

Shields, Gerald R. "The FBI Creates an Awareness of Librarian Ethics: An Opinionated Historical Review," in *Ethics and the Librarian*, ed. F. W. Lancaster, Urbana-Champaign, IL: University of Illinois Graduate School of Library and Information Science, 1991, 19–30.

Wyatt, Anna May. "Do Librarians Have an Ethical Duty to Monitor Patrons' Internet Usage in the Public Library?" *Journal of Information Ethics* 15 (Spring 2006): 70–79.

LIBRARY 2.0

Bell, Lori, Kitty Pope, and Tom Peters. "Who's on Third in Second Life?" *Online (Weston, Conn.)* 31 (July/August 2004): 14–18.

Berry, John N. III. "Library 2.0 Comes into View," *Library Journal (1876)* 132 (April 15, 2007): 10.

Bolan, Kimberly, Meg Canada, and Rob Cullin. "Web, Library, and Teen Services 2.0," *Young Adult Library Services* 5 (Winter 2007): 40–43.

Casey, Michael E., and Laura C. Savastinuk. "Library 2.0," *Library Journal (1976)* 131 (September 1, 2006): 40–42.

———. *Library 2.0: The Librarian's Guide to Participatory Library Service*. Medford, NJ: Information Today, 2007. For a review, see Boatwright, Susanne, [Library 2.0] *The Journal of Academic Librarianship* 33 (December 2007): 719–720.

Casey, Michael E., and Michael Stephens. "Living Out Loud," *Library Journal (1876)*: 132 (June 1, 2007): 34.

Cohen, Laura. "A Librarian's 2.0 Manifesto." *Library 2.0: An Academic's Perspective* (November 2006), http://www.tinyurl.com/ybwq6s. For mash-up versions of the manifesto, go to http://www.myplus.ca/manifestofinal.html (produced and set to music by Pickering Public Library, Ontario) and to http://www.youtube.com/watch?v=ZblrRs3fkSU (a version by Soren Johannssen).

Murley, Diane. "What Is All the Fuss about Library 2.0?" *Law Library Journal* (Winter 2008): 197–204.

Stephens, Michael. "Web 2.0 and You," *American Libraries* 38 (December 2007): 32.

Tenopir, Carol. "Web 2.0: Our Cultural Downfall?" *Library Journal (1976)* 132 (December 2007): 36. [discussing Keen, Andrew, *The Cult of the Amateur: How Today's Internet Is Killing Our Culture*. New York: Doubleday/Currency, 2007].

Wyatt, Neal. "2.0 for Readers," *Library Journal (1976)* 132 (November 1, 2007): 30–33.

INDEX

About the Author

JEAN PREER is Professor in the Indiana University School of Library and Information Science—Indianapolis. A graduate of Swarthmore College, she earned her MLS degree at the University of California—Berkeley and a JD and PhD in American Civilization at George Washington University. Before joining the Indiana University faculty in 2002, she taught at the library school at The Catholic University of America where she also served as Associate Dean. At IU SLIS—Indianapolis she teaches Perspectives on Librarianship, Collection Development and Management, and Library Philanthropy.

In 2005, Dr. Preer received the Indiana University Trustees Teaching Award and in 2006 the Association for Library and Information Science Education (ALISE) Award for Excellence in LIS Teaching. In 2007, her essay, "Promoting Citizenship: Librarians Help Get Out the Vote in the 1952 Presidential Election," won the Justin Winsor Prize for Library History awarded by the Library History Round Table of the American Library Association. Among her many publications on library science, history, and law is *Lawyers v. Educators: Black Colleges and Desegregation in Public Higher Education* (Greenwood, 1982).